march co

Barbary
Pirate

9

!

BARBARY PIRATE

The Life and Crimes of
JOHN WARD

GREG BAK

Suffolk County Council	
30127 07570985 2	
Askews	Feb-2010
364.164	£12.99

First published 2006
This edition published 2010

The History Press
The Mill, Brimscombe Port
Stroud, Gloucestershire, GL5 2QG
www.thehistorypress.co.uk

British Library Cataloguing in Publication Data.
A catalogue record for this book is available from the British Library.

ISBN 978 0 7524 5161 9

Typesetting and origination by The History Press
Printed in India by Aegean Offset Printers, New Delhi

For Grace,
Ruby and Fiona

Contents

Plates

(Between pages 114 and 115)

1. Frontispiece from William Okeley, *Eben-ezer, or, A small monument of great mercy: appearing in miraculous deliverance of William Okeley, John Anthony, William Adams, John Jephs, John —, carpenter, from the miserable slavery of Algiers,* London, printed for Nat. Ponder, at the Peacock in Chancery-Lane, near Fleet-Street, 1675. *(Courtesy of the Beinecke Rare Book and Manuscript Library, Yale University)*

2. Title page from *Ward and Danseker, two notorious pyrates, Ward an Englishman, and Danseker a Dutchman. With a true relation of the piraces by them committed vnto the sixt of Aprill,* London, for N. Butter 1609. *(With permission of the Bodleian Library, University of Oxford)*

3. Title page from Andrew Barker, *A True and Certaine Report of the Beginning, Proceedings, Ouerthrowes, and now present Estate of Captaine Ward and Danseker. As also the firing of 25. saile of the Tunis,* London, W. Hall [for] I. Helme, 1609. *(With permission of the Bodleian Library, University of Oxford)*

4. Engraving of a janissary from Nicolas de Nicolay, *The nauigations, peregrinations and voyages, made into Turkie,* imprinted at London, [at the cost of John Stell] by Thomas Dawson, 1585. *(Courtesy of the Beinecke Rare Book and Manuscript Library, Yale University)*

5. Engraving from Nicholas de Nicolay, *The nauigations, peregrinations and voyages, made into Turkie. (Courtesy of the Beinecke Rare Book and Manuscript Library, Yale University)*

6. Engraving of Leonardo Donato from Thomas de Fougasses, *The generall historie of the magnificent state of Venice: From the first*

foundation thereof vntill this present, London, printed by G. Eld and W. Stansby, 1612. *(Courtesy of the Thomas Fisher Rare Book Library, University of Toronto)*

7. Map of Venice from Thomas de Fougasses, *The generall historie of the magnificent state of Venice. (Courtesy of the Thomas Fisher Rare Book Library, University of Toronto)*

8. Detail of map from Martin Cortes, *The arte of nauigation: conteyning a compendious description of the sphere, with the making of certayne instruments and rules for nauigations, and exemplifyed by many demonstrations*, at London printed [by Abell Jeffes] at the charges of Richard Watkins, 1589. *(Courtesy of the Beinecke Rare Book and Manuscript Library, Yale University)*

9. Detail of engraving from John Smith, *The True Travels, Adventures, and Observations*, London, printed by I[ohn] H[aviland] for Thomas Slater, and are to bee sold [by Michael Sparke] at the Blew Bible in Greene Arbour, 1630. *(Courtesy of the Beinecke Rare Book and Manuscript Library, Yale University)*

10. Detail of map from George Sandys, *A relation of a journey begun An: Dom: 1610*, London, Barren, 1615. *(Courtesy of the Thomas Fisher Rare Book Library, University of Toronto)*

11. Engraving of Lithgow in regalia from William Lithgow, *The Totall Discourse of the Rare Aduentures and Painefull Peregrinations of long nineteene Yeares Trauayles, from Scotland, to the most famous kingdomes in Europe, Asia, and Affrica*, imprinted at London by Nicholas Okes, and are to be sold by Nicholas Fussell and Humphery Mosley at their shops in Pauls Church yard, at the Ball, and the white Lyon, 1640. *(Courtesy of the Thomas Fisher Rare Book Library, University of Toronto)*

12. Engraving of Lithgow in Fez from William Lithgow, *The Totall Discourse. (Courtesy of the Thomas Fisher Rare Book Library, University of Toronto)*

13. Woodcut of a hanging at Wapping from Thomas Heywood, *A true relation of the lives and deaths of the two most famous English pyrats, Purser and Clinton*, London, I. Okes, 1639. *(With permission of the Bodleian Library, University of Oxford)*

Engravings

Acknowledgements

This book could not have been written without the work of all of the archivists, librarians and scholars, past and present, who have helped to organize and make available the documentary and print history of the United Kingdom.

Early readers of the book included Megan Butcher, Paul Dechene and Grace Sheppard. Thanks are owed for their insightful comments. Susan Martins, Cathie Bergeron, Sandra Kehoe and Megan: thanks for your help in the completion of the book. My agent, Christopher Sinclair-Stevenson, played a key role in the early stages of the writing. It has been a pleasure to work with Jaqueline Mitchell and all of the staff at Sutton.

The first time that I wrote on John Ward's life was in my doctoral dissertation. I owe a special debt to Dr Daniel R. Woolf, my academic supervisor, for developing my skills as an historian and for his contributions to the dissertation.

Thanks for the music, Air and Madrid.

But the greatest debt of all is to Grace, who gave me the opportunity to start writing this book, and to our lovely twin daughters, Fiona and Ruby, who encouraged the finish.

For whosoever commands the sea, commands the trade; whosoever commands the trade of the world commands the riches of the world and consequently the world itself.

Sir Walter Raleigh

ONE

A Fish Day for Sir William Cecil

The year of our Lord 1603: exchanging the folly of youth for the wisdom of age, John Ward, tired of the short wages of the Royal Navy, marked a half-century of life by leading a mass desertion from the service, stealing a civilian vessel and defecting to the Ottoman Empire's outpost at Tunis. From Tunis he devilled the sea lanes of the Mediterranean for years as a captain among the Barbary Corsairs before converting to Islam and, finally, retiring. Meanwhile, back in England, in the forced rhymes and broken metre of popular ballads, Ward's reputation skittered between admiration for a commoner made good (or at least rich), and vituperation for the most infamous infidel of the age. Why such a life at such an age? Poor financial planning. Two years before revolting from the ranks of the navy and heading for Tunis, John Ward had been a master at sea and lordly on land, a sea captain during the greatest age of English privateering. Nonetheless, when a royal decree unexpectedly brought an end to privateering, Ward was penniless.

Ward's life, inevitably, was shaped by the political and social forces of his age. More than most, John Ward seems to have lived in reaction to official policy, especially navy policy. His story cannot be told without delving into naval history, for the two twine like hemp in an anchor rope, twisting into the early years of the reign of Elizabeth I. Ward's story begins not with his birth – an event unrecorded by midwife or priest – but with the submission

1

of a parliamentary bill that would revive the prospects of English mariners even as John Ward, perhaps ten years old, was just of an age to begin to work the boats.

In 1563 Sir William Cecil gambled his authority and reputation on the passage of one particular bill through Parliament. Elizabeth I had been on the throne for five years and Cecil's place as her chief minister was established, though not unassailable. Nonetheless, Cecil, a member of the House of Commons, boldly opened debate on what he knew would be the most contentious, but believed with all his heart to be the most important, issue of the session. It might be expected that this would be a bill on religion, as Elizabeth was in the process of steering her beloved England back to the Protestantism of her father, Henry VIII. The nation had briefly but violently been compelled towards Catholicism under Elizabeth's half-sister, whose bonfires of Protestants had earned her the sobriquet of Bloody Mary. In fact, when Sir William rose in the chamber it was not to pick at the festering sores of religion. He had cod, not God, on his mind.

Cecil, born in 1520, had witnessed personally the decline of fishing among the English. He could recall when the nation's coastal waters had teemed with small craft, while larger vessels had made their way to the North Sea and the rich Grand Banks off Newfoundland. Results of the decline in fishing were as ominous as the causes were clouded: dilapidated ports and harbours, few English ships plying the waves, and a dearth of mariners in England. For an island nation, Cecil knew, the situation could be deadly, stifling economic growth and inviting foreign invasion. As he stood to speak on that day in 1563 Cecil was determined to illuminate both cause and effect.

'The causes of the decay of fishing,' intoned Sir William, 'must be divided into two parts: small eating of fish in the realm and no selling of it abroad.' A fine starting point, but as Cecil developed his argument he described a more tangled skein than just these two factors. Cecil instructed those members of Parliament who could to cast their thoughts back twenty-seven years and consider the state of England then, when fish was eaten by 'the great multitude of people in the realm for superstition'.

The mathematics are obscure now but could not have been mistaken on that day in 1563: twenty-seven years back was 1536, the dawn of the Protestant Reformation in England. Between 1532 and 1536 Parliament had recognized the divorce of Henry VIII from his first wife, the mother of the future Bloody Mary, in spite of the fact that the divorce had been refused by the Pope. Henry had then married Anne Boleyn and a second daughter, destined to rule England as Elizabeth I, was born. Between 1536 and 1539 the Reformation, initially a reality only at the royal court and in Parliament, was forcibly extended into the countryside. Monastic religious communities were violently disbanded, their wealth and property seized by the state. Prayers were rewritten to exclude all mention of the Pope and to recognize the king of England as the principal religious as well as secular authority. The ceremony, iconography and language of religious services were made to assume a national outlook.

Ten years of Protestantism under Henry VIII were followed by six more under his son, Edward VI. Five years of fanatical and authoritarian Catholicism under Queen Mary were hardly sufficient to rekindle a love for the old religion, but quite long enough to drive Protestantism further into English hearts. Elizabeth inherited a nation that was ideologically Protestant. Now, several years into her reign, the young queen and her advisors, Sir William Cecil foremost among them, had to deal with an unintended and potentially disastrous effect of Reformation: a massive decline in fish in the national diet.

Roman Catholicism had required the consumption of fish in place of meat on numerous fast days, thus providing a steady market for English fishermen. This market had been especially rich among monasteries and convents, where fast days were observed rigorously and additional days of abstention were frequent. The Protestant Reformation had wiped out England's monastic communities and all but eliminated fish consumption among the general population. As the Reformation penetrated the countryside common folk began to sneer at what they now called the superstitious practices of Roman Catholicism, including the observance of the Pope's numerous 'fish days'.

Refusing to eat fish became a measure of religious commitment, and even patriotism, in the popular culture of the day. England was soon ringed with collapsing piers and crumbling moorings, the profession of fisherman all but abandoned owing to a lack of markets. Not that English coastal waters were no longer exploited: Cecil burned with resentment that God's bounty continued to be harvested, but by French and Dutch rather than English fishermen. Even worse, these foreigners were bringing fish caught in English waters to English tables, selling a portion of their catch to those English who had not given up fish entirely (as indeed some had not given up the old religion entirely), whatever the 'superstitious' associations.

Meanwhile, Cecil was in the midst of engineering an economic boom. The mid-sixteenth century had witnessed prolonged economic recession, a crisis that forced English merchants to look for markets ever further afield. During the 1550s Englishmen made their way to Russia, Newfoundland, Africa and throughout the Mediterranean Sea. Previously content to allow the merchants of Venice to supply them with the silks, spices and drugs of the Orient, Englishmen now began to appear in the ports of Italy and the Middle East, their vessels' hulls crammed with English wool and tin, and ready to trade. Cecil was pleased with the gains that English merchants had made in diversifying their ports of call, but recently progress had slowed on account of two rather substantial difficulties. There was a shortage of ships and a lack of men to work them.

The construction of ships was not an insoluble problem, but in his plea to the House of Commons Cecil cautioned against subsidizing shipbuilding. 'To multiply ships and to lack mariners is to set armour upon stakes at the sea coast and to provide no people to wear it, or to build castles and put no soldiers in them', he insisted. It also would have placed an intolerable drain on the royal coffers, a point that Cecil did not raise. Instead, he advocated an organic solution to the problem, identifying the root cause and seeking its remedy. If, Cecil reasoned, the market for fish could be increased, then Englishmen would cast nets once more. To cast their nets, fishermen would build ships: first small coastal vessels, but eventually great ocean-going ships to plunder the seas off Iceland and Newfoundland. These ships would need moorings; therefore ports would be maintained. Shipping would increase and a new generation of mariners would ride the waves, all at no cost to the crown.

Cecil proposed a number of measures to stimulate the market for fish. Foreigners would be forbidden from selling fresh fish in England, and the salted or dried fish that they supplied would be taxed heavily.* The export of fish from England would be tax-free, so long as it was carried in English ships. And finally, shockingly, every Wednesday and Saturday would be declared days on which all English men and women would eat fish and only fish. Two days of every week would be given over to patriotic fish-eating. It was this last proposal that provoked controversy, for to earnest Protestants it smacked of a return to Roman Catholicism.

Sir William Cecil was not a man to be trifled with. As a member of the Privy Council and Elizabeth's chief minister, he was the most powerful man in a realm governed by an unmarried queen. And he was determined. Through all of the debates that followed that first speech, the shuttling of the bill from house to committee and back, Cecil gave ground on wording but not principle, and certainly not on the declaration of Wednesdays and Saturdays as fish days. In the end Cecil rammed the bill through Parliament by sheer force of will. His primary concession to his opponents – a clarification, really – appears in paragraph twenty-three of the act that entered the statute books. To prevent confusion about the intentions behind the bill, Cecil wrote that the fish days were 'purposely intended and meant politically', not religiously, their sole function 'the increase of fishermen and mariners and repairing of port towns and navigation, and not for any Superstition'. The act goes further: 'whosoever shall

---

* Salted and dried fish were a necessity in any long-distance venture at sea, for these, along with salt pork and the hard-as-iron ship's biscuit, were the seamen's staples of the day. Until the English fish industry had returned to health, Cecil knew that it would only harm English shipping to prohibit the importation of salted and dried fish altogether.

by preaching, teaching, writing, or open speech, notify that any eating of fish and forbearing of flesh mentioned in this Statute is of any necessity for the saving of the Soul of Man, or that it is the Service of God . . . then such person shall be punished as [a] spreader of false news.'

The need had been sufficient for Cecil fully to exert his authority, standing up in the House of Commons and insisting on the bill's passage. The newly created Protestant fish days became known, derisively, as 'Cecil's Fast'. They were grumblingly and sporadically observed, but observed nonetheless. England began to eat fish again. And, just as the Reformation had had effects that Henry VIII could never have foreseen, so did Cecil's Fast have implications that eluded Sir William's sharp intellect. The revival of fishing brought new life to England's ports and shipyards, but it also launched the career of the man who would become the most notorious English outlaw of the next century: Captain John Ward.

In 1563, the year that Cecil's Fast became law, John Ward – or Jack, the familiar name by which he was then known – was ten years old, of an age to help his father on the family boat, and of the generation that had arrived at Elizabethan Protestantism via the blood-stained Catholicism of Queen Mary. There is a woodcut picture of Ward, perhaps at the age of fourteen or fifteen, printed in a news pamphlet of 1609 (see p. 1). The woodcut shows two men in one of the sturdy, broad skiffs favoured by English coastal fishermen. An older man (Jack's father, presumably) grimaces and hauls line as the younger man, Jack, strains and heaves at a net filled with fish. Overhead, clouds swirl as a storm rolls in. It is a cheerless image but one that would have brought a smile to the face of Sir William Cecil. The men are fishing.

This would hardly have been surprising in pre-Reformation times. Faversham, the town of Ward's birth and early life, had deep traditions of Catholic devotion and a long history of coastal fishing. King Stephen so loved the town, nestled in the Kentish countryside along the banks of a tidal inlet, that in the twelfth century he founded a monastery where he and all his family were duly interred. Also in the town's church was a chapel, dedicated to St Thomas à Becket, that attracted pilgrims as they made their way to the saint's principal shrine 10 miles down the road in Canterbury. Equally important to the local population was the chapel to Saints Crispin and Crispianus, who, it was said, had come to Faversham in ancient times to escape the persecutions of the Roman Emperor Diocletian. The fishermen of Faversham were kept busy supplying fish for the monks, and for the general population, during holy days, religious festivals and periods of personal and communal penance.

Whatever its traditions, during the sixteenth century Kent was at the forefront of the English Reformation. In 1538 Canterbury Cathedral was purged of all 'superstitious' Catholic relics and paraphernalia, including England's principal shrine to St Thomas à Becket, who was now reviled as a defender of papal authority against royal supremacy. The cathedral became the epicentre of England's Protestant Reformation, the headquarters of the new national church. In Faversham King Stephen's monastery was closed after some 400 years, the monks expelled, their lands and buildings seized by the state. The shrines to Saints Thomas, Crispin and Crispianus were purged from Faversham's church, the relics desecrated and destroyed. And fish dropped out of the local diet.

Among fishermen this new Protestant zeal was a bitter pill. There are no records of how the Ward family survived the crisis, but it is easy to guess. They, like other fisher folk, lived outside of the systems of communal charity and personal obligation that served for a social safety net in Tudor England. They were masterless men, men who lacked a feudal lord to whom they swore allegiance and who, in exchange, promised to protect them and provide aid in times of dearth. Nor did the fishermen belong to one of the trade guilds, the civic organizations that had evolved among urban craftsmen to take the place of feudalism's bonds of personal loyalty. In good years it was a boon for fishermen to be outside these structures, for it spared them much taxation, but in hard years they could look for no assistance. They would survive or perish by their own effort and wits.

Fishermen of all times and places practise a patchwork economy, and this certainly was the case in mid-sixteenth-century Kent. The Kentish fishery had never been a rich one: William Lambarde, writing in 1576, described it as furnishing 'neither so much in quantity nor in variety as some other coasts of the realm'. Even in good times the fishermen of Faversham were quick to seize other opportunities as they arose. The nature of such 'opportunities' is easy to guess.

Daniel Defoe described the county early in the eighteenth century, noting that 'after I have mentioned the tombs of King Stephen and his Queen, in Faversham, I know nothing else this town is remarkable for, except the most notorious smuggling trade'. According to Defoe the fishermen of Kent 'have carried on the smuggling trade for years, for which this creek [i.e. the Swale, a tidal inlet] lies very convenient'. Defoe offers a tip to prospective travellers: 'Brandy, and often French wines, are sold here at very low rates, especially at such times as the smugglers have been apprehensive of discovery.' In exchange for the wine and brandy of France the smugglers of Kent practised what Defoe calls 'owling', the illegal exportation of Kent's principal commodity, wool.

In addition to smuggling, the fisher folk of Kent fell back on another traditional mainstay of coastal communities, salvaging or wrecking. Often such work began with children like Jack Ward ranging over the beaches and into the coves after a storm, eager to find wreckage or jettisoned cargoes. And, of course, when dearth and temptation grew too strong, it was sometimes necessary to give a little assistance to the foundering of a ship. When the fish rotted at market, when smuggling and salvaging were not enough to sustain a family, piracy was a last recourse of the fisherman.

We do not know how Jack Ward spent his boyhood, but we can imagine him walking the coast as a wrecker, half-playing and half-scouting, searching for washed-up cargoes either abandoned by smugglers or lost at sea during storms. As he got older he would have accompanied his father in the family's boat, pulling an oar or helping to manage the simple rigging that was designed by coastal fishermen to hoist a single sail above their skiffs. Perhaps young

Jack even made his way across the Channel, setting foot in a new country and hearing a strange language while exchanging illicit wool for bootleg brandy.

Through it all the sea surges and flows. Sir William Cecil's revival of English fishing came as Ward was about ten years old. We can imagine him at sea with his father, old enough to remember the horrible poverty and terrible anxiety that had prompted secretive night voyages. No doubt the boy was thankful to cast a net by day. But did he miss the excitement?

As the boy became a fisherman, the lessons he learned on his father's skiff would prove invaluable. Jack was inducted into the dangerous practice of coastal navigation, an art that in those days relied as much on intuition as information. Fishermen work in all conditions, at all times of the day, and Ward learned to navigate through fog and night by the presence and behaviour of seabirds, animals and plants, the sound of surf on rocks, beach and cliffs. An instinctive awareness of the tides was essential to the fisherman who ventured without charts or books. This instinct was inculcated through observation and repetition, slowly attuning the body to the rhythms of the moon and sea instead of those of the sun. Such accumulated wisdom, learned at his father's hand, would later set Ward apart from socially superior captains who studied the sea through professional apprenticeship and books.

As Jack Ward acquired the arts of the fishermen he was absorbed into their fraternity. These men were masterless and they formed a distinctive band, a breed apart, complete with their own costume – rough jackets, loose trousers, oiled cloth – and their own dialect, the argot of the sea, too salty for the God-fearing burghers of Faversham. This sense of being apart from mainstream culture, of belonging to a restricted brotherhood, remained with Ward his entire life.

It is not clear when Jack Ward stopped working the coastal fishery in Kent, but it is safe to assume that he was not there for long. Cecil's Fast was successful in reintroducing fish to the English diet, but even more successful were those measures that Sir William had taken to favour the exporting of fish from England. These included prohibitions on the importation of foreign-caught fish and the elimination of tariffs on English-caught fish sold abroad, measures that created a favourable environment for an export boom in dried fish. During the 1560s and 1570s English Protestants became primary purveyors of fish to Catholic tables on the continent, once again profiting from the many fast days of the Roman religion. As Sir William Cecil had foreseen, English fishermen and merchants soon outgrew the coastal fishery, and the North Sea and New World fisheries beckoned.

As expeditions to Iceland and Newfoundland were financed and outfitted, coastal fishermen became highly prized crew members. Already seasoned in the ways of the sea, they took to the ropes and sails of ocean-going ships with ease. Arriving at a distant fishery, they proved equal to the brutal work that followed, their callused hands tirelessly hauling nets while exhausted landsmen collapsed and nursed bloody wounds inflicted by the rough hemp of rope and net. Fishermen like Jack Ward were the men of the moment, and the sure wages offered on ocean-going voyages were sufficient to lure them from the vicissitudes of coastal fisheries and the fluctuating returns of local markets. Did Jack Ward, not one to shirk adventure, abandon the coastal fishery of Faversham and cast nets in the trans-oceanic harvest of the legendary Grand Banks of Newfoundland? There is no record of it, but it is easy to imagine: Ward, perhaps sixteen years old, unfurling sails and hauling rope on his first voyage to the New World.

This was Ward's apprenticeship: a childhood of poverty rooted in nationalistic religious fanaticism, relieved only by wrecking, smuggling and hauling nets to feed England's enemies. It is impossible to imagine better training for a man who would regard the laws of nations as flexible rather than fixed, nationality mere affectation, religion a convenience.

TWO

'Through All Ranks of the Service'

 Sir Francis Drake's most famous voyages and battles occurred while he was a pirate. John Ward, despite isolated acts of piracy, was a privateer for virtually his entire life. The difference? The privateer's assaults are made under the aegis of a sovereign power, a practice recognized within international law, while a pirate is a thieving miscreant who operates outside the law. Nonetheless, history celebrates Drake for his patriotism and condemns Ward as a lawless renegade.

Between 1577 and 1580 Drake circumnavigated the globe. When he set forth on this voyage he had no intention of charting new lands, encountering new peoples, or even claiming valuable natural resources in the name of queen and country. From the start his goal was simply to plunder and pillage, and his decision to take the long way home from the New World was made solely out of fear of capture. As he sailed through the Caribbean, down the Atlantic coast of South America, through the Straits of Magellan and back up the Pacific coast, he pillaged Spanish ships and settlements in South America, Central America and Mexico: acts of piracy, for there was no declared war between England and Spain, and Drake did not carry letters of marque or letters of reprisal, documents that license privateering. That he dedicated his actions to Queen Elizabeth is of no moment, nor is the fact that Drake gave his monarch a generous share of the plunder when he finally returned to England. Had Drake's circumnavigation occurred a decade later, after 1585, things would have been different.

Throughout the 1560s and 1570s Protestant England under Elizabeth I was poised for war with the Catholic Spain of Philip II – Elizabeth's sworn enemy, but also her brother-in-law, for he had been husband to her half-sister and predecessor, Queen Mary. Whatever the personal relations between the rulers, King Philip had declared himself the leader of the Roman Catholic Counter-Reformation, a militant movement designed to check the spread of Protestantism in Europe and foment Catholic rebellion where Protestantism had taken root. As Elizabeth set about undoing Mary's attempts to rekindle Catholicism in England, Philip began to encourage Catholic rebels in Ireland and sought, as much as possible, to hamper the new queen's movements on the European stage. In the process Philip not only established Spain as the defining foreign policy challenge of Elizabeth's reign but also delivered the queen the credentials she needed to reinvent herself as the de facto head of Protestant Europe. Already the open enemy of the leader of the Counter-Reformation, Elizabeth needed only the censure of the papacy to clinch the admiration of continental Protestants. In 1570 Pope Pius V graciously aided Elizabeth's political ascendancy by singling her out for excommunication.

For her part, Elizabeth encouraged Protestant rebels in the Netherlands, which was Spanish territory at the time, and pretended to be unable to do anything about hot-headed English pirates like Sir Francis Drake who preyed upon Spain's shipping and New World colonies. Nonetheless, though happy to accrue prestige by having powerful enemies and willing enough to replenish state coffers with ill-gotten Spanish booty, Elizabeth was not foolish enough to bait Philip and his globe-straddling Spanish empire into open warfare.

This changed in 1585 when a Spanish treasure fleet, bound for the Netherlands to provide overdue payment to Spanish forces fighting Protestant Dutch rebels, was forced on to English shores by a storm. Elizabeth's admirals detained the ships and claimed their treasure. In response, Philip ordered his officials to seize all English shipping and goods in Spanish territories, thus injuring the large number of English merchants for whom commerce knew no religion. To make good their losses Elizabeth ordered her lord admiral to issue letters of reprisal to the affected merchants. These letters licensed merchants to outfit privateering voyages with the stated intent of attacking Spanish shipping, private or state, to recover the value of goods and investments lost in the Spanish seizures of 1585. In practical terms the queen had declared war, though she would maintain to the end that English privateering was nothing more than private citizens recovering the wealth that had been stolen by Spain.

Truth be told, English letters of reprisal were issued judiciously at first. Merchants applying to the lord admiral had to provide convincing evidence of their losses in the illegal seizures made by the Spanish crown. Letters of reprisal, valid for six months, were issued only for that amount. Within a year the system had fallen apart. Lord Admiral Nottingham had begun issuing letters to his friends, his friends' friends, and anyone who could afford to bribe him and his subordinates. It is no mystery why Elizabeth did nothing about this situation: in addition to satisfying her subjects' calls for war against Spain, privateering was enormously profitable to the state, and all the more attractive given that the financial risks were assumed by private investors and the personal risks by England's civilian seamen.

Through customs tariffs the queen received 5 per cent of the value of every prize brought back to England. The lord admiral received an additional 10 per cent as recompense for administering the privateering system. This included managing the High Court of Admiralty, where neutral or friendly foreigners might plead cases against English privateers whose enthusiasm had led them to attack non-Spanish shipping. Operating expenses notwithstanding, the lord admiral earned himself a tidy profit, without any personal or financial risk whatsoever – even when he was not bribed.

We know very little about John Ward before 1603, the year that he became an outlaw, for Ward belonged to the lowest orders of English society. These are the hardest people for historians to study, for they left few traces. Almost entirely illiterate, they kept no diaries or journals. Having little property, they did not draw up the complex wills that provide modern researchers with snapshots of the household goods of the upper orders of society. Disenfranchised from the local court system (on account of having neither master nor guild), they left few records of their disputes and crises. Attempting to track individual members within this population is hopeless.

Hopeless, that is, if they remained anonymous their entire lives. The fact that John Ward eventually became a celebrity means that information about his early years became a commodity. People interested in exploiting Ward's story for personal profit found eager buyers among newsmen, balladeers, playwrights – and the English authorities. Much of our information about Ward's life before 1603 comes from these sources, and it is to one particular report, purchased by the English ambassador to Venice and shuffled among his papers in the Venetian archives, that we owe the titbit that Ward 'rose through all ranks of the service of our wars with Spain'.

This report corroborates what we otherwise know of Ward. His skill as a seaman, his intimate knowledge of ocean sailing from ropes to rudder, his ability to manage men, his grasp of naval gunnery, and his mastery of the strategy and tactics of small-scale naval warfare – all of these qualities point to his experience as a commander among the Elizabethan privateers. More than this, when Ward made his move from England to Tunis he replicated there the political and practical organizational structure of English privateering, demonstrating knowledge not only of maritime command, but of virtually every aspect of English privateering from provisioning to the division of prizes.

In 1585, when the lord admiral began to issue letters of reprisal licensing English privateering, John Ward was about thirty-two years old. If it is true, as is likely, that Ward had already made the transition from the Kentish coast to the richer North Sea or New World fisheries, then he would already have mastered coastal sailing and attained experience as an ocean-going mariner. What would he have learned during his years as an English privateer? This is the question that makes privateering's economics and culture of moment here.

One of the unusual aspects of the privateering culture of Elizabethan England was the ease with which ships' crews were replenished. Privateers of other nations and other times might resort to forcing men into their service, abducting them from taverns or seducing them with promises that overstated both the abundance of treasure and the share to which new crew were entitled. In Elizabethan England the popular press, combined with late-century economic doldrums, furnished the privateers with an inexhaustible supply of volunteers.

Mariners were the action heroes of the Elizabethan age. During the 1580s and 1590s stories were told and songs rang out describing their adventures around the globe, and especially their bearding of the Spanish lion. Canny businessmen exploited the craze by having scribes copy down these stories and songs, using pen and paper to make physical that most fleeting form of communication, the spoken word. Clutching their papers, these men approached the printers of London and had the sea shanties and travellers' tales printed, transforming dockside gossip and tavern revelry into neat stacks of verse ballads and prose pamphlets. These were then offered up for sale by the booksellers who clustered in and about St Paul's churchyard.

What began as a phenomenon within London soon spread into the countryside. Moving throughout England at this time was a small army of itinerant pedlars, men and women who, like John Ward, came from the lowest ranks of society, the masterless men. William Shakespeare has left us a portrait of one such pedlar in his play *The Winter's Tale*. Shakespeare's pedlar is an unrepentant rogue, a shameless scam artist who cheats those not wise enough to avoid him. The pedlars' reputation for dishonesty was not limited to the playhouse. English statute books of the day include many laws intended to circumscribe the movements of these men and women, or even to apprehend them and punish them by flogging or expulsion from the community. Among honest folk pedlars were often considered to be scarcely better than vagabonds, the rootless social exiles who often figured as villains in popular ballads of the day.

In a society where social prestige hinged on whose name you invoked when you identified your master – the most powerful serving only the queen, the less powerful serving local potentates – itinerant pedlars, the fishers of Faversham and other men and women who claimed no master were feared. This independence was dangerous, for it meant that there was no master who could be called to account for the actions of these men and women. But more than this, masterless men like John Ward and the rogue pedlar of Shakespeare's *The Winter's Tale* were viewed as having renounced the very ties that bound society together, even though their status was more usually determined by birth or misfortune than choice.

Despite their seamy reputation, the pedlars, like Faversham's fishermen, provided an essential service. Fishermen supplied cheap, protein-rich food for their communities, while pedlars carried into the countryside inexpensive commodities that were otherwise available only in cities and towns. Shakespeare's pedlar in *The Winter's Tale* enters his big scene singing a song that describes his wares:

> Lawn as white as driven snow,
> Cypress as black as [ever] was crow,
> Gloves as sweet as damask roses,
> Masks for faces and for noses,
> Bugle-bracelet, necklace-amber,
> Perfume for a lady's chamber,
> Golden coifs and stomachers
> For my lads to give their dears,
> Pins and poking-sticks of steel;
> What maids lack from head to heel –
> Come buy of me, come, come buy, come buy;
> Buy, lads, or else your lasses cry; come buy.*

---

* Lawn and cypress were varieties of cloth, purchased by the woman of a home to be fashioned into 'good' clothes, as opposed to the rough homespun used for daily wear. Perfumed gloves, masks, bottled scents and inexpensive jewellery (a 'bugle-bracelet' was made of cheap glass beads) were all courting gifts for 'lads to give their dears', as were the caps ('coifs') and other ornaments ('stomachers')

Single-page news ballads and narrative pamphlets formed a perfect complement to these small luxuries and cheap wares, for they were light to carry and easy to sell. Shakespeare's play gives a sense of what sort of stories passed as 'news' among these pedlars and their rustic audience.

Male Villager: What hast here? Ballads?

Female Villager: Pray now, buy some. I love a ballad in print, a-life, for then we are sure they are true.

Pedlar: Here's one to a very doleful tune, how a usurer's wife was brought to bed of [i.e. gave birth to] twenty money-bags at a burden, and how she longed to eat adders' heads and toads carbonadoed [i.e. flayed and grilled].

Female Villager: Is it true, think you?

Pedlar: Very true, and but a month old.

Second Female Villager: Bless me from marrying a usurer!

Pedlar: Here's the midwife's name to't, one Mistress Taleporter, and five or six honest wives that were present. Why should I carry lies abroad?

Female Villager: Pray you now, buy it.

Male Villager: Come on, lay it by, and let's first see more ballads. We'll buy the other things anon.

Pedlar: Here's another ballad, of a fish that appeared upon the coast on Wednesday the fourscore of April forty thousand fathom above water, and sung this ballad against the hard hearts of maids. It was thought she was a woman and was turned into a cold fish for she would not exchange flesh with one that loved her. The ballad is very pitiful, and as true.

Second Female Villager: Is it true too, think you?

Pedlar: Five justices' hands at it, and witnesses more than my pack will hold.

---

that the pedlar also offered for sale. Pins and poking sticks were used to make and care for the 'good' clothes that were created from the 'fine' cloth that the pedlar sang of off the top.

So it goes. The pedlars must have memorized the contents of their ballads and pamphlets before leaving London, for it would be very surprising if even one of them could read. This did not stop them from singing out great tracts of text, the better to draw an audience and hawk their wares.

Mixed in with the tales of greedy usurers and cold-hearted maids were songs and stories praising English naval assaults on Spanish tyranny, extolling the selfless bravery of seamen and the riches that had been won: bars of gold and silver from the New World, sacks of pearls, rubies and diamonds, thick golden doubloons and shining Spanish reals. And, proving that gullibility is at least as old as the printing press, there have always been people like Shakespeare's bumpkin who loved 'a ballad in print . . . for then we are sure they are true'.

The flood of print ballads and pamphlets that pedlars humped on their backs from London and into the English countryside did more than give small-time operators one more chance to fleece hard-earned cash from naïve rustics. They also proved to be a potent recruiting tool for the privateers. The transformation of sea shanties and travellers' tales into a printed product that was carried inland from the ports coincided with a downturn in the rural economy, the effects of this recession multiplied by a series of crop failures. So, while villagers toiled in the dust for scant return they heard tales of the brave men who struck a blow for Protestantism and God while reaping treasure whose only limits were the imagination of the scribes who penned the ballads and the pedlars who recited them.

Men flocked to the docks. There they found ready reception. Unlike soldiers and other seamen, the men who worked privateering voyages were not paid wages. Instead, they were offered shares in the prizes they captured. If no prizes were captured, they received no money. This system furnished strong motivation for bravery and risk-taking among privateering crews, but it also meant that it was in the interests of the promoters of the voyages to cram as many as possible on to the decks. Extra men resulted in no additional costs for the promoters, though it did mean that individual prize shares would be smaller on account of the larger number entitled to a cut.

At sea these extra men were worse than useless. The green landsmen who were drawn to the privateering ports from far inland were
capable of only the least skilled shipboard duties. For the most part
they got in the way of the experienced seamen who made up the core
of the sailing crew, crowding the decks and making dangerous inroads
into the stingy provisions allowed by the investors of the privateering
venture. Worse, the crowded, unsanitary conditions below decks
promoted the spread of sickness and lice among unwashed bodies.
Privateering ships became notorious carriers of disease, and the
English were so strongly associated with privateering that some
Mediterranean ports refused to allow any Englishman ashore without
a period of quarantine. The privateers themselves, hoping to stem the
spread of disease, were known to abandon diseased men on foreign
shores at the first hint of illness. Even so, privateering voyages often
reported the deaths of as much as one-third to one-half of a crew to
disease and malnutrition, even before a shot was fired.

Once battle was met the landsmen were more favourably looked
upon, for they made excellent cannon-fodder. Man-to-man combat,
conducted by boarding parties largely composed of landsmen, was
the preferred method of taking a prize, for attempts to bombard
enemy ships into submission risked damaged cargoes or, worse,
sunken prizes. If prize ships were seaworthy after capture, seasoned
crewmembers of the privateer could be divided between the vessels,
their ranks filled out by semi-trained landsmen, and both ships
navigated back to England. This precluded the labour of transferring
cargoes and increased the value of the capture by bringing home the
additional ship. Enemy crews were landed at the nearest port of call
or absorbed into the crew of the privateer if they were willing to lend
a hand (as often they were).

Seamen like John Ward were usually sufficiently generous to let the
landsmen absorb the first, and worst, volleys of cannon and small-
arms shot, but were loath to allow them pride of place in capturing
a Spanish vessel. Judged by his later behaviour, Ward would have
ignored the danger and joined the first ranks of rail-jumpers to storm
a prize. It was neither glory nor duty that drove him on to enemy
decks. It was the time-honoured right of pillage.

Among the privateers, pillaging was limited by some standard rules. These rules excluded from pillage anything valued over 40 shillings, established that nothing was to be removed from the cargo proper, and demanded that all pillage was properly to be brought to the privateer's mainmast after the battle to be shared out by rank among seamen and soldiers. These rules were designed to ensure that the seasoned seamen consigned to the riggings during an assault received equal share of the plunder.

It was a nice theory. In practice it was every man for himself. Much pillage would be brought to the privateer's mainmast, but even more made its way below decks in the pockets and under the clothing of the boarding party. And while formal convention excluded cargoes from pillage, in the late stages of battle it was not difficult for members of boarding parties to slip below decks and into a ship's hold. This is the origin of embezzlement as a concept and as a term – the stealthy breaking into and spiriting away of prize cargoes by the boarding parties of privateers.

When a prize was brought back to England, the value of its cargo would be calculated, and the first order of business was to ensure that the queen's customs officers received 5 per cent on behalf of the crown. Next, agents of the lord admiral would take his 10 per cent. Full 15 per cent gone, the remaining value of the prize was divided into three. The ship owner, or owners, received one third, while the investors who had outfitted the venture received another third. In general, ship owners would number from one to three individuals, rarely more than five. There were larger numbers of investors, for most privateering voyages were provisioned by having bakers, victuallers, sail-makers and carpenters of the home port provide goods and services as their contribution to the venture. These lesser investors held a smaller stake in the voyage than the three or four merchants who had provided the capital to purchase powder, ordnance and small arms. Whatever the quantity of investors, their total was insignificant next to the numbers in the crew – the men who risked their lives to capture the prize – among whom was shared the final third of the value of the prize.

As a rule of thumb, privateering voyages were crewed by just over one man per 2 tons burden (i.e. carrying capacity) of a ship. Thus, an 80-ton vessel measuring perhaps 20 feet at its widest point, 10 feet at its deepest, and 40 feet in length, would have fifty men or more crammed above and below decks. Most privateering voyages employed 100- to 150-ton vessels – perhaps 20 feet wide, 10 to 12 feet deep, and 40 or 45 feet long – with crews that ranged from sixty to ninety men.

These men did not earn equal shares. Poorest paid were the unskilled landsmen who swelled the ranks of boarding parties. Experienced mariners like John Ward received greater shares, and might look to earn between £12 and £15 during a successful cruise. In contrast, a seasoned sailor could earn 10 shillings per month in the Royal Navy. To put this in perspective, a vagabond hired by a farmer as casual labour to bring in the harvest would be paid a shilling per day. In other words, in three months a man such as John Ward could earn £1 10s in the Royal Navy, £4 10s as a masterless agricultural worker (provided he found steady work), or £15 as a privateer, if the voyage was moderately successful. This was a fraction of what ship owners and investors, who risked only money, might earn from an expedition. Nonetheless, viewed in comparison with other work available to masterless men, the attractions of privateering were obvious.

Even given that privateering voyages might be drawn out to a year or longer, and always bearing in mind the chance that a man might earn nothing at all or lose his life to sickness, starvation or battle, the potential profits ensured a ready supply of men of all abilities. Historian Kenneth R. Andrews has summed up the comparison between the Royal Navy and the privateers thus: English seamen 'had nothing to lose but their lives, and who can blame them for valuing themselves at more than ten shillings a month?' Nonetheless, neither common sailor nor petty officer on board a privateer was likely to get rich fast – or even at all. It is true that while at sea they did not have to pay for their victuals or their accommodation, thus creating enforced savings, but these savings were obliterated in the epic revels that rocked port towns whenever privateering crews returned home and received their shares.

Being at sea did not always mean that a man had no expenses on shore. At some point prior to 1603 John Ward married and set up home in the West Country port of Plymouth, far from Faversham, the village of his birth. That Ward and his wife settled in Plymouth speaks to the nature of Ward's work. The port prospered through two industries: the Newfoundland fishery and privateering. The importance of the one is attested by the region's famous son, Sir Walter Raleigh, who accounted the fishery 'the stay of the West Country'. Sir Walter's own career as pirate, privateer and rogue speaks to the importance of the other.

To construct this part of Ward's story we need to fall back on the social history of the lower orders. In 1585, at the dawn of English privateering, it is likely that Ward (perhaps thirty-two years old) was already married or soon would be, for English commoners of the day generally married in their late twenties or early thirties. As in every period, family life for seamen was fraught with difficulties, the constant threat of financial ruin not the least among them. Wives had to eke out an existence while their men were away, and there was always the terrible risk – some might say the inevitable likelihood – of death or maiming at sea, especially among the privateers. There is a reason why literary seamen like Long John Silver and Captains Hook and Ahab are missing limbs, and that reason is to be found equally in accidents amidst the rigging, the perils of hand-to-hand combat, and the gruesomely rudimentary techniques of pre-modern naval surgery.

Supporting a wife and perhaps a family – there are no references to children, but their existence is assumed to be possible – meant that Ward, a boy no longer, had to think of his wages in terms different from his younger crewmates. Home port revels undoubtedly continued, but carelessly spending the whole of his shares could reduce his wife to beggary until he returned from his next venture. In addition, the shares that Ward earned as a common seaman would have been inadequate to meet the needs of two and to pay his Plymouth landlord throughout the year. Ward had a strong motive to work his way through the ranks of privateering seamen. No doubt he felt entitled to hold shipboard office, as he had spent his life on the sea, was able to manage rowdy seamen with dexterity and was a fearless fighter to boot. But it was not enough to be ambitious, capable and deserving. Ward had the misfortune to live in the era that witnessed the birth of the professional mariner.

Ward had known nothing but the sea since a boyhood spent on the Kentish shoreline in search of washed-up treasure. He felt the sea's moods in his blood and could navigate by intuition. But towards the end of the sixteenth century, the highest shipboard officers – captains, ships' masters, pilots and master gunners – began to take apprentices. Seamanship, raised from its mid-century doldrums through the intervention of statesmen like Sir William Cecil and on account of the romance and riches of privateering, had so grown in the national esteem that minor gentlemen and wealthy burghers began to view it as an appropriate vocation for their younger sons. These boys were schooled in letters and their rise created a demand for costly technical literature that was doubly inaccessible to poor and illiterate men like John Ward. Richly illustrated publications such as *The Arte of Navigation* (1561, and at least seven more editions before the end of the century), *The Mariner's Mirrour* (1588) and *The Arte of Shooting in Great Ordnaunce* (1578) provided theoretical guidance to those who lacked experience. But it was not only this abstract learning that thwarted the ambitions of bred seamen like Ward in order to promote this newly founded professional class. It was money.

Apprentices were paid wages, but these were very low, and the recruits were not expected to work any less than other boys or young men on the ships. Vessels that took apprentices therefore acquired cheap labour. The officers who supervised apprentices were paid by the parents of the boys to do so, thus earning money above their own wages and shares. The boys themselves learned advanced technical skills, such as the use of navigational tools like the sextant and Jacob's staff to find latitude, and were groomed for shipboard office. Ship owners received cheap labour, officers earned extra cash and some few boys with the good fortune of moderately wealthy parents leapfrogged into professional sea careers.

John Ward and other bred seamen who had only decades of experience to recommend them, rather than money and connections, paid the price. Bred seamen could work their way into shipboard office, but as the century drew to a close they often found their progress stalled among the quartermasters, pursers and other petty officers, denied promotion to the top ranks of their trade. That John Ward attained the rank of captain must be recognized as a mark of achievement, a recognition of his valuable skills.

The professionalism of seamanship during the sixteenth century can be overstated. Professionals did not completely monopolize the upper ranks of the trade until the late seventeenth or eighteenth century. Nonetheless, this was the trend. Previously, men of John Ward's ability and ambition had routinely worked through the ranks and into the captain's cabin, the most ambitious eventually owning the ships they commanded. Over the course of the seventeenth century this changed, with senior officers increasingly belonging to a professional caste that was socially superior to the common seamen but still inferior to the merchants, gentleman investors and ship owners who hired them. Seamanship, one of the few meritocratic English professions of the early sixteenth century, was becoming, like the rest of English culture, socially stratified.

But John Ward could not be held back. 'Through all ranks of the service' he most surely did rise. That he made it to the pinnacle of the profession – captaincy – is attested by a run-in he had with the officers of Elizabeth's lord admiral, Lord Howard of Nottingham. Before he became a notorious corsair it can be difficult to identify Ward in records of the day, for his is a common enough English surname and there was more than one Ward involved with the privateers. Nonetheless, in 1602 the first likely reference to our John Ward crops up in the High Court of Admiralty records.

Privateering was a murky business and the privateers were unafraid to work the grey areas to their own advantage. To the privateer it was not necessarily the nationality of the ship, or the ship's captain, that mattered, it was the ownership of the cargo. Thus, goods owned by a Spanish merchant that were being shuttled between Venice and Marseilles were a fair prize for an English privateer, even if they were carried by a Dutch ship with an Irish captain. Shipping was an international affair, with vessels often taking one-way cargoes and then looking for more work at their destination. Ship personnel jumped from ship to ship without regard for nationality or even national enemies. A good example of the international, opportunistic outlook of English seamen is found in the autobiography of Edward Coxere, a professional mariner of the mid-seventeenth century. 'I served several masters in the wars between king and parliament at sea', writes Coxere.

> Next I served the Spaniards against the French, then the Hollanders against the English; then I was taken by the English out of a Dunkirker; and then I served the English against the Hollanders; and last I was taken by the Turks, where I was forced to serve then against English, French, Dutch, and Spaniards, and all Christendom. Then, when I was released from them, I was got in a man-of-war against the Spaniards, till at last I was taken prisoner by the Spaniards.

Commercial carriers took advantage of the confusion that resulted from these random alliances, with captains using their own nationality or the flag they were sailing under to disguise the nationality of their cargo. English privateers often exploited the vagaries of the prevailing international situation to take cargoes that belonged to neutral or friendly powers. Such cases were routinely examined in the High Court of Admiralty, which was presided over by the judge and lawyer Sir Julius Caesar (who owed his unlikely name partly to his Italian father and partly to the age of Renaissance in which he lived). Caesar was appointed by, and beholden to, Lord Admiral Nottingham. The lord admiral and Sir Julius sat at the pinnacle of a network of Admiralty officials spread throughout England. The various regions had local chief administrators who went by the title of vice-admiral. And so it was that on 25 August 1602 Christopher Harris, a vice-admiral in England's West Country, sent a letter to Sir Julius Caesar concerning the case of Reynold Symonson, a Dane, who alleged that Captain John Ward of Plymouth had committed an act of piracy by seizing his ship in Spanish waters a year previously. A warrant was issued, but Ward was not arrested.

Taken far more seriously was a breach with which Ward was charged later that same year, when a group of privateering investors, led by William Neele, brought a second suit against Captain John Ward. The charge is unspecified but can be guessed, for privateering captains very often were suspected of embezzling entire cargoes before bringing prizes back to England. This was usually done by taking a prize into Morocco or Ottoman North Africa, where the local authorities were not excessively concerned with the finer points of law so long as neither ship nor cargo belonged to a subject of the Ottoman Empire or Morocco. Once in Salé, Safi, Tunis or Algiers it was a simple matter to sell part or all of a cargo with no one in England the wiser, cheating the crown of its 15 per cent and depriving the ship's owners and investors of their two-thirds of the prize's value. A clever captain would ensure that his crew was well paid to keep quiet, return to sea, take another prize and then make for England. It was an ingenious scheme for the men who worked the ships, though not so popular among the oligarchs who controlled English privateering. And it was out-and-out piracy.

This new charge against Ward quickly resulted in his incarceration. While he was in prison, Sir Julius Caesar served warrant for Ward's arrest for piracy in the case of Reynold Symonson, putting Ward under even more pressure. Then we lose track of Neele's suit against Ward, which seems to have been settled by private arrangement between the two men. Ward was fined £50, a substantial sum, but not much compared to what a captain might make through embezzlement. We may assume that this was not the full extent of what Ward paid to Neele and the other English investors, but only the official fine. Far more interesting is what happened once Neele and Ward reached their agreement. Neele's suit settled, Sir Julius Caesar dropped Symonson's case, leaving the Dane frustrated and failing in one of the basic responsibilities of the High Court of Admiralty. Captain Ward was released. Whether all of this is evidence that it paid for Neele to have friends at the High Court of Admiralty or that Neele paid to have friends there hardly matters.

It reveals how run-of-the-mill cases like that of Reynold Symonson were managed.

This is the extent of the hard evidence that we have of John Ward's career as an English privateer, and it is at least as damning of his social superiors as it is of Ward himself. Within a decade it would become much easier to chart Ward's course. In the early seventeenth century English privateering was a massive industry, with thousands of civilians outfitting well over 100 military ventures against Spanish shipping each year, many such ventures involving three to five ships. That all of this activity was about to come to an abrupt halt on account of a new direction in English foreign policy was the last thing that could be expected. Nonetheless, it was this sudden policy shift that would transform the nearly-anonymous Captain John Ward of Plymouth into the infamous corsair Captain John Ward of Tunis, converting the mariner who worked 'through all ranks of the service in our wars with Spain' into 'the greatest scoundrel that ever sailed from England'.

THREE

The Thief's Path

Sir Robert Cecil and Captain John Ward shared these things: both men succeeded far beyond what might reasonably have been expected of them at birth; both men trained in their chosen fields of endeavour during the reign of Elizabeth I; and both reached their greatest power and material success under James I. This is the full extent of their similarities. Among their differences is the fact that Ward was a notorious outlaw while Cecil was a political insider. Also, John Ward is rarely mentioned in histories of the English nation, but it would be inconceivable to describe either the late reign of Elizabeth I or the early reign of James I without reference to Sir Robert.

Sir Robert Cecil was the second son of that redoubtable English gentleman, Sir William Cecil. Sir William had been chief minister to Elizabeth and the political force behind the creation of the Protestant, patriotic fish day known as Cecil's Fast. Towards the end of the queen's reign Sir William had received the great and rare honour of being elevated from the ranks of the gentry and into the English peerage. As Lord Burleigh, William Cecil had reached his apogee of honours and wealth.

Under the rule of primogeniture the greatest part of Lord Burleigh's lands and wealth, in addition to his title, would devolve to his spendthrift eldest son, Thomas. The old man's political acumen, however, proved to be the far more valuable gift, and this was given by nature to the baron's second son, Robert. While Thomas made himself busy spending the fortune even before the old man's death in 1598, Sir Robert set about creating a political empire that would eclipse the accomplishments of his father. He did so by being the consummate political insider, a power-broker who manipulated affairs of state so that, somehow, the interests of England always ended up in alignment with the interests of Sir Robert.

Sir Robert's accomplishments are all the more remarkable given that he was not merely a younger son, but was born a hunchback as well. To men who interpreted physical abnormalities as missives from God, the sight of a hunchback rolling and limping through the corridors of power caused some alarm. Robert's profligate and care-free elder brother, Thomas, seemed to spring fully formed from the sweating nightmares of their repressed, circumspect father. Robert seemed a ghoul from the collective anxieties of the nation, and he was often portrayed as a conniving and crafty statesman in the tradition of Machiavelli, the dark and twisting habits of his mind alleged to be made plain in his deformed body. 'Robertus Diabollus', or 'Robert the Devil', was whispered behind his back.

Comparisons between Sir Robert and Richard III, the manipulating hunchbacked king of English history, were inevitable. This was all the more true after the memory of the fifteenth-century monarch was made fresh by William Shakespeare's wildly popular play *Richard III*, in which the king is depicted as a man of monstrous ambition, a villainous, murderous machiavel with an insatiable appetite for political intrigue. Incidentally, the play was first performed in 1591, the year of one of Sir Robert's earliest public triumphs, when he was sworn into the queen's Privy Council despite his relative youth. By the time Sir Robert Cecil died, in 1612, comparisons with Richard III were commonplace, made with less subtlety by authors less eloquent than Shakespeare – as in this mock eulogy, penned by an anonymous versifier:

> Here lieth Robin Crooktback, unjustly reckoned
> A Richard the Third, he was Judas the Second . . .
> Richard or Robert, which [was] worse?
> A Crooktback great in state is England's curse.

Queen Elizabeth did not share this prejudice and Sir Robert, despite enmity, jealousy and physical deformity, would become, by the end of her reign, the most powerful man of the realm – much as Robert's father had been Elizabeth's most powerful courtier at the beginning of her time on the throne. Like his father, too, by the time of his death Sir Robert had been elevated into the peerage. But while Sir William had attained only the modest rank of baron, his younger son would rise much higher, eventually becoming Earl of Salisbury.

Sir Robert Cecil had managed the Anglo-Spanish war ever since the lord admiral, at the queen's behest, had begun to issue letters of reprisal to English privateers in 1585. Sir Robert's involvement in the conflict, as in other state affairs, was not limited to his role as a senior government official. He also profited as a private citizen. The Cecil family archives reveal that Sir Robert was a regular investor in privateering voyages, often in conjunction with the lord admiral himself. Between them Sir Robert and Lord Admiral Charles Howard shared control of the progress of the hostilities: that they also invested as war profiteers might beg some questions about ethics. Worse, as we shall see, modern historians have also suggested that these men not only profited from inside knowledge, but may also have misappropriated state funds to underwrite their investments. Be this as it may, in 1603, the year that Elizabeth died and James ascended the English throne, it was his inside knowledge of state affairs that proved to be of greatest benefit to Sir Robert. While the soldiers and sailors who worked the privateers were caught at a disadvantage by the end of English privateering, Sir Robert was not.

In 1602 Sir Robert Cecil, already familiar to King James VI of Scotland as the chief minister of the queen of England (James had once referred to Cecil as 'king there, in effect'), addressed the issue of succession to the English throne in a set of secret letters between the two men. The final years of Elizabeth's reign were a time of great anxiety for the English, for the Virgin Queen lacked a biological heir and had refused to name a successor. The House of Tudor had risen amidst the terrible dynastic struggles of the fifteenth century, the Wars of the Roses, and none in England wanted to see a return to strife when the Tudor line ended.

While counsellors and ministers pleaded with the queen to name a successor for the good of her realm, Sir Robert surveyed the potential candidates and struck on the Scottish king as the most likely. Through his clandestine correspondence with James, carried on without the knowledge of Elizabeth, Sir Robert laid the groundwork for the smooth transition of the English crown from the queen to her Scottish cousin.

Elizabeth, however, continued to refuse to name an heir, even when it was apparent that she was to die within days, if not hours. On 21 March 1603, as select members of her Privy Council gathered around her bed, the queen, who was too weak to speak, was called upon to listen to a list of possible successors and signal with her hand when she heard the name she favoured. Reports of the outcome of this parlour game varied: some maintained that the dying queen made no signal at all and some held that she 'put her hand to her head when the King of Scots was named to succeed her', while others described how she turned her hand 'in the form of a circle' at the reading of James's name. She died within hours.

Whether the queen was delirious or lucid; whether she had a headache, a spasm or really did favour King James as her heir – this is unknown and irrelevant. Sir Robert Cecil had, several days previously, written the proclamation that would name James as heir to the English throne and had even sent a copy north for the putative king's approval. The story goes that James first read the draft proclamation on the very day of the queen's death, perhaps even as a core group of royal councillors and noblemen signed the proclamation in the English capital and Sir Robert himself read it out to the crowd that quickly assembled in the streets of London.

Sir Robert proved prescient not only in the matter of the royal succession. Most of the king's English subjects were surprised when one of James's first acts was to revoke the letters of reprisal that had been issued under Elizabeth, the documents that provided a legal basis for English privateering. Sir Robert Cecil, however, was not caught wrong-footed, for he was well apprised of the new king's wish for Anglo-Spanish peace and had already divested himself of war investments. And, in addition to the financial benefits Cecil realized by being a foreign policy insider, the new king of England, recognizing the debt that he owed Cecil, bestowed upon Sir Robert his first aristocratic title, naming him Baron Cecil of Essingden.

In his *History of the Administration of the Royal Navy*, published in 1896, Michael Oppenheim wrote that 'the first wish of the new monarch [James I] was to obtain peace with Spain, a desire for which modern historians have unanimously praised him'. Noting this praise, Oppenheim goes on to signal his dissent, suggesting that 'it may be at least a matter for debate whether the continuance of war until Spain was bled to death would not have been ethically justifiable, politically expedient, and commercially profitable'.

There is no question that the conflict had been politically expedient, for Elizabeth's subjects had demanded military operations against Catholic Spain as insistently as the Spanish king had himself assaulted the queen's Protestant co-religionists on the European continent. That Anglo-Spanish hostilities had been commercially profitable is also true, at least for the crown, ship owners and investors, if not always for the seamen who worked, and often died, on the privateers. Nonetheless, that the tiny island of England could ever have bled the mighty Spanish Empire to death is entirely unlikely, a fantasy projected back from a position of British naval superiority in the nineteenth century. It is a similarly fantastic notion that ethical justification could be found for the war itself, especially given the means with which it was fought.

In 1603 England had been in conflict with Spain for almost two decades. The war, rooted in religious prejudice, pitted the king of Spain – master of an immense empire that embraced all of modern

Spain and Portugal as well as parts of the Netherlands, Italy, North Africa and the majority of the Americas – against England, whose imperial grandeur all lay in the future. It was, to quote historian A.L. Rowse, 'the clash between the Spanish world-empire and the heretical half-an-island'.

That the English were able to stand against the Spanish at all is largely due to the queen's rejection of traditional naval actions in favour of privateering. Staged encounters like the Battle of the Spanish Armada of 1588 or the 1596 English assault on Cadiz occurred periodically throughout the war, but only when Elizabeth was left without options. And despite the signal English victory of 1588, in which the English fleet broke and routed the larger Spanish Armada, Philip of Spain had an infinitely more powerful navy than Elizabeth. In 1588 it was not modesty but incredulous gratitude that compelled the queen, far from gloating, fervently to attribute victory over the armada to God alone, who had sent a 'Protestant wind' to blow with the English ships and smite the Spanish.

It was far less chancy to leave the work of fighting the Spanish in the hands of private citizens than to hope that God would repeat this performance. And it was cheaper, too. Nonetheless, English privateering was a ruthless, ugly system. Whatever the patriotism and valour of individual commanders and seamen, the privateers as a lot were as savage as the wolf-pack that feeds upon the sick and the weak. English privateers haunted Spanish sea lanes to the New World and trading routes in the Mediterranean, melting away at the approach of military ships, re-forming into deadly groups and surrounding vessels that lagged behind convoys or were battered in storms. Coming upon such helpless prey, the English sea dogs were merciless, firing chain shot into riggings and using mortars (all too appropriately called murderers) to scatter round shot and jagged fragments of lead, stone and glass among Spanish crews. In this brutal, thuggish combat the highest strategic objective was the richest prize. Fighting the Spanish by these means saved the queen much expense, and it may well have won honour and wealth for the individuals who served on and financed the voyages, but it was not an honourable war.

Sir Robert Cecil had been elevated to the peerage as reward for delivering the English crown to King James, and he would be further elevated for negotiating the end of Anglo-Spanish hostilities. Never mind that Cecil himself had reaped substantial profit from the conflict over the preceding decade: with single-minded determination he set about brokering the peace. In August 1604 a Spanish delegation arrived in England and the Treaty of London was signed. War was over.

Cecil was again showered with titles, honours and riches. The recently created Baron Cecil of Essingden was now made Viscount Cranborne, a title he held for less than a year before he was made Earl of Salisbury, his highest elevation and the title he held until his death in 1612. These titles were not the only plums given by the king to his faithful servant. Peace, for the Earl of Salisbury, also brought generous grants of lands and riches, commercial monopolies on luxury products, and lucrative bureaucratic posts.

The accession of James I to the English throne had served Robert Cecil well, and in truth he served the crown and commons of England diligently too.

But so did other men, men who lacked the politesse and connections that came from high birth. These men had served their country by going into battle believing propaganda about Spanish tyranny and Jesuit plots. For these men no allowance was made and no care taken as the nation was thrown, abruptly, from war into peace. The professional mariners – those who had entered the trade as apprentices to officers rather than by working through the ranks – found work on the commercial ships that continued to sail, money and connections serving them well once again. But for those who had only the experience of war to recommend them, whose skills included the forcible boarding of other ships, and the ruthless murder and oppression of the crews they fought against, for these men there was no work.

Several months after King James VI of Scotland became King James I of England the mayor of Plymouth wrote to Sir Robert Cecil with the following complaint:

Now of late, since our late Queen's death, there do daily resort hither such a great number of sailors, mariners and other masterless men that heretofore have been at sea in men-of-war [i.e. fighting ships], and being now restrained from that course, do still remain here and pester our town, which is already overcharged with many poor people. And some of them do daily commit such intolerable outrages as they do steal and take away boats in the night out of the harbour.

Little wonder that the mayor should be alarmed that so many were milling about his port. In the hearts of these coarse, ragged and hungry men desperation and betrayal fermented into resentment and discontent. Of such men, men who had known the horrors of sickness and hunger on board the privateers, who had doled out and received the violence of brutal hand-to-hand combat, and who had rejoiced in the looting and pillaging of other seamen: of such men anything could be expected, and their presence was to be feared.

The end of privateering had left Captain Ward ragged, like so many other seamen. His best years were gone: balding, thickset and battle-scarred, he seemed stagnant as ballast bilge. Near Plymouth harbour he and his wife kept house, rent in arrears. Regardless, Ward made the rounds of the alehouses where 'he would never out of their damnable pit if there were either money in his purse or creditable chalk in his host's hand'. The same witness, writing six years after the fact – when John Ward had long left the tumbledown harbour taverns of Plymouth behind – also offers a colourful description of Ward's behaviour:

Oaths were almost as ordinary with him as words, so that he seldom spoke a sentence but one was a syllable. He would sit melancholy, speak doggedly, curse the time, repine at other men's good fortunes, and complain of the hard crosses [that] attended his own. . . . He was commonly called by the name of Jack Ward

[and] was welcome into any tap-house more for love of his coin than love of his company.

It beggars the imagination to conceive how a man who had attained the post of captain among the privateers could be brought so low so fast. Nonetheless, to escape mounting debt Ward swallowed his pride and enlisted aboard the *Lion's Whelp*, a Royal Navy vessel. Neither the work nor the discipline suited him. As a privateer he had been king at sea, captain of a private vessel. To return into the ranks at his age was an ignominious retreat. Worse, whereas on the privateers decisions on strategy and destination were discussed with the crew and put to a vote, providing at least an illusion of consultation, aboard the *Lion's Whelp* there were only orders and the lash. The money – what little there was – must have been welcome, but it is impossible that Ward could have counted himself fortunate to get it. While his soul soured John Ward kept himself alive to opportunity. One night, late in 1603, his chance came.

After a hard day of idleness the men of His Majesty's Ship the *Lion's Whelp* liked nothing better than to retire to the taverns of Portsmouth, the vessel's home port. The officers, themselves tired of lingering in port without sailing orders, were willing to let the seamen squander their wages ashore rather than have discontent below decks.

Andrew Barker, mariner, was an acquaintance, though no friend, of Ward's from Queen Elizabeth's wars. He tells us that it was during one of these unofficial shore leaves that John Ward first sowed sedition among his shipmates. Once the men were well into their cups, Ward tested the waters. 'My mates,' he began, 'what's to be done?'

Here's a scurvy world, and as scurvily we live in it. We feed here upon the water, on the king's salt beef, without ere a penny to buy us bissell when we come ashore. Here's brine, meat good for ravening stomachs, but where is your brim cup, and your full carouse that can make a merry heart? Where are the days that we cried 'Cargo in'? . . . God's blood! What would you have me say? Where are the days that have been, and the seasons that we have seen, when we might sing, swear, drink, drab, and kill men as your cake-maker doth flies? When we might do what we list, and the law would bear us out? Nay, when we might lawfully do that we shall be hanged for [if] we do now? When the whole Sea was our Empire, where we robbed at will, and the world but our garden where we walked for sport?

The response of the sailors was to berate the old man for reminiscing on better times when those days were gone.

Foh, por! quoth the whole knot. What should we talk of that now? To think of those happinesses past is as much for a man to remember his mother's flesh, and the favour of her countenance, seven years after her bones are rotten. The days were then clear, and they are now cloudy. . . . To speak of that golden world is but like knocking our lips against cherries while others sweeten their mouths with the meat.

Ah but, Ward assured them, there could be a return to those heady times. He blamed the current state of affairs on the timidity of the new generation.

'Tis certain, quoth Ward, but if true resolution were not bankrupt in England, if we had not women's hearts to bearded faces, nay, and we were not all cowards, but of my mind, manhood should not be thus fubbed as it has been. I know a redress. I know a means – and yet, 'tis no matter for it.

His appeal touched a nerve.

Having licked over their lips, the whole gang set agog. And now there was no persuasions nor protestations lacking till they had digested the whole dish, no vows to the furtherance of the business, no oaths wherein they were not bound to be constant and confident, no desperate, drunken means wanting to the sealing up of the bargain.

Ward laid out his plan: 'Brave hearts, since you have this voluntary sworn to me your resolutions, know then, there is a gentleman of this country, who being a recusant hath sold the whole estate of his living to a gentleman of Winchester.' Ward doled out details of how the recusant, a secret Catholic, had cashed in lands and goods in preparation for flight to France, where he and his family could practise their religion openly, without fear of persecution. Even now, Ward continued, the man had purchased a small ship of some 25 tons burden and was ballasting it with English gold.

Ward's approach was inspired. Recognizing that, like him, any man working the *Lion's Whelp* had deliberately stoppered his ears to the siren song of piracy, Ward cast his appeal in terms of a lark, a harmless adventure, a brief, nostalgic return to the days when Protestant Englishmen enriched themselves even while punishing faithless Catholics. Ward concluded his speech by stressing the temptation of ready cash and delivering a final dig at the virility of men who chafed under the witless leadership of the Royal Navy.

I speak it of mine own knowledge. He hath embarked above two thousand pound in ready clinks, besides plate and household provision. If we shall strike a hand, say. You see how easily it is to be done. If not, show yourselves cowards and faint hearted still, and live as beggars and fools, under the check of every knave all the days of your lives.

The next day: idle drudgery aboard the *Lion's Whelp*. In the evening Ward led his shipmates in a rowdy protest over their scant supper and weak ale, accusing the steward of lining his pockets while the men starved. Sensing an ugly mood, the officers allowed the crew shore leave once again, letting them sup at their own charge. They made for the same tavern, hooting and laughing as they laid plans for the capture and, sweeter yet, the spending of the recusant's fortune. Perhaps they even told themselves that they could take the recusant's money and be back to the *Lion's Whelp* with no one the wiser. Back in their chairs from the previous night, the tavern master's fine ale before them, the confederates started down the slippery slope, taking a page from the pirate's book and holding a free election of captain. To nobody's surprise Jack Ward was voted into the office. In keeping with the mood Captain Ward confirmed his appointment by draining a brim pot of ale even as his raucous crew fell to their knees in mock deference. They acted with the opposite of discretion.

Also dining at the tavern, a townsman noted the ugly tone of the proceedings and bent an ear to the mariners' talk. It was not long before he had a fair idea of their plans, realizing with a start that the ship they intended to bring under the command of their shabby captain was none other than that of his country cousin, ready to flee on the next tide. Coins clanked and flashed amidst a half-finished meal and the man hurried into the darkening evening.

Late into the night Ward and his crew continued their revels, slipping out to the nearby brothel in small groups but mostly drinking away the last of their short wages. Around midnight several passed out on their benches, and two hours later all were scattered about the small tavern, snoring. Ward, successfully initiated into his command, had nursed his beer, sipping while others gulped, and kept his wits about him. By the time the tavern master retired to his own quarters only Ward was awake to nod to him, promising not to let his men ransack the room if they should awake.

That night might fairly be considered a turning point in the latter years of John Ward's life. More, it was that rare thing, a moment in which it is impossible for a man not to be aware that he is making a life-altering choice. John Ward, mariner, could let his friends sleep off their revels, watch dawn break the darkness, and with them shuffle back to the *Lion's Whelp*, suffering only the mild embarrassment of having let drunken boasts outstrip good sense. Or, Captain John Ward could rouse his crew of pirates before dawn and lead them into an unknown future, one far more likely to bring death in battle or at the hangman's noose than to end in freedom and riches.

It was well before sunrise when Ward roused his crew and led them out of the tavern. Through dark streets a small band of ragged men made their way to the port. Liberating two skiffs, they rowed to the recusant's anchorage.

The decks of the recusant's ship – only a barque, really – were dark, quiet, deserted. Ward snorted in amazed contempt to find no watch awake. Silently, gently, he led his men out of the rowing boats and on to the decks of the ship. Signalling them to various posts, he led a small party to the ladder below decks. In the darkness they found two bleary mariners, shocked out of sleep by Ward's men. A cursory inspection turned up no other guard. Binding these two, Ward raised anchor and, fisherman's instincts perfectly tuned, rode the tides out of the harbour. With Captain Ward in command, the sails of the barque unfurled in the morning wind. Ward gazed in satisfaction as the sweating men, heads throbbing and stomachs acrid from the previous night's revels, were gilded by the rising sun.

The idyll was not to last. Ward's command as a pirate captain very nearly brought him to ruin not once but twice in those early days. The first crisis came while the tiny barque was still within sight of the Isle of Wight, barely out of Portsmouth harbour. The tale that follows comes from the report of the two seamen who had been discovered asleep below decks by Ward's men.

As day spread across the sea the sails of the barque were tugged west. Ward directed his men to follow the wind and make good their escape. Safely at sea, Ward sent for the two captive mariners, sole guardians of the barque during the night watches. He demanded of them why they were the only men aboard a ship so richly freighted, and the news they delivered nearly incited a mutiny against his nascent captaincy. Ward must have cursed his own stupidity and the carelessness of his crew as the captives explained the situation.

While Ward and his co-conspirators drank and whored the previous night the rich recusant had been warned of their intentions. Learning of the threat, he had brought his treasure back to shore and placed it under lock and key at an inn named the Red Lion. There it was diligently guarded by his servants, including the majority of the seamen. The two left on board had been ordered to watch over the provisions, the ship's supplies and the barque itself. These men shook with fear as they told their tale, lamenting their irresponsibility in falling asleep. Had they been vigilant they could have roused the harbour watch at the approach of the thieves, or, at the very least, they themselves could have escaped.

Captain Ward manned himself better than the distraught prisoners, but he, too, must have felt the cold creep of fear. To any observer, the condition of the trussed captives could not have seemed further removed from that of the pirate captain who stood over them. In reality it was almost identical. The bound men were at the mercy of the crew who had caught them sleeping, and so was Ward. Like any pirate captain Ward had nothing but reputation to bind his men to him. The crew had elected him captain and these same men could revoke this authority, granting it to another. Captains so deposed did not often last long among the crew they had formerly commanded. If Ward hoped to witness another sunrise he would have to salvage the situation without delay.

A thorough search of the barque bought Ward a few minutes but confirmed the story told by the captive seamen. 'The rogues all began now to be rank-mad,' the captives later testified. 'There was then such cursing, such swearing, such banning. There was a pox of thee, a pox of thee, and a plague of us all.' Ward watched his men, letting them indulge their discontent and expressing a bit of his own ('Ward raps out oaths like pellets out of a piece,' we are told), while he took stock of the situation and prepared to reassert his command.

The search of the barque, while failing to turn up money, jewels, plate or any other valuables, had yielded much rich food, provisions laid in by the gentleman for the voyage and to cushion his family's arrival in France. Ward had these carried on to the deck. As the men cursed their misfortune, Ward's voice rang out in an unexpectedly cheerful tone. 'Come, let's be merry, my hearts!' he called out. 'The goldfinches we came for are flown out of their nest. Little succour is to be found here, and to go ashore we shall be sure to be hanged there. Here we are fallen desperately into the pitfall, and there we have brought our necks just to the noose. . . . Come, let's be merry and freely fat ourselves with their fodder.' Gesturing at venison and turkey pies, choice meats, fresh loaves, bottles of fine vintage and casks of ale, Ward affected an air of great generosity, as if it were his alone to share or withhold at his own pleasure. 'Here is good cheer.' Making an absurd reference to the biblical parable of the Good Samaritan (who, hearing a plea for help, saved the life of a man who had been beaten and robbed by thieves), Ward delivered his peroration: 'It is bootless these days to lie in a ditch and cry for help, since every man is bound to thrust out his hand to help himself. Therefore, my hearts, let us frolic with this and live in hope that our fortunes will be better.'

As the men accepted Ward's largesse in sharing the goods that they themselves had stolen, he piped up again, bidding them to compare their current fortunes with navy life. 'What say you, my bloods! Who would be aboard the *Lion's Whelp*, with bare and hungry allowance of cold fish and naked cheese?' Prising open a crate of excellent wine, Ward passed the bottles around. It was not yet noon, but they fell to drinking with vigour. 'Here, my mates,' he called out, raising a bottle in toast. 'Here is a health to our good fortunes, and to the poor [fortunes] of the hangman. We know the worst, and let's therefore hope for the best.' Sails set, the ship ran steadily west along the southern coast of England as the fledgling pirates drank deep.

Ward had postponed rebellion, but no more. If he failed to come up with a plan that would justify his command, he knew that his as yet obedient men would turn on him. Like the wretched watchmen from the previous night, Captain Ward was captive to the contempt of the pirate crew.

As Ward drank and feasted with his men, he continued to drop references to the hangman, for only fear of retribution and a bit of luck could save his captaincy. They spent that evening and night off the rocky coast of Cornwall. The next morning dawned fair. As the stolen barque continued its progress along the coast Ward kept keen watch for another, any other, ship. It was not long before he spotted one, a smallish ocean-going craft of about 70 tons' burden, bearing six cannon for defence against pirates and flying the French flag. Such a ship was by no means easy prey for the over-manned and under-armed Channel runner that Ward commanded, but he was not in a position to be choosy.

Ward called the men together on the barque's deck, outlined the grave state of their current fortunes and proposed a way forward. He painted a grim picture. By abandoning their posts on the *Lion's Whelp*, he alleged, they had all become treasonous deserters, derelict in their duty to the king. On top of this, the theft of the recusant's ship was out-and-out piracy. They were outlaws.

My comrades, quoth he, you know we have proceeded so far into the thief's path that to return back we shall be stopped with a [hangman's] halter. To trust to the mercy of the law is as good as for a man to chop his hand upon a Razor and see if it will cut. Therefore, since to retire can allow us no safety, it will be wisdom here to provide for our safeguard.

Ward proposed that the seamen continue down the thief's path, with him still at their head. Pointing to the French ship approaching from the east and drawing on his experience in privateering, he outlined a daring plan of how the tiny barque, lacking cannon or even small arms, could capture the larger ship, fully armed for defence. So persuasive was Ward that the men accepted his account of the perils of surrendering to the English authorities, despite common knowledge that deserters and pirate crews were not often sent to the gallows: that fate was reserved for ringleaders and commanders. Having won this rhetorical battle, Ward easily persuaded his men to go along with his desperate plan for the capture of the French merchantman.

The captain of the French vessel must have viewed the approaching barque with apprehension, despite its small size. Since the accession of King James, Cornwall had become well known as a haven for petty pirates, many of whom worked from small barques and skiffs not much different from the English ship before him. The Frenchman's fears were reduced as the undersized vessel drew near, for it was unarmed and its entire crew consisted of the captain on deck and four men in the rigging.

As the barque came within hailing distance of the French merchantman it identified itself as an English ship making the run from Plymouth to the south of Ireland. The captain of the barque, a short, bald old man speaking mangled French, declared himself undermanned and desperately afraid of being overtaken by pirates. This was his first command, he explained, and he was not yet skilled at navigation or defence. Enquiring where the merchantman was bound, he asked whether the barque might accompany them, the better to provide protection against pirates. The French captain laughed; it was obvious that the ageing Englishman was none too skilled, for even during this short parley the English barque moved in and out of shouting range. The captain and his scanty crew could barely govern the tiny vessel. The Frenchman agreed to accompany the barque to Ireland, where he himself was bound.

Whatever apprehension the first appearance of the barque had raised dissipated over the next several hours as its men continued their struggle for control of the ship. As the day passed the garrulous captain of the barque, identifying himself as John Ward, exchanged news with the French captain, the two of them speaking the fluid seaman's lingua franca that combined gabbled fragments and scraps of various Western European and Mediterranean tongues, a bizarre amalgam that was clear enough to men who shared decks and hammocks with shipmates of all nations. Captain Ward spoke of the coming of a Scottish king to the English throne, the end of English privateering, and the hard times for English seamen that followed, while the French captain told of the affairs of seamen on the continent. By the time the sun began to descend the crew of the merchantman had grown accustomed to the erratic course of their companion vessel, and had hardly noticed that, over the last couple of hours, it had begun to stray out of shouting range less and less often and was now more likely to make sudden jags in towards the French ship.

The sun was showing red when the English ship veered in, the hull of the barque bumping the merchantman. Ward, halfway through his recitation of a ballad of the recent arrest of the great English seaman Sir Walter Raleigh, gave a powerful shout of 'Now, my masters, for us!' Men swarmed out from the hatches and on to the barque's deck, while the barque's small crew lashed the ships together. Drawing a knife with one hand and grasping a cudgel with the other, Ward led his men over the rails, catching the French captain and crew entirely off guard.

The man who minutes earlier had seemed but an incompetent fool promoted beyond his merits had revealed his true identity: Captain John Ward, soon to be notorious. Armed only with knives and clubs, outnumbered and outgunned, Ward and his men captured the larger ship. 'It is without question', reported the two seamen who were Ward's first victims, 'that this was the original and first beginning of Ward's piracy, even so base and so low.' As evening turned to night, the French crew found themselves trussed below the decks of their ship, sharing company with the two 'poor snakes' who had slept through their watch on the recusant's barque. As the men from the barque told of how they were caught, Ward, now in command of two ships, his crew working the riggings of both, turned east. The small convoy headed for Plymouth, a town familiar to all as the chief port of English privateering during the Anglo-Spanish war.

Putting in to Cawsand Bay, just east of Plymouth harbour, the pirates guarded the prisoners while their captain made his way into the town. Two days had elapsed since they had deserted the *Lion's Whelp* in Portsmouth. Ward was not yet a wanted man in these parts, but he soon would be. Hurrying into taverns and flophouses, Ward scouted out his old privateering mates before making his way towards home. He woke his wife and they spoke briefly. Then Ward led a ragged band of mariners to where the merchantman and barque were moored.

The men Ward had enticed back with him had not had an easy time of it since the accession of King James, and they looked like the filthy beggars and vagabonds they had become. Their clothes worn to rags, none needed more than a small bag to hold his worldly goods. To the mayor of Plymouth these were derelicts and vagrants, a triple threat to the king's peace, the property of men and the virtue of women. But to Captain Ward these impoverished men were alchemists, powerful magicians who could take the iron of cannon and the lead of shot, the steel of knife and sword, and turn it into purest gold.

Returning to his boats, Ward had his captives carried from below decks and rowed to shore. There they were left, ashamed to have been made to submit before a weak foe but thankful to be alive. Ward's luck still holding, his crew, with renewed faith in their captain, took advantage of an early morning wind. The merchantman and barque turned south-west, making for the Straits of Gibraltar and the Mediterranean.

Ward had weathered the first challenge to his captaincy. But it would only be a matter of weeks before the better part of his crew would be locked in an Ottoman prison, Ward himself a condemned man thrust before the all-powerful pasha of Algiers. The second, and far greater, crisis of Ward's command was looming.

FOUR

Barbary Pirate

 During the Anglo-Spanish wars Captain Richard Gifford had served under Sir Francis Drake and Sir John Hawkins and held commissions issued directly from Sir Robert Cecil and Sir Julius Caesar; after the wars he became a pirate-hunter, a freelance mercenary hired by the grand duke of Florence to extirpate the infamous nest of sea rovers at Algiers. John Ward, on the other hand, is infamous for betraying his nation, first by deserting his post aboard the *Lion's Whelp* and turning pirate, and afterwards by sailing with the Barbary Corsairs, eventually converting to Islam. On the face of it, Gifford seems the honourable man, Ward an opportunistic rogue. Appearances can be deceiving.

While it is true that Gifford was often associated with state-sanctioned enterprises, it is also true that he used these for personal advancement, even at the cost of the lives and fortunes of his countrymen. Captain Ward, on the other hand, betrayed England only if you consider England an abstract concept. As for individual Englishmen, and especially English mariners, time and again Ward proved to be a faithful friend, even at risk to his own life and to his own impoverishment.

This would be nothing more than a study in contrasting person-alities were it not for the fact that Captain Gifford's lack of personal honour, having already resulted in the execution of some dozen Englishmen at Algiers, was also the cause of the detention and torture of Ward's men, and very nearly of Ward himself. The two men's stories inextricably, if briefly, intertwine at Algiers.

British histories of the Anglo-Spanish hostilities of 1585 to 1603 generally follow two courses. One is a story of state-financed military ventures against the forts and settlements of the Spanish mainland, in the Americas and on Spanish territories in Europe. The other tells of privateering expeditions, financed by civilian investors, in which the greatest tactical objective, like that of any commercial venture, was to maximize profits. It is the former, the one which most resembles legitimate military action, that has received the greatest attention from historians, while the latter usually is given only brief mention. The story of Captain Richard Gifford demonstrates the folly in treating these histories separately.

In 1595 Gifford served in the last stand of two of the greatest mariners of the previous generation, accompanying Drake and Sir John Hawkins on their disastrous final expedition in the Spanish Caribbean. This state-sponsored venture, it was hoped, would replicate the astounding success of Drake's strike against Spanish America in the late 1570s, or even the moderate outcome of his foray into the Caribbean in 1585. Instead, it seemed that the law of diminishing returns doomed the expedition from the start; the voyage yielded sickness and calamity in place of riches and honours. Drake and Hawkins, both old men, succumbed to the often fatal combination of shipboard enervation and tropical disease.

Gifford, a captain in the fleet, survived disease but was taken by the Spanish during one of several engagements that the English provoked and lost. After four years of shuffling through various Spanish prisons, he escaped and found passage to England. Arriving in London in March 1600, penniless and bedraggled, he immediately contacted the most powerful man in the realm: Queen Elizabeth's secretary of state, Sir Robert Cecil. Cecil evidently took pity on the man, for less than a year later Gifford was once again at sea, now captain on a privateering mission whose investors included Cecil himself and Thomas Sackville, Baron Buckhurst, both members of the queen's Privy Council.

Cecil personally approached Sir Julius Caesar, judge in the High Court of Admiralty, to secure the letters of reprisal necessary to license Gifford as a privateer. In this, as in all else connected with Gifford, Cecil maintained a cloak of secrecy that concealed his actions for over three and a half centuries. Only since the 1960s has the Cecil family allowed historians to peruse all of Sir Robert's papers. After a comparison between these and the state papers housed in the National Archives at Kew, the story of Sir Robert's wartime investments was pieced together by historians including Lawrence Stone and K.R. Andrews.

Caesar authorized Gifford's letters of reprisal on the pretext that Gifford was sailing on a top-secret mission to gather anti-Spanish intelligence. It is odd that Cecil invented such an elaborate fiction, for his political influence was such that Sir Julius would gladly have issued letters of reprisal for the asking. Cecil's motive is stunning even by the standards of the corrupt bureaucratic culture of the day. By pretending that Gifford's mission was to spy for the English crown, Cecil, one of the wealthiest men in England, was able to provide his stake in the voyage out of state funds allocated for intelligence work.

In any event, Captain Gifford ignored his purported mission, which would have had him haunt the Atlantic coast of Spain to intercept ships and communications. Heading directly for the Straits of Gibraltar, Gifford entered the Mediterranean and joined company with Captain Hugh Griffith, a known pirate already indicted *in absentia* by the High Court of Admiralty. Gifford and Griffith captured a ship carrying grain from Sicily to Spain. The fact that Sicily at this time was part of the Spanish Empire made this fair prize for English privateers, though such action clearly lay beyond the terms of Gifford's official brief. Taking their prize to Algiers, the English captains extorted a ransom for men, ship and cargo. This must be counted an act of piracy, for English privateers were required to bring prizes home to England. Captain Gifford had now abandoned his mission, deserted the service and broken English law.

Incredibly, Gifford's next move was to offer, for a fee, to escort from Algiers to Livorno the ship and crew that he had just bullied and blackmailed. This northern Italian port was part of the territories controlled by the grand duke of Florence, a Spanish ally. Arriving at Livorno the Sicilian captain reported directly to the authorities, who had Gifford and his men arrested and imprisoned. From his cell Gifford piteously wrote to his influential English investors, pleading for help.

Instead of disavowing knowledge of Gifford or rebuking him for exceeding his brief, the privateer's patrons exerted their influence on his behalf. Back in Tuscany, the grand duke, though describing Gifford and the pirate Griffith as 'herrings of one barrel', nonetheless professed himself unwilling to 'offend any of the signors of England'. The duke held his nose and freed Gifford, who now could boast of having been imprisoned by both the Spanish and the Florentines.

Gifford returned to England and in 1602 shipped out to sea once more, financed by the same backers and charged with the same spurious mission. Once again sailing past Spain's Atlantic seaboard, where, as before, he was supposed to intercept Spanish communications, Gifford made his way through the Straits. This time he committed acts of open piracy, capturing French and Dutch commercial shipping and selling the plunder to English merchants at Algiers and, of all places, Livorno. So clear-cut was the case that when the French and Dutch merchants took the matter to the High Court of Admiralty, Gifford was apprehended and imprisoned. Nonetheless, Sir Robert Cecil once again acted behind the scenes, and in short order Sir Julius Caesar reassigned responsibility for Gifford's crimes to the English merchants who had purchased his booty in Algiers and Livorno. Gifford walked a free man, leaving the merchants to suffer the consequences.

So far Captain Gifford's story furnishes but more evidence of how English privateering, as administered through the offices of the Admiralty, was rigged to benefit insiders, even in the face of blatant wrongdoing. When Gifford next sailed, however, in the early months of 1603, Cecil was absent from his backers. The Secretary of

State was at that moment engineering the transition of the English crown from Elizabeth to James of Scotland, and he knew that James favoured peace with Spain. For once Gifford was not on the inside track, and the end of privateering in 1603 caught him, like other English seamen, off guard. When word caught up with him, Gifford ordered his men to return to England, but not before they had dropped him – once again – at Livorno.

Unlikely though it may seem, Gifford was warmly welcomed in the port. Perhaps his connections to the former queen's Privy Council impressed the Florentines. At any rate, no sooner had he arrived than he received a military commission from the grand duke. The sometime privateer, sometime pirate, sometime inmate of the duke's own prison, was to lead an undercover raid against the Barbary Corsairs at Algiers.

In 1603 Algiers, Tunis and Tripoli were the principal ports of the Barbary Corsairs, a confluence of Muslim privateers sailing in the service of the Ottoman Empire. Algiers was the largest and westernmost of these ports, and it served as the base from which the Barbary Corsairs launched their attacks upon Spanish, French and Florentine shipping. As we have already seen, Gifford had used Algiers as a dumping ground for illegitimate booty in 1601 and 1602. The Ottoman pasha there tolerated such activity on the grounds that, so long as Gifford and his ilk did not attack Ottoman shipping, it was no concern of his if Englishmen broke international laws. Given that the privateers still had to pay Algerian port fees and customs duties on their booty, the Algerian state made good profit by looking the other way, while Algerian merchants benefited by buying looted cargoes at cut-rate prices. With the end of privateering, when many English sailors turned to piracy, the pasha at Algiers was content initially to have them work their trade from his port.

Then, in 1603, Captain Richard Gifford, secretly in the pay of the grand duke of Florence, arrived under the entirely believable pretext that he had turned pirate. The port authorities allowed his ship a berth. That night Gifford repaid the pasha's hospitality by setting fire to the Algerian galley fleet. He then fled under cover of darkness, in his haste stranding members of his crew in the port they had just assaulted.

The raid caused little harm to the Algerians, who were able to douse the flames before they spread, but did result in considerable material and physical suffering for other Englishmen. So annoyed was the pasha that he banned English ships from his port. Janissaries, the hardened Ottoman soldiers whose very name inspired terror throughout Western Europe, swept through city and port, seizing any and all English citizens. English merchants were arrested and had their goods confiscated as reparations for damages caused by Gifford. John Bannister, an officer on board an English merchant-man named the *Hopewell*, later testified before the High Court of Admiralty that he was arrested and tortured. Even Bannister, however, would have counted himself among the fortunate, for he lived to return to England. Less fortunate were a dozen other Englishmen captured in the sweep, including the crewmen abandoned in Algiers by Captain Gifford. All were executed.*

Enter John Ward.

Captain Ward and his men had been busy en route from Plymouth to Algiers. On the Atlantic side of the Straits of Gibraltar they captured a Dutch flyboat, a large commercial carrier that was, incidentally, quite well suited to piracy. Ward crammed the Dutch crew into the recusant's barque which the men of the *Lion's Whelp* had liberated from Portsmouth, and left them to make their own way. Continuing in command of the flyboat, Ward captured a setty, another commercial carrier. With three ships under his command (the French merchantman captured off Cornwall, the Dutch flyboat and the setty), Captain Ward arrived at Algiers.

---

* Gifford may have left these men 'on the hook' literally as well as figuratively. One of the ways in which executions were carried out at Algiers at this time was through 'ganching', in which a man was impaled on a huge iron hook, hoisted into public view and left to bleed to death.

The convoy put into port, intent on selling prizes and cargoes. Ward left the ships, presumably to report to the harbourmaster and customs officers, and so was absent when a contingent of Ottoman soldiers arrested the crew of all three vessels – some eighty men, according to one account. Ward was not captured, suggesting that he learned of the arrests before he reached the port offices.

The truly surprising turn of events is what John Ward did next. He did not abandon his countrymen and crew. Instead Ward made his way to the kasbah, or citadel, of Algiers and attempted to negotiate their freedom. Ward was an international outlaw by this time, having robbed several ships since deserting the Royal Navy. He could hardly pretend to be a law-abiding foreigner caught up in a bad situation – though, given the pasha's response to Gifford's raid (an act of war by the duke of Florence that was only incidentally carried out by an Englishman), which included the detention and financial penalization of legitimate English merchants, even if Captain Ward had been a loyal English subject he need not have expected to be treated with justice and fairness.

In most Ottoman territories the administration was firmly bound to the sultan's palace in the imperial capital of Istanbul. This was not the case in Algiers, where the pasha – the nearest English equivalent might be 'lord' or 'commander' – sat at the pinnacle of the local power structure. Algiers was not so much the regional centre of an Ottoman territory as a besieged Ottoman enclave, constantly threatened equally by the revolt of the tribes of the interior and by attack from Spain or some other Christian power. In the face of these threats the pasha could not wait for orders from Istanbul before reacting to the feints, shifts and attacks of his opponents; his independence was tolerated by Istanbul because it allowed the Ottomans to retain a base in the western Mediterranean, and also because the Barbary Corsairs, in addition to carrying out guerrilla campaigns against the Spanish, French, Maltese and various Italian powers, served as a highly effective auxiliary fleet that was available for Ottoman sea campaigns. Within Algiers, where the pasha deprived even citizens – never mind foreigners – of basic rights and freedoms through a century-old tradition of martial law, his iron rule was tolerated because of the tremendous material benefits realized through Ottoman privateering. The pasha was not an imperial bureaucrat; he was a regional warlord.

Several sources mention the arrest of Ward's men in Algiers, but only one describes Ward's interview with the pasha. Here it is, quoted in full, from its anonymous source: 'Ward, having [got] much money at sea, and greatly enriched himself with unlawful purchase by the setty, promises a sum of money, joins with certain janissaries, and so procures the peace and enlargement of his followers.'

The account is maddeningly brief, but we can fill in some of the blanks. The pasha would not have been moved by protestations of innocence, nor could his anger be assuaged by the offer of the prizes whose 'unlawful purchase' Ward and his men had made en route from Plymouth to Algiers. These goods and ships had been confiscated by the Algerians before Ward made his appearance in the kasbah, and the pasha undoubtedly already considered them his. Ward therefore offered future prizes – or, to quote our anonymous report, Ward 'promises a sum of money'.

Allowing a pirate like John Ward to venture out and bring prizes into Algiers was not a novel notion. To secure these prizes, however, Ward would need the freedom of his men and the use of a ship. How, then, to ensure that he and his men would return to Algiers with these prizes, and faithfully render them to the pasha? What better way than to place Ottoman soldiers on board the ship? And so, Ward 'joins with certain janissaries'. The result: Ward 'procures the peace and enlargement' of his men, who are released from the Algerian prison so that they can prowl the Mediterranean, working in concert with the janissaries of Algiers.

This was an unorthodox arrangement and an historic one. Janissaries routinely sailed with the Barbary Corsairs; indeed, the janissaries were essential to the success of the Ottoman privateers. The mere sight of these dreaded warriors, whose fierce devotion to a literal interpretation of jihad and personal loyalty to the sultan were well known, was sufficient to unman most Christian sailors.

As far as we know, Ward's privateering excursions of 1603 – for his work now must be counted privateering, sailing under the authority of the pasha – were the first time that janissaries had sailed with a non-Muslim, non-Ottoman captain. Within Algiers, as at Tunis and Tripoli, privateering was the sole preserve of captains, called *raïs*, who were required to be members of a professional association called the *taifa*. The work of the Barbary Corsairs was accomplished in the name of Islam, purportedly an expression of jihad. Jihad is a complex concept and is not a direct equivalent to the Christian concept of Holy War. Holy War focuses on accomplishing a specific goal – perhaps the conquest of territory or the conversion of a people. Jihad, on the other hand, focuses on the process of the struggle. It may be possible to articulate a desirable end point – for example, to bring all human civilization into Islam – but the struggle itself is beneficial to the believer, regardless of the outcome. Jihad, unlike Holy War, cannot be subcontracted. As we shall see, the Barbary Corsairs' claims to be faithful jihadis had already been undercut, long before Ward's arrival in Algiers, by the incorporation of free Christians as shipboard officers into the operations of individual *raïs*. Nonetheless, for the pasha to appoint a Christian as a *raïs* was another level of hypocrisy altogether. The pasha's agreement with Ward went against the privateering monopoly of the Algerian *taifa* and against the guiding principles of the corsairs. As in England, so in Algiers: when it came to privateering, greed trumped legal, religious and moral scruples.

Captain Ward and his men soon found themselves at sea, once again sailing the great Dutch flyboat that they had captured on the Atlantic side of the Straits of Gibraltar. It is unlikely that the janissaries spoke English, but any English mariner with a modicum of experience would have had some facility with several other European tongues, including French, Dutch, Spanish and Italian. The soldiers and sailors undoubtedly established a bastard lingua franca to allow rudimentary communication, though it is unlikely that they struck up any particularly strong bond of friendship. Ward and his men were the inmates of a floating prison, working off their debt to the state, and the janissaries were their gaolers. Unsatisfactory as this arrangement was, it may well have planted a seed in Ward's imagination. It would not be long before mixed crews of

Christians and Muslims would become a distinguishing feature of Ward's command, damning him in the eyes of many contemporaries.

Captain Ward had successfully weathered the second major crisis of his command. Once again his persuasive charisma had carried the day, and once again the well-being of his men was his ethical lodestar, in stark contrast to the behaviour of Richard Gifford. Gifford aligned his own interests with those of his employers and then faithfully served those interests, thinking nothing of the lives of the men who served under him, evidently taking comfort in the fact that, in all his exploits, he acted under the sanction of Sir Robert Cecil, the Duke of Florence or other such grandees.

We can only assume that John Ward squared a life that encompassed the murder, plunder and enslavement of countless men at sea against a determined dedication to the welfare of his crews. Certainly Ward's decisions make little sense if he is viewed, as many historians have viewed him, as an unexceptional opportunist. In the days and years to come, Ward would demonstrate loyalty to his men time and again, often to his personal cost. Given the choice between betraying his country or his compatriots, Captain John Ward would betray his country every time.

In 1604 Richard Parker, merchant tailor, sailed from London for Morocco on a merchantman named the *Blessing*. Parker had been contracted to exchange a cargo of lightweight English woollens for cone-shaped loaves of Moroccan sugar – an assignment never completed, for Parker defected from the *Blessing*, sailing from Morocco with Captain John Ward and his crew of pirates. Parker, in later years, would twice be summoned before the High Court of Admiralty to account for his dealings with Ward. The depositions he sweated out in 1608 and again in 1613 were given with the intention of clearing his own name, but they also cast light on Ward's operations.

Morocco was the one region of North Africa that was completely free of Ottoman influence. Unlike English trade into the eastern

Mediterranean, which was controlled by the monopolistic, royally chartered Levant Company, the Anglo-Moroccan trade was managed by independent merchants who pooled their resources to fund individual voyages, like that of Richard Parker and the *Blessing*. Moroccan independence was also vital for Captain John Ward, who, fresh from the débâcle at Algiers, required a non-Ottoman port in which to attend to ship, men and booty during a shore time interlude.

Daily life in the cosmopolitan Moroccan centre of trade, worship and learning of Salé was not like anything Richard Parker had experienced in England. The climate of the region meant that buildings, often three storeys high or taller, were clustered along narrow streets and twisting alleys, offering welcome shade to the labyrinth they lined. North African Moors, Berber tribesmen, Arabs, black Africans from south of the Sahara, swarthy European and African Mediterraneans and pasty north Europeans all met in the streets of Salé, and Parker could be forgiven if he came to believe that they traded religion and culture as freely as their commodities. The call to prayer of the muezzin floated across the city, while itinerant peddlers hawked strange breads and rogues offered incomprehensible services. Strange though all of this was, Parker would also witness something far more alarming: the sight of fellow Englishmen being exchanged for silver and gold.

Slavery was part of daily life in the Mediterranean throughout the sixteenth and seventeenth centuries. A steady supply of slaves was needed to row the galleys that criss-crossed the sea. During the winter storm season, these same men were put to work on farms or on civic projects such as maintaining breakwaters and other port structures. This culture of slavery transcended even the divisions of Christianity and Islam. Mediterranean Catholics, including the French, Spanish, Maltese and those from various Italian states, felt no scruples in enslaving Muslims, foreign Christians or even criminals of their own faith and nation. The Moroccans and Ottomans enslaved Christians of all denominations and even a few Muslims. Under Islam the enslavement of Muslims by Muslims was prohibited – a frequently misunderstood prohibition which led some Christian slaves to convert to Islam, only to find that the prohibition did not extend to those who were enslaved *before* they were Muslims. And so Islam, too, allowed the enslavement of some co-religionists.

Most slaves, however, were captured in the longstanding conflict between Christian Europe and the Ottoman Empire, which provided both sides with a ready supply of prisoners of war and served as pretext for slaving raids on civilian settlements throughout the Mediterranean. Nonetheless, English merchants, trading factors and seamen who fell afoul of local laws, or who had the simple bad luck to be in the wrong place at the wrong time – for instance those who were in Algiers at the time of Captain Richard Gifford's raid – might find themselves with a price on their backs and shackles on their legs. English archives include narratives from Englishmen enslaved by Catholic nations such as Spain, France and Malta, as well as by Morocco and the Ottoman Empire.

Over the course of three months in Salé, as Parker sought a Moroccan investor to buy his masters' cloth and worked out the details of the next leg of his voyage, to the sugar-producing regions around Sus in the south of Morocco, the officers and crew of the *Blessing* had ample opportunity to explore the city themselves, and to become familiar with the comings and goings of the port. Before long they noted the arrival of an English crew under the command of Captain John Ward.

Parker's testimony would be invaluable to our story for no reason other than that it fixes Ward's presence in Salé in 1604, but as we shall see, it also provides fascinating details of Ward's operations. First, however, it is worth noting how much information we can conclude merely from the captain's appearance at this location. His arrival at a port on the Atlantic coast of Morocco without any Ottoman soldiers on his ship establishes that Ward had, by this point, worked off his debt to the pasha of Algiers. In addition, Parker states that Ward's crew were English, which suggests that he was successful in his attempt to ransom his men back from the pasha. And finally, Parker mentions that Ward came to Salé to sell booty, which means that Ward must have captured at least one further prize after having worked off his debt.

Like Parker, Ward had pressing business in Salé. Parker was in Salé as part of the legitimate and ongoing English cloth-for-sugar trade, a trade that had been established several decades earlier. Ward, on the other hand, was in Salé as part of an emerging trade in piratical contraband. By 1615 Salé would be a notorious pirate haunt, particularly known for the community of exiled European outlaws, called the Sallee Rovers, who made it their home base for raids throughout a vast region that encompassed Europe's Atlantic coast, the western end of the Mediterranean and even extended across the Atlantic Ocean to the Spanish New World and the Grand Banks of Newfoundland. But this lay a decade in the future: in 1604 Salé was primarily a legitimate commercial port and only a few pirates in the know, men like Captain Ward, made their way there.

As in Algiers and Tunis, it is not difficult to understand why these men were tolerated by the authorities. By offering sanctuary to European pirates Islamic leaders could demand that they limit their attacks to Christian shipping and so provide relief to Muslim vessels even while claiming that the depredations of the pirates contributed to jihad against imperial Spain and other Christian aggressors. Behind this façade of righteousness, the financial advantages of allowing commerce with pirates were tremendous, through customs and port fees as much as baksheesh. Meanwhile, every boatload of pirate booty allowed local merchants to earn vast sums on relatively small investments. Men like Captain John Ward were not keen to drive a hard bargain; they would rather dump their spoils and fetch more than haggle over prices. This suggests no lack of commercial cunning, but stems from a longer-term need to cultivate a network of friendly merchants on land. A seasoned pirate knew that his own best fortune lay in the opportunity to sell future prizes rather than to extract every pennyworth from any one cargo.

Richard Parker tells us that John Ward did not come to Salé solely to sell off booty, though this was one of his first acts upon arrival. Once Ward had placed a jingle in the pockets of each of his men, and once his men had sown their oats ashore, Ward and his crew refocused their attention on outfitting their ship for further adventures at sea. Or, as Parker related to the High Court of Admiralty,

Ward and his men set about 'to victual and trim' their ship, 'having sold all their goods.'

Ward and a few of his officers looked after securing food and other supplies. If, as is likely, Ward ordered his boat like the Elizabethan privateers, he would have appointed a purser and steward to monitor and replenish the store of food, candles, rope, sailcloth and other sundries that were necessary to life at sea, while the ship's carpenter would have been concerned with making sure that the vessel had sufficient stock of lumber of various types and cuts so that damage from sea, storm or battle could be repaired quickly and efficiently. Ward's role was that of manager over these men, ensuring that their monies were well spent and that sufficient store of supplies was secured. As with any successful enterprise, criminal or legitimate, the devil was in the detail. Our perception of pirates has long been conditioned by the gothic horrors described in story-books like Daniel Defoe's *General History of the Pirates*. The reality is that derring-do by sea and inspirational leadership were but two of the necessary skills of a successful pirate captain: he also needed an accountant's sense of cash flow and a stock-boy's awareness of supplies.

While Ward and his officers went about their business, the rest of the crew set to the drudgery of trimming the ship. Trimming, also called careening, involved hauling the ship on to a gentle beach and laying it over ('careening' it) first to one side and then the other while the seamen set about prising off ('trimming') barnacles and scraping away accumulations of algae and seaweed. Though not strenuous, the work was tedious and uncomfortable, especially under a blazing Moroccan sun. Nonetheless, no pirate worth his prize-share had to be urged on to thoroughness: all knew that their ability to win future booty, and to preserve their very lives, depended upon a clean hull.

Pirates were more likely to use a lumbering merchantman than a sleek man-of-war to ply their trade, and they relied upon a well-maintained hull to reduce drag and therefore increase speed and manoeuvrability, to give them the edge in pursuing prizes and eluding captors. The merchant tailor Richard Parker, like other observers, notes that Captain Ward typically sailed in a Dutch flyboat. One naval historian, commenting on the flyboat design in general, ventured the opinion that these mid-sized commercial carriers were 'about as warlike as a coal scuttle'. This is accurate, and therein lay the attraction for a pirate like John Ward. The most effective pirates and privateers did not want to engage in open combat with their victims but rather sought to use surprise to force a surrender, preferably firing only warning shots. If a man-of-war is cutting through the sea with cannon extended and fighting nets at the ready, it is not very difficult to discern its intentions. If a flyboat merchantman comes bobbing through the waves, apparently seeking a companion with whom to sail in convoy, far fewer suspicions are raised.

Some peculiarities of flyboat design made them especially attractive to pirates. The ships were notoriously plain, lacking ornamentation or other distinctive features. This made them easy to care for and difficult to identify, attributes that were sought after by pirates who, unlike their fictional counterparts, were more interested in harvesting booty at sea than establishing a known identity. Flyboats also lacked the distinctive structures, called castles, that were built above the decks of many men-of-war. This made them lighter in the water. And finally, flyboats were designed to be 'floaty', their keels tracing a softer u-shape instead of the sharp v of the classic man-of-war. This gave them more of a rolling motion on the waves, and it also made it harder to gauge whether a flyboat was laden or empty – enabling a pirate, secretly towing a sea anchor, to appear to be floundering under a heavy load when in fact he was ready to shoot off in pursuit of prey.

But he could shoot off only if he had a clean hull beneath him. So, a canny pirate careened his hull at least once every three or four months, a far more rigorous schedule than that followed by most merchantmen. For such work the beach at Salé offered a gentle slope and soft, fine sand. Physically the setting was ideal, but more was required to make Salé the pirate haven that it would become by 1615. A pirate ship on a beach was a turtle on its back: unable to escape, unable to fight. Pirates such as John Ward, willing to sell cargoes at cut-rate prices and enrich local officials with bribes, now extracted their precious *quid pro quo*. And so, under the very gaze of the Moroccan forces that protected the twin ports of Salé and Rabat, Ward and his men beached their flyboat and careened it, confident that they would be neither arrested by the authorities nor assaulted by their foes. This confidence was not misplaced. In one incident, Moroccan sultan Mulay Zidan arrested a group of Dutch pirate-hunters who had attempted to abduct several English pirates from his port of Safi.

Selling booty, replenishing stores and trimming the hull – each of these was an essential task. But as Parker's own story makes clear, Ward had one further purpose in putting into Salé: attracting new recruits.

During the Anglo-Spanish wars English privateers customarily sailed with as many crew as could fit into their holds. Such cramming was necessary, in part, because the demand for sailors and soldiers outstripped supply, with the result that most ships carried a substantial number of 'green', or untried, men. In 1604 Captain John Ward did not sail with green men. Thanks to the lack of work for the ex-privateers, Ward was usually able to recruit well-seasoned crews whose experience in battle and efficiency among the sheets meant that he did not have to maximize the number of bodies on his ship. Nonetheless, piracy, like privateering, was dangerous work and there was a constant need for a captain to replenish his crew, as much to account for death and injury as for those who chose to move on to less risky employments.

During his stop in Salé in 1604 Ward began his search for new recruits among the English mariners currently in port. Richard Parker reports that he found many willing volunteers among the men of the *Blessing* – so many, in fact, that Parker himself began to panic that the *Blessing* would not have sufficient hands to sail to southern Morocco, lade sugar and return to England. That so many men should abandon their positions with the *Blessing* is not surprising. At a loose end in Salé while Parker looked to his commercial negotiations, the men of the *Blessing* had plenty of time to contemplate their return to the uncertain employment market in England. Sailing with a pirate was not without its physical, legal and moral dangers, but it was paying work – as was temptingly demonstrated by the booty-fuelled debauches of Ward's men about the port.

Nor were economic prospects the only attraction for men to sign up with John Ward. Seamen were a gossiping bunch among whom news travelled faster than a merchantman on the Levant wind. By the time that Parker arrived at Salé it is likely that word had spread of Ward's singular exploits, including his tenacious loyalty to his men. And, if Ward's peculiar zeal for aiding the common English seaman was not already familiar knowledge among the men of the *Blessing*, they were provided with further evidence even as they sat in port.

The most remarkable part of Parker's account of Ward's activities at Salé comes as he relates Ward's attempts to purchase the freedom of certain enslaved Englishmen. Parker states that Ward and one of his senior officers – one Richard Bishop, of whom we will hear much more – pooled their shares to 'redeem a countryman'. Finding that they still did not have enough, they pleaded with another English pirate who was then at Salé, John Muckell, to contribute further cash.

Mediterranean nations like France and Spain, long accustomed to having citizens enslaved by the Muslims of North Africa and the Ottoman Empire, had religious societies that were devoted to relieving the misery of the slaves. There was no equivalent among the English. If the family of an English slave did not know of his fate, or was unwilling or unable to raise funds to purchase his freedom, or had no way of conveying those funds from England into Islam, then for that man there could be no hope of escaping bondage. No hope except the kindness of pirates.

In his depositions before the Admiralty court Parker swore that he joined Ward only to escape the 'heathen country' of Morocco. According to Parker, so many of the men of the *Blessing* were seduced into piracy that he was convinced he would be stranded in Salé unless he, too, joined Ward. He tried to minimize his sins by saying that he only sailed with the pirates for a matter of months, after which time Ward's flyboat encountered the *Centurion*, an English merchantman. Parker requested to tranship to the *Centurion*, a vessel that Ward did not attack. Permission was granted and Parker soon found himself back on English soil.

Admiralty court records abound with stories of men who became pirates under duress, or because they were tricked, or because they feared being marooned. In Parker's case this familiar tale seems even less likely than usual. Salé was a regular port of call for English merchantmen and, at any rate, Parker was legally obligated to remain with the *Blessing* to protect the ship and his masters' wares.

We do not know the outcome of Parker's trial; nor do we know whether Parker helped to capture any prizes during his brief career as a pirate under Captain Ward. But we do know that John Ward did not remain a pirate for very long after he visited Salé. Upon leaving the Moroccan port Ward made for the Straits of Gibraltar and returned to the Mediterranean, making his way east. Perhaps his brief stint sailing with the janissaries of Algiers had planted the seed of an idea in his mind, for Ward seems to have made directly for the other major Ottoman outpost of central North Africa: Tunis.

FIVE

Barbary Corsair

If joining the king's navy in 1603 was John Ward's attempt to go straight, then the two years of piracy that followed his desertion were a euphoric howl of freedom, the inevitable binge of an inveterate drunk. Ottoman Tunis was the place where Ward sobered up, took a hard look at fifty-odd years of life and climbed back on the wagon. Tunis, like Portsmouth, represents a turning point in John Ward's life. At Portsmouth Ward turned pirate; at Tunis he rejoined the ranks of privateers.

That John Ward became an Ottoman privateer shortly after his arrival in Tunis in 1605 has been misunderstood. In the 400 years since, Ward has almost invariably been described as an English pirate. This characterization follows a blinkered logic: if Ward is considered as an English citizen, a subject of James I, then his actions at sea most assuredly were piracy. While there were many European captains, including Britons, who worked as pirates from various ports of Ottoman North Africa, John Ward's arrangements at Tunis were categorically different from theirs. Before Ward became an Ottoman privateer, he became an Ottoman subject. Christian pirate or Muslim privateer: it is not just a matter of perspective; it is also a question of legal status.

During his time among the Barbary Corsairs John Ward did not hesitate to attack English shipping, though there were always old friends who were allowed to pass unmolested. Not counted among these old friends was Andrew Barker, an English ship's master (the equivalent of captain on small or mid-sized merchant shipping). Barker was captured by William Graves, one of Ward's men, probably in 1608. He was then taken to Tunis and ransomed rather than enslaved. Held for some months, Barker returned to England after his ransom was paid. During his time in Tunis he was a privileged prisoner, roaming the port and swapping tales with his captors, many of whom he had known in England, including Graves and John Ward himself. By 1608 Ward's followers included several hundred Englishmen, most of whom had been part of the English seafaring community for a decade or more. A fresh English captive such as Andrew Barker represented the opportunity to hear news from home, and, upon being ransomed, Barker undoubtedly carried to England tidings and gifts from certain of Ward's followers for wives, families and friends.

Shortly after his return to London Barker published a leisurely description of John Ward's operations entitled *A True and Certaine Report of the Beginning, Proceedings, Overthrowes and now present Estate of Captaine Ward*. Barker states that Ward approached Tunis in 1605 determined to make an impression. Upon putting into the port, Ward sent gifts to the kasbah, 'Where with small suit to the *king*, in respect he brought Merchandise with him, beneficial to the state, [Ward] had leave to find safe harbouring for himself, his ships and his followers. Where having made sale of his Commodities [he] presented diverse acceptable gifts to the *king of Tunis*.' In other words, upon arrival at the port and selling his cargoes, Ward observed Mediterranean custom and presented gifts to his hosts. But whereas a merchant might be content with making gifts to port officials only, Ward sought to ingratiate himself with the man Barker calls 'the king of Tunis'. There is an inaccuracy here, if an understandable one. Barker should have known that Tunis was part of the Ottoman Empire and not an independent monarchy. Like Algiers, Tunis was subject to rule by a pasha appointed by Istanbul; but as in Algiers, the Ottoman sultan tolerated a considerable degree of independence in Tunis. An Englishman of Barker's day, accustomed to royal rule, inevitably would think of the pasha as 'the king of Tunis'.

Ward's gifts had their desired effect, and it was not long before he came to the attention of an official that Barker calls 'the Crossyman'.

'[Ward] received some outward graces of the *Crossyman*, which is as much to say, the *Lord Admiral* of the Sea, and the man that hath ever since held share with *Ward* in all his Voyages, Prizes and Shipping. [The Crossyman was] the only supporter in all [Ward's] designs.' Again, there is a mistake here, not in substance, but involving titles. 'Crossyman' does not mean 'Lord Admiral', nor is it a title of any sort. It is a name. Or rather, it is the bastardized version of a name. The man that Barker is referring to was nicknamed Kara Osman, which Barker has slurred into a single word. But Kara Osman was not his proper name; he is known to historians as Uthman Dey and he was a very powerful figure in Tunis – more powerful, even, than the Istanbul-appointed pasha. Uthman's power, however, was exercised in secret, and Barker, unaware of the true hierarchy, has cast Uthman as the pasha's lord admiral. The important point is that, by making Uthman his business partner, Ward shared wealth with the chief power broker of Ottoman Tunis.

Having secured powerful friends, Ward set about advancing himself from the peripheral social position afforded to Christian pirates at Tunis. Backed by the good will of Uthman, '*Ward*, growing bold . . . was at length a suitor to the [pasha]' and asked to become a captain among the Tunisian privateers, but first to 'be received as [the pasha's] subject, or if not so, yet at all times . . . be ever sanctuaried under his princely protection.' He sought no less than to become a subject of the pasha and a citizen of the Ottoman Empire.

Ward's extraordinary petition had not yet ended. He now requested a complement of Ottoman soldiers to sail under his command 'with whom [Ward] doubted not to return, [making] of *Christian*'s goods so worthy a spoil that hereafter [Ward's] name should be held [by the pasha] in more regard, and his service more acceptable.' In Tunis such an arrangement was unprecedented. Ward's experience with the Algerian janissaries had evidently left him impressed with their effectiveness in persuading the surrender of prizes.

Barker's report acknowledges the key role that Uthman Dey played in securing for Ward privileges as an Ottoman citizen and as a privateering captain, noting that Ward's suit 'being granted at full', Uthman henceforth was 'an aider and furtherance in all his expeditions . . . [and] in all [Ward's] profits [Uthman] was a full sharer.'

John Ward had absorbed more than tactics and naval prowess among the Elizabethan privateers. Despise though he might Captain Richard Gifford and his ilk, Ward had learned from them. But for the support of men of influence, a seaman could only be a pawn in the wargames of the powerful. With Uthman Dey as his ally Ward possessed the endorsement of the most powerful authority in Tunis – much as if he had secured the goodwill of Sir Robert Cecil in London. Captain Ward had joined the Barbary Corsairs.

There were many reasons for John Ward to prize his newfound status as an Ottoman citizen. Other Englishmen, younger ones, might turn pirate to amass riches, lie low for a spell and then return to England. But for a man of John Ward's age and history this was not possible. Ward was already an old man when he deserted his post in the Royal Navy and became an outlaw; he could hardly spend years waiting for his sins to be forgotten. He needed security and he needed it immediately if he were to enjoy his filthy lucre in peace. More than a home port, Ward needed a home.

Though the advantages for Ward were undeniable, it is not immediately apparent why Uthman Dey and the pasha were willing to accord him extraordinary privileges. If they merely sought riches, they could have extorted contraband and baksheesh from him in exchange for use of the harbour and market at Tunis, as they did with other European pirates. The Tunisian authorities wanted something more.

During the sixteenth century Tunis had been a focus of Christian–Muslim warfare, swapped between Spain and the Ottomans or the local proxies of one side or the other. It was not until 1576 that the port was decisively brought into the Ottoman ambit. With stable Ottoman rule the citizens of Tunis hoped that civil society would flourish once more, allowing a return to the diverse and thriving economy that had preceded the wars, an economy that balanced agriculture and textiles manufacturing with the legitimate trading of various commodities through an excellent natural harbour that served as a regional transportation hub.

The Tunisian economy was far more robust than that of Algiers, which, since the ascendancy of Kheir ed-Din Barbarossa in the early sixteenth century, had become dangerously reliant upon a single industry: privateering. Nonetheless, the Ottomans sought to replicate the success of Algiers in Tunis, forcing upon the Tunisians the political structure that had been created at Algiers: a rule of martial law that repressed the rights of citizens even as it glorified privateers and the janissaries who sailed with them. At Algiers this political system had held together for the better part of a century, but at Tunis it came apart after fifteen years, in 1590. The crisis of 1590 was the result of discontent among the tribes who farmed the richly fertile lands immediately beyond the city walls, the cloth workers within the city, and the merchants who participated in the legitimate import/export trade. Surprisingly, however, when the system finally broke down it was neither the rural tribes nor the urban workers who led the rebellion: it was a common soldier named Uthman, nicknamed Kara Osman.

Uthman was a janissary, an infantryman sent to Tunis by Istanbul. Prior to the rebellion of 1590, Uthman's fellow janissaries had elected him *dey*, but this title was not official. Janissaries elected *deys* from their ranks to act as intermediaries between soldiers and their officers. The *deys* offered an alternate path to pursue complaints and grievances about regimental life, one that kept petty problems outside official channels of power.

During the 1580s the janissaries had become restless. While the senior command of the *ojaq*, or garrison, remained obedient to the pasha, the rank-and-file felt the strain of exerting martial law over a resentful population. As the men who were ordered into the city streets to break up meetings of cloth workers, or into the country-side to track down insurgents, the janissaries knew that Tunis was simmering with discontent. Still the pasha continued to accumulate power into his own hands, refusing to share authority with civic or tribal leaders even as the chaos of a popular rebellion threatened to engulf the region. Pashas, appointed to three-year terms by Istanbul, were more concerned to maximize their own profits from this dangerous but lucrative posting than to bring long-term stability to Tunisian governance.

In 1590 the janissaries, tired of serving as pawns in a game that was being misplayed, rose in bloody rebellion against their senior officers. The entire command structure was destroyed, with every officer ranking captain or higher hunted down and executed. As the pasha looked on in horror, the forty deys of the Tunisian garrison presented themselves as the new power brokers. In keeping with the process that had seen each of them elected from among their peers, these forty deys elected Uthman Dey to oversee government at Tunis. This election was the foundation of the rule of Uthman Dey, who held sway at Tunis until his death in 1610.

As bloody as the rebellion was, and despite its radical after-effects, this was a rebellion and not a revolution. The deys, and the janissaries that they represented, were quite content for the pasha to continue to rule as a figurehead. Back in Istanbul the Ottoman authorities, long accustomed to viewing North Africa as virtually ungovernable, accepted this new arrangement as the price for keeping control over the Tunisian galley fleet and a strategically valuable port. Uthman, though in essence a dictator, succeeded in bringing civic and tribal leaders into his government councils, creating a modicum of political diversity as a weak complement to the robust economic diversity of the port and region.

When John Ward arrived at Tunis in 1605 Uthman Dey had been ruling for fifteen years. Uthman, not himself appointed by Istanbul, was careful to exercise power in the pasha's name. Never mind that the pasha was virtually a captive in his palace, delivering pronouncements scripted by Uthman and following only those policies that Uthman had devised. To the outsider Uthman appeared a shadowy figure, in possession of significant influence yet seeming to bow to the will of the pasha.

Uthman Dey was able to satisfy or otherwise suppress the demands of the local population, but he did not rule by their authority. Tunis was a province of the Ottoman Empire, and Uthman's experiments in governance were tolerated because he delivered to the empire a strong navy that would answer when called upon. The *taifa* of the *raïs* and the *ojaq* of the janissaries remained constituencies whose demands had to be satisfied if Uthman's rule were to survive. More, though Tunis possessed a community of merchants who participated in the legitimate import/export trade that had long been part of life at the port, there were also merchants who made their profits by trading in the spoils of privateers and pirates. Uthman allowed the natural diversity of the Tunisian economy to flourish, but Tunis remained, like Algiers, a corsair state. And it was precisely in the last quarter of the 1500s, the same period in which the rebellion of the deys brought Uthman to power, that the effectiveness of the Barbary Corsairs began to slump.

Unsurprisingly, a man who could walk the fine line between rebellion and revolution did not take an ideological approach to this new problem. Instead of viewing the activities of the privateers in religious terms, Uthman seems to have considered their political and economic effects. The *dey* did not seek to promote jihad: he sought to revive a revenue stream. If he were to transform his fleet of corsairs, Uthman needed a seasoned sea captain who was not stuck in the traditional mode of North African privateering. It did not take him long to realize that in John Ward he had found that man.

Did Uthman Dey recognize a kindred spirit in John Ward? The two men shared a willingness to break with convention and rewrite the rules. Both had entered the service of their respective rulers and rebelled, albeit Uthman's rebellion was far more bloody and radical than Ward's. Both were fundamentally populist figures who, initially at least, accepted authority only when it was freely given by the men who served under them – as demonstrated in the Plymouth tavern when Ward was elected captain, and in the bloody aftermath of the janissary rebellion when Uthman was elected to represent the deys. Both Ward and Uthman were charismatic leaders, and this fact alone makes it remarkable that they could become business partners and even friends without clashing. One further similarity helps to explain why these strong-willed men got along: they were, above all, pragmatic. Each built political alliances to accomplish clear-cut objectives and shared material benefits to retain loyalty, rather than grooming a cult of personality.

Uthman's willingness to break with tradition served John Ward well, and eventually resulted in new opportunities for rogue Christian seamen throughout Ottoman North Africa. Soon after Ward's admission into the *taifa* at Tunis the Dutch pirate Simon Danziker began to sail as a *raïs* under the pasha of Algiers. John Ward's arrival at Tunis was a pebble tossed in a pool, causing ripples throughout the region. From this point forward the Barbary Corsairs were a heterogeneous body, and therefore one with a renewed capacity to change and adapt. By allowing their claims to jihad to be shown up as utter hypocrisy, the corsair states of North Africa flourished well into the eighteenth century.

Uthman Dey's shrug at the jihadi tradition of the Barbary Corsairs was nothing more than a pragmatic man's acceptance of a sea change that had already occurred. A century and a quarter earlier the North African coast was ruled by a patchwork of competing minor rulers, each too busy scheming to effect local alliances and betrayals to pay attention to the growing power of Spain throughout the western Mediterranean. Spanish expansion included an ambitious agenda of building fortified presidios along the North African coast. The small-time sultans and sheiks of the region accepted these developments as just another point in a kaleidoscope of potential allies and enemies, but the local people nursed a potent hatred for the Spanish. This hatred redoubled after 1492 when King Ferdinand and Queen Isabella, the 'Catholic Kings' who unified Spain and launched its empire, completed the Reconquista by offering generous terms, including religious toleration, to the Muslims of Granada in exchange for their surrender. Ferdinand and Isabella then embarked upon a campaign of anti-Islamic religious persecution, including the eventual expulsion of Muslims from the Iberian peninsula, openly contravening the terms of surrender of 1492. The exiled Muslims of

Granada were welcomed into North Africa, where they fanned the already smouldering hatred of Spain into open flame.

Despite such popular resentment, the feckless local potentates of North Africa continued their dynastic wars against one another, applying the corrosive logic which states that the enemy of an enemy must be a friend. Exploiting such conflicts, the Spanish created puppet regimes to advance their own interests. Among the most hated of these was the local Muslim dynasty that suffered the Spanish to construct a presidio overlooking Algiers harbour.

The internecine struggles of North Africa offered plenty of opportunities for mercenaries, and in 1504 there arrived in Tunis a trio of brothers, Ottoman adventurers, from the island of Lesbos. Known to western historians as the brothers Barbarossa, Aruj, Ishaq and Kheir ed-Din invented themselves as committed jihadis who, under the leadership of Aruj, sought the total annihilation of Spanish power in North Africa. After an attempt upon the presidio at Algiers failed, ultimately resulting in the deaths of both Aruj and Ishaq, Kheir ed-Din turned to the only power that was a match for Spain: the Ottoman Empire. Agreeing to terms with Istanbul that placed a contingent of janissaries under his command, Kheir ed-Din returned to Algiers and defeated both the Spanish and their Muslim puppet regime. The Spanish presidio that had loomed over the port was destroyed, its rubble employed to construct an enormous breakwater that transformed Algiers harbour from a minor port, open to the elements, into a protected haven capable of hosting large numbers of galleys. Literally from the rubble of the Spanish occupation Kheir ed-Din laid the foundations of the pre-eminent corsair state of North Africa.

Garnering esteem as a local champion who had defeated the Spanish and as a commander in the service of the mighty Ottoman Empire, Kheir ed-Din began a concerted sea war against the Spanish and all Christians, his ships crewed by North African and Ottoman seamen, carrying janissaries to do the heavy fighting. This war was financed through privateering but Kheir ed-Din won glory by assaulting Spanish warships and fortresses. His actions were governed by an intoxicating blend of idealism and opportunism, and it was not long before Algiers became the rallying point for *raïs* who had previously commanded ships under the authority of local potentates or engaged in open piracy. The Barbary Corsairs, born of political chaos, were unified and reinvented as Ottoman privateers who sailed under a fierce and effective commander known to Christians simply as Barbarossa.

Barbarossa had arrived at Tunis in 1504; John Ward presented himself to Uthman Dey in 1605. In the intervening century much had changed. Barbarossa's success had encouraged the Ottomans to create corsair-dependent administrations at Tunis and Tripoli modelled upon Barbarossa's regime in Algiers. Among Christians Barbarossa had his imitators, too, with corsairs launching their galleys from France, Malta and various parts of Italy. Life in the Mediterranean had settled into a state of permanent sea war, but a sea war of a peculiar sort: given the choice, the combatants avoided fighting each other, reserving their best energies for the lucrative sacking of merchant shipping. Slave traders grew rich throughout the region, since ongoing galley warfare required vast numbers of slaves to pull the oars.

By 1605 Mediterranean merchants had evolved strategies for minimizing their risks. For example, it had long been common for wealthy merchants to hire a few armed bravos to watch over their investments. Over the sixteenth century this practice became formalized, so that it became normal for mercenaries to sail on galleys that carried goods of sufficient value. This was expensive, and not merely on account of wages paid to these soldiers. More personnel meant more space devoted to passengers, less to cargo, as well as greater expenditure on food, water and other supplies.

In addition to carrying mercenaries to beat off pirates and privateers, merchant traffic became far more likely to sail in groups. By the late sixteenth century the Serene Republic of Venice – the state most direly affected by Mediterranean piracy – not only compelled its merchants to travel in convoy, but deployed state war galleys to accompany commercial convoys on the most valuable trade routes. Even without such an escort, however, three or four merchant galleys sailing together often were sufficient to discourage attack, given that the golden rule of privateering calls for victims who are obviously weaker than their attackers.

Merchant galleys, moreover, had changed. Cargos of pedestrian goods, such as olive oil, wheat, barley and so forth, continued to be moved in light galleys, but by 1605 cargoes of silks, spices and other rare materials were transported aboard a new generation of super-galleys. These larger ships could carry more cannon than light galleys and were more difficult to storm, on account of their higher sides. Captains in command of these larger vessels nearly always maintained a complement of mercenaries on board.

By 1605 the political context had also changed from Barbarossa's day. The success of the Barbary Corsairs had inspired emulation by various Christian military orders. The Knights of Malta, founded as the Knights of St John during the medieval Crusades, had reinvented themselves as Christian privateers whose operations mirrored those of the Barbary Corsairs at Tunis, just as the operations of the Barbary Corsairs at Algiers were mirrored by the Knights of St Stephen, who operated under the protection of the grand duke of Florence, sailing from the port of Livorno. Meanwhile, the Reformation had riven Christendom, pitting Catholics against Protestants in terrible wars of religion that divided nations and made enemies of neighbours. The English and other northern European nations, which tended to be Protestant, began to develop navies for defence and trade, and started to penetrate into the Mediterranean world with their ships, instead of allowing Italian and French merchants – Catholics – to supply them with the fruits of international commerce.

The design of the ships sailed by these northern Europeans was very different from the galleys of Mediterranean nations. Galleys were long, open and low to the water, and so were not suitable for the stormy conditions of the North Atlantic, where routine swells could be higher than those produced by many Mediterranean storms. The new northern vessels quickly became known as round ships because, when viewed in comparison to galleys, their tall sides, closed decks, shorter keels and wider beams gave them a rounded appearance.

The same qualities that made round ships impervious to Atlantic swells and gales also made them difficult to storm from a galley. To the dismay of Catholic privateers such as the Knights of Malta, as well as the Muslims of the Barbary Corsairs, it was found that round ship crews often held off attackers by using their greater elevation to rain small-arms fire into the low, open holds of a galley. Round ships, moreover, were made for transoceanic voyages, and had been designed to maximize the use of the winds through a highly complex system of square, rectangular and triangular sails that collectively were referred to as square-rigging. In contrast, galleys generally had only a few lateen-rigged triangular sails. These were sufficient for the relatively short distances typical of most Mediterranean voyages. In combat, galleys relied on oar-power, supplied by rank upon rank of galley slaves. This offered the galley great manoeuvrability, independence from the wind and the ability to put on tremendous bursts of speed. But in any extended chase the advantage inevitably went over to the inexhaustible wind, captured by the very efficient sails of the square-rigged round ship. The combination, then, of tall sides and highly efficient sails gave these ships a defensive advantage over the galleys of the Mediterranean.

Finally, in the century between the landing of Barbarossa at Tunis and the arrival of John Ward, the ideological motivations of the Ottoman privateers had slowly eroded. Barbarossa had cast himself as a jihadi and had relied upon religious principles to motivate his men, but his reputation had always been complicated by the vast profits that were realized by the corsairs under his command. During the sixteenth century the greed of individual *raïs*, combined with the avarice of pashas on limited appointments to Tunis, Algiers or Tripoli, rendered the Barbary Corsairs' claims to jihad increasingly dubious. The decision to allow Christian pirates to sail from Ottoman ports made sense economically, but was politically and religiously indefensible. What's more, Christian crewmembers were becoming more and more common on the ships of the Barbary Corsairs. It started with pilots, recruited to guide the corsairs' galleys into waters that the pilot knew intimately – the sea coast of his home state or an archipelago that he knew well through work on commercial galleys. Some of these men were drawn into service with the Barbary Corsairs in order to escape the bonds of slavery, but many were attracted by the money, or by the possibility of using the Muslim privateers to settle old scores. Once Christian pilots were accepted into the crews of various *raïs* it was not long before skilled Christians, though still uncommon among the corsairs' crews, had been known to hold virtually every post on board the corsairs' galleys. The exception to this was the post of *raïs* itself, which, by the rules that governed the monopoly granted to the *taifa* at Algiers, Tunis and Tripoli, had to be Muslim.

John Ward temporarily had sailed as a *raïs* under the pasha of Algiers. Nonetheless, the decision by Uthman Dey to allow him to sail from Tunis as a *raïs* on an ongoing basis was a major departure from the North African privateering tradition established by Barbarossa. But it was also the logical evolution of trends among the corsairs that had long predated Ward's arrival. In exchange for breaking this final taboo, Uthman Dey gained a commander who could diversify corsair operations at Tunis. John Ward and his band of English exiles, drawing on skills developed during the Anglo-Spanish wars of Elizabeth's reign, would create a parallel fleet of round ships that complemented and extended the operations of the Tunisian galley fleet.

Uthman Dey recognized that he needed a means of preying upon the increasing numbers of round ships in the Eastern Mediterranean, but it was probably John Ward who realized just what a powerful instrument of terror could be forged of a round ship under an English crew with Ottoman janissaries to serve as a boarding force.

The English were notorious as bloodthirsty sea bandits on account of the potency and lawlessness of the Elizabethan privateers. During the 1590s England was often described as a nation of pirates, and the double character of much English merchant shipping before and after the end of the Anglo-Spanish wars – carrying cannon for defence, but also for privateering or piracy if the opportunity presented itself – meant that all English ships were looked upon with fear and mistrust.

The janissaries had their origin as the palace guard of the Ottoman sultans, and during the sixteenth century most were recruited from the Anatolian peoples of western Turkey. Trained from boyhood in the arts of war, they experienced continual combat as the Ottomans constantly sought to defend or expand their empire and this kept their battle skills honed to a fine edge. They were drawn from the lowest social order, the agrarian peasantry, and as a consequence bore a lifelong debt of gratitude to the sultan who had rescued them from poverty. Moreover, their training in exclusive military schools in Istanbul stressed the importance of absolute loyalty to the sultan and the Ottoman state. Recruited as children, the boys received a general education until they were old enough to begin military training. They were then streamed into two groups. Those who showed more academic than military potential continued their studies and eventually formed the core of the Ottoman bureaucracy. Those who showed more physical prowess than mental agility began an intensive schooling in combat and deep religious indoctrination that stressed the importance of jihad. Upon graduation, this second group joined the janissary corps.

It would have been sufficiently unnerving to face a band of meticulously trained and battle-seasoned warriors whose fanaticism for jihad was matched only by their loyalty to their sultan. But the horror was heightened by the knowledge of how some janissaries were recruited. During the sixteenth century Christian Europe learned that the Ottomans were practising a peculiar form of taxation upon the Christian populations of their territories in Greece and the Balkans: the *devshirme* or child levy. Through the *devshirme*, Christian boys were removed from their homes and families to receive military training and Islamic indoctrination alongside the sons of Muslim farmers. These boys were always a minority among the trainee janissaries. Nonetheless, the very concept of the *devshirme* – that Christian boys were trained into jihadis who then pushed Ottoman frontiers ever further into Christendom – seemed created to be sensationalized by Christian preachers and the popular press in non-Ottoman Europe.

These were the men who stood as soldiers on the decks of John Ward's ships. During the roaring days of Elizabethan privateering, men like Ward were known to be unscrupulous, remorseless and devastatingly effective. The ships that were jointly chartered by Uthman Dey and Captain Ward combined the ruthlessness and seamanship of the English privateers with the most disciplined, efficient and feared fighting force in Europe.

John Ward offered Uthman Dey a means to tap the flow of round ships through the Mediterranean, but Ward did not restrict himself to taking these vessels. Instead, he used his tremendous grasp of privateering tactics to lay siege to virtually any vessel that he met upon the waters: round ships of all sizes and all nations, commercial galleys from light galleys through to super-galleys, and even the war galleys of Venice and Malta.

This accomplishment has not been well understood by naval historians until recently. During the past thirty years, the long-held assumption of the inherent superiority of round ships over galleys has been slowly overturned. It has been noted that nations with Atlantic and Mediterranean fleets were more apt to use galleys outside the Strait of Gibraltar than they were to use round ships in the Mediterranean. Recent research by N.A.M. Rodger argues that English ship design during the sixteenth century consisted of a series of attempts to adapt the advantages of the galley to round ships. Rodger concludes that successful adaptation of galley design lies at the root of the eventual naval superiority of the British.

These findings make John Ward's story more complicated. Until recently it was suggested that Ward was a merely competent round ship captain who revitalized the Barbary Corsairs by betraying his nation and delivering superior British naval technology to them. Now that it is understood that the sailing technology he used was not categorically superior to the galleys already in use among the Barbary Corsairs, the story cannot be this simple.

Every technology has its strengths: we have already seen that the tall sides and efficient sails of round ships gave them a defensive advantage over galleys, making them difficult to storm and allowing them to flee faster. These defensive advantages meant that, for the most part, the round ships of the Barbary Corsairs would be used to capture other round ships, while the corsairs' galleys preyed upon other galleys. Nonetheless, the galley remained the preferred warship of the day in fleet actions and staged naval battles, on account of its advantages in hull design, gun deployment and locomotion.

Galley hulls were long, narrow and low to the water while round ships had higher sides, were shorter in the keel and broader in the beam. The sides of galleys were reserved for ranks of oars, while ordnance was deployed in the bow and stern. Round ships, driven across the seas by the winds alone, presented ranks of cannon instead of oars. The high sides of these vessels meant that the cannon either were at a very high elevation or had to be on a special gun deck, with hatches cut into the hull to allow them to poke through. The hull design of round ships prevented gun ports from being cut into the bows; as a result, forward-facing guns on round ships could only be fired from high elevation. Round ship cannon were principally arranged broadside not because of the advantages of the broadside charge, but because there was no other choice.

Having cannon arranged broadside placed round ships at a disadvantage when confronted by galleys in a staged naval battle. To allow his gunners to be effective a round ship captain had to turn his vessel sideways to a target, thus exposing maximum profile to his enemies' guns. Galley ordnance was forward- or rear-facing, which allowed galley captains to fire freely while exposing only the minimal, head-on profile of the vessel to their opponent's weapons. The greater elevation of round ship cannon also placed them at a disadvantage. Galleys sat low in the water, allowing gunners to point and shoot, thundering away directly at the waterline of their adversaries. Round ship gunners, when firing at the low, narrow profile of the galleys, had to calculate the physics of arcing payload into the open hold of the ship – the difference between throwing a ball at a wall and trying to lob a ball into an open basket.

But even before the round ship gunners could start firing their weapons had to be brought to bear, an operation made all the more difficult and dangerous by the nearly total reliance of round ships on wind power. The disadvantages of relying on this means of manoeuvring became obvious whenever the wind died or blew in the wrong direction. The round ship's *raison d'être* lay in allowing a relatively small crew of skilled mariners, managing complex configurations of square-rigged sails, to voyage around the world, requiring little in the way of supplies and therefore maximizing the ship's carrying capacity. This was irrelevant, however, when a round ship found its adversary was upwind and there was no way to bring its broadside cannon to bear without exposing the entire vessel to withering fire.

Galleys were principally powered by the wind, too, for even the relatively shorter distances of Mediterranean travel were too great to be crossed solely under the strength of the oar. Managing the simple, lateen-rigged triangular sails of galleys did not require the degree of skill necessary for the efficient sailing of a square-rigged round ship. Though galleys most often moved by sail, galley captains relied upon oar power to provide a nimbleness that round ship captains, blown by the winds and tugged by the currents, could only envy. Round ships might tack back and forth all day, fruitlessly seeking to bring their broadside cannon into play, while a galley could move with the wind, against the wind, or rotate on one spot. Keeping round ships in fleet formation was something akin to herding cats, but galleys could move in perfect unison. In a staged battle a galley could serve as a floating gun platform, to be positioned at will.

Finally, galleys carried far more powerful cannon than round ships. This, too, was on account of their superior hull design. Galleys mounted their cannon parallel to their keel, the foundational element of the vessel. Upon firing a cannon a galley was pushed back through the water, the force of the shot dissipated into the waves. Round ship ordnance, mounted broadside, was fired at or near perpendicular to the ship's keel. Instead of sliding and dissipating the force of the recoil, the round ship keel was held in the vice-like grip of the sea, and the force of the shot had to be absorbed by the ship's timbers. The firing of very powerful cannon, or the repeated firing of even moderately powerful guns, inevitably resulted in stress to the ship's structure, causing timbers to buckle and twist, and in extreme instances to crack and shiver. Repeated firings at the very least would force the caulking from between the planks of the hull, allowing sea water into the hold and reducing the mobility of the ship. As a result, while galleys could carry massive 'ship-killing' cannon, round ship ordnance tended to be lighter. In open combat a square-rigged man-of-war not only had to rely on the inconstant winds while trying to close in on a war galley, but had to suffer the ravages of the more powerful cannon of the galley while attempting to do so.

Despite the advantages of galleys over round ships, John Ward was able to develop a strategy of privateering that relied on terrifying his enemy into submission rather than taking them through overwhelming force. Ward's terror tactics allowed him to steal victory from much stronger adversaries – galleys, super-galleys and large round ships that, by rights, should have been able to hold off his assault or defeat his forces in hot battle. In his own day John Ward was recognized as a prodigiously gifted naval commander, a man who was unreasonably successful in battle.

One account of Ward's arrival in Tunis in 1605 states that as he made his way east across the Mediterranean, a war galley of the Knights of Malta set forth from Valletta with the intention of capturing or killing him. The knights hovered in the narrow seas between Tunis and Sicily, trusting the bottleneck to direct Ward into their trap. What happened next provides a vivid illustration of how Ward used psychology and tactics to defeat a theoretically stronger foe.

As he made his way east, Ward had word of the knights' intentions from a friendly ship passing westward. Another man might have taken the opportunity to make a strategic retreat back to the safe ports of Morocco, but we are told that Ward 'began to bestir himself, for his desires admitted no limitation, nor could he persuade his mind to accept any servile yoke'. Calling his men on to the deck of his ship, Ward presented the situation to them, arguing that it would be cowardly to turn tail, and stating that he himself was confident they could fight and beat any galley of Malta. 'The law of nature (quoth he) allows every man to defend himself, being assailed, and to withstand force by force.' Ward's men agreed with this view of the cosmos, and the ship prepared to fight.

The account of the battle is maddeningly brief, but between its broad brushstrokes we can infer some details. Given the relative strengths and weaknesses of galleys and round ships, the most surprising aspect of the account is that it describes a combat in which Ward triumphed through the use of his cannon. 'Many assaults were made, and several showers of shot sent forth on both sides, yet the forces of *Ward* did so disanimate [i.e. render immobile] the *Maltan*, as the edge of his [i.e. the Maltan's] courage was clean taken away, and forc'd to submit himself to the mercy of his enemy.' Galleys held an advantage over round ships in staged naval battles in which the goal was to destroy the opponent. Ward, like any privateering captain worth his command, specialized in taking ships while inflicting a minimum of damage.

Ward's cannon were elevated so high above the waterline that it was difficult to use them to inflict structural damage upon an enemy's hull, but the last thing that he wanted was to sink a prize. Yet these same cannon were ideally situated to scatter chain and bar shot into riggings, and so 'disanimate' his opponent, who, his masts destroyed or stripped of rigging, could now *only* move by oar power, and whose slaves would eventually tire or be whipped into collapse. Meanwhile, Ward could use the short-range snub-nosed mortars that were all too appropriately named 'murderers' to rain jagged pieces of stone, metal and rubbish into the open holds of the galleys, inflicting ghastly wounds and sowing panic. A few such passes and most opponents could be induced to surrender.

The most dangerous part of the combat would be the first passes, when the galley was still able to play its powerful cannon against

Ward's hull. There was no way for Ward to avoid this phase of battle. It is likely that he simply took his gamble, sailing directly for the galley, keeping as narrow a profile as possible, and hoping that the notoriously poor galley gunners would fail to make a solid hit. English gunners had earned a reputation for being highly skilled during the Anglo-Spanish wars, and it is likely that Ward particularly drilled his men on the rapid loading, firing and reloading of his guns. Every pass of Ward's ship left him open to potentially hull-breaching damage from the cannon of the Maltese galley, but with every pass he would have his men fire and reload quickly, maximizing the damage to the galley's rigging and personnel.

Ward's besting of the Knights of Malta upon his approach to Tunis in 1605 is unlikely to have been the first time that he had triumphed over a war galley, and it certainly would not be the last. He was so successful in making war against all nations and all types of ships that in time Ward was persuaded by Uthman Dey to create a school for North African seamen and gunners. Andrew Barker, Ward's sometime captive, reported that while in former days the Barbary Corsairs posed virtually no threat to English traffic in the Mediterranean, 'yet of late, to my own woeful experience, I can witness [that] they have been so readied by the instruction of our apostate countrymen (I mean of Ward and others, who have been their commanders) to tackle their ships, to man and manage a fight.' Another account, written by a merchant's factor who had worked in the eastern Mediterranean, stated that, when not at sea, Ward 'practiseth the casting of ordnance, & in training up those Turks . . . in military discipline'. In years to come, Ward's name would be reviled not primarily because of the damage he personally inflicted by becoming a *raïs* among the Barbary Corsairs, but because of the enduring legacy of his instruction.

Barbarossa had relied on jihad to unify the forces under his command. In place of jihad, John Ward relied upon the universal desire to get rich to unite his crews and best his enemies. The outcome of the battle with the Knights of Malta in 1605, we are told, was that the knights were 'forced to submit [themselves] to the mercy of [their] enemy', the pirate John Ward. What would this have meant for the Maltese? To comprehend it, we must first consider the diverse populations on the war galley. Surrender to an English pirate would have meant different things for each of these groups.

First, there were the oarsmen, whose ranks would have been filled primarily by enslaved Muslims, men captured either as prisoners of war during naval encounters or in slaving raids that the knights had made on to the North African coast and islands. These slaves could hardly be dismayed at the defeat of their captors, and would have been heartily relieved when the fighting stopped. Contemporary depictions of galley warfare show battle raging over the heads of the oarsmen, whose benches ringed the outer edge of the deck. There was a very real danger that the slaves would be killed by random cannon and mortar fire, small shot, crossbow bolts and so on. Worse, if the hull of their galley were breached, slaves had no hope of survival, for they would be dragged below the waves by their chains. With the end of battle the immediate danger to their lives lifted. At worst, the slaves would continue on in their slavery. At best, they could hope for freedom. English privateers-turned-pirates like John Ward were known to be on friendly terms with the corsair states of North Africa. Capture by English pirates held out the possibility of a return to Islamic lands, and perhaps freedom. It is tempting to believe that Ward's gift to the pasha upon arrival in Tunis, which Barker mentions but does not describe, was nothing less than the freedom of the slaves taken with the Maltese galley. Few other gestures would be nearly so effective in capturing official attention and popular acclaim.

Next, there were the sailors. These were the men who navigated the galley at sea, managing the sails, keeping the vessel on course, and looking to the daily maintenance that kept a ship seaworthy. These men were part of the free population of Malta, for whom galley warfare against infidels and Protestant heretics was either an economic necessity or a religious obligation, depending on whether they had sworn fealty to the Knights of Malta or had been hired for their skills. Such men could reasonably hope that they might be allowed to go free after the battle, provided they did not resist the boarding of the galley and did not attempt to conceal any part of the cargo.

The final population on a war galley was the soldiers who played small-arms fire against their enemies and engaged in hand-to-hand combat. The soldiers who sailed on galleys were perceived to be the chief opponents of their enemies, and they could expect no mercy. Death or enslavement awaited them upon capture, unless they acted as complete cravens and put up no resistance whatsoever.

Ward, however, made an unusual offer to the men of the Maltese galley. Taking possession of the ship and preparing to sail it into Tunis, he gave the soldiers and seamen two options: they could die or join with the pirates. Our account describes Ward's offer and the response to it. '[Captain Ward] left it to the choice of such as were taken in her, either to be resolved to subject themselves to his service, or to submit their necks to the stroke of death. Of the two, they rather chose the first.'

This is a remarkable episode in a remarkable career, and it demonstrates many of the qualities that made Ward the success he was. Not only did he rely upon cunning to overcome the greater firepower and manoeuvrability of his enemy, but he evidently viewed the defeat of his enemies as an opportunity for recruitment. It is one matter to conscript the crew of a captured commercial ship, who were not so much adversaries as unfortunate bystanders to the business of the privateer or pirate. In this instance, however, Ward sought to augment his own crew by drafting pirate-hunters who had intended his own death, either in hot battle at sea or back in Malta at the end of a hangman's rope. Why did Ward think he could trust them, and why did he bother? It would appear that, as in days to come, he relied on the transcendent, universal human qualities of greed and self-interest to keep his heterogeneous crew focused on the common goal of becoming uncommonly rich.

SIX

'The Greatest Scoundrel that ever Sailed'

 The years from 1605 to 1608 were John Ward's most active during his tenure among the Barbary Corsairs, a period when he rejuvenated the fortunes of the Muslim privateers and made a fortune for himself. His operations were predominantly in the eastern Mediterranean. This, combined with Ward's propensity for attacking round ships and galleys indiscriminately – so long as they were owned, freighted and manned by Christians – meant that he inevitably became the scourge of Venice, still the most important trading nation in the region, and the bane of English merchants who chartered voyages into the Levant.

The records of England and Venice provide considerable evidence about his activities during this period, in particular identifying some of his prizes and providing information about how he set about capturing them. Perhaps the most remarkable aspect of his operations was how quickly he moved from being a lone operator to becoming the admiral of a fleet and then to coordinating operations from shore. Ward was born in the early 1550s; it is evident that by his own mid-fifties he was less keen to set forth himself and increasingly content to place trusted lieutenants in command of single ships and even small fleets that issued from Tunis in his name. That Ward was able to build a fleet of privateers, attract sufficient numbers of seamen to crew them and highly effective commanders who would rather raid the seas in his name than under their own banner, is testimony to his success and charisma.

The Serene Republic of Venice maintained a network of colonies and naval bases throughout the eastern Mediterranean, staffed by officials who were careful to keep the doge and senate of the republic apprised of local developments. The island of Zante was a key link in the chain. Located just off the coast of Ottoman Greece, it was an incredibly important way-station for Venetian shipping as well as a centre for espionage and observation.

The period of Ward's rise at Tunis was also an era of English piracy generally. Unlike John Ward, most English pirates would not dare to attack war galleys, preferring to prey upon the much weaker merchant shipping of the region. The governor of Zante was accustomed to hearing tales of woe in which Venetian merchant galleys were assaulted by English round ships (which the Venetians called 'bertons'), battered into submission, and then hauled into Ottoman ports where ship, cargo, crew and passengers were sold to the highest bidder. The governor did his best to keep up with this activity, interrogating officers and seamen who had had hostile encounters with English bertons, pressing them to recall distinguishing features of either ship or person of the pirates or would-be pirates. These reports were then forwarded to Venice where they were digested by bureaucrats for the senate or presented as raw data to the various committees that looked after commercial and military affairs.

The reports that flowed out of Zante are remarkable in their quantity, but also in the range of encounters that they described. For example, over the course of two days in 1604 the governor forwarded to the senate four reports of English assaults on Venetian shipping. Two of these describe brief skirmishes which resulted in no or only minimal damage to the Venetian galleys. The third is more consequential, describing a brief encounter in which a pirate was interested only in ready cash, while the last deposition describes a dreadful encounter that left the Venetian ship broken and smouldering, thirteen corpses strewn about the deck, violently subdued by the English boarding party.

Deposition of Marco Salamon of Irakleiou, Crete, supercargo of the *Spelegato*

Left Irakleiou for Venice. Put into Souda for water and to wait for fair weather. Sailed again on the 26th of last month. On Thursday last, the 11th of October, off Strivali, we were boarded and captured by an Englishman. Our mizzen mast and sails were set on fire. Thirteen people were killed between crew and passengers, and five taken prisoners. Our crew numbered thirty-one, and there were about fifteen passengers; the berton was of about two hundred tons burden, and had one hundred and twenty people on board.

He cannot give her name; but it was said that two Knights and two Captains were on board, and one of these was called Formin, a man of about forty years of age, black beard, medium stature, well built; the other squinted, but deponent remembreth not with which eye, thinketh it is the right; well built; about forty; thick brown beard, ordinary moustaches. Of the Knights one was thickset, pale, black beard, about thirty; has a mark on one lip; short; fat; called Saint Andrew. The other is short; thin; blond; deponent does not know his name. The ship had a variety of flags, and used them as suited her.

Enclosed in the governor's dispatch from Zante, 19 October 1604

Such encounters became ever more common. Amidst this general confusion and ruin the specific threat posed by Captain John Ward was slow to be perceived.

Towards the end of 1606 a rich Venetian merchant galley named the *Rubi* mysteriously disappeared. Ever diligent, the governor of Zante began to interrogate the seamen who passed through his port, hoping to learn of the vessel's fate, already suspecting the worst. On 3 December 1606 the governor wrote to the doge and senate stating, 'I have news that at Sapientza there is a prize brought in by an English berton. This prize I conjecture to be the ship *Rubi*, which was recently captured by a privateer.'

The governor sent a spy to Sapientza to determine whether this ship was the *Rubi*, and soon learned otherwise. 'My messenger, sent to get news of the ship *Rubi*, returned yesterday and reports that he found no traces of the ship', he wrote on 10 December 1606. Having crossed the narrow channel that separates the island of Sapientza from the town of Methoni, the governor's spy reported that 'the people of Methoni declare that they witnessed a fight at sea between two ships, which separated as evening fell'. The governor reasonably concluded that this fight was between the *Rubi* and its captor. The fact that the *Rubi* did not then end up in Sapientza, the governor suggested, 'leads one to the conclusion that the privateer was either Maltese or Spanish, for if she had been English she would have taken shelter in one of the Turkish ports'. The governor's logic here suggests that he was not yet aware of the change that had begun with Ward's appointment to the *taifa* at Tunis: that English captains might not be pirates looking to dump booty in the nearest Ottoman port that came to hand, but rather Ottoman privateers with a home port to which they must return.

Two months passed, during which time the governor kept his file on the *Rubi* open even as the trail apparently ran cold – a sure indication that the *Rubi* must have had quite a valuable cargo. Then, in February, he wrote of the plundering of the *Carminati*, a Venetian merchant galley that had the misfortune to be taken and sacked not once but twice. Setting out from Naples, the *Carminati* was attacked and plundered by a Tuscan pirate who flew the flag of Malta in order to catch the vessel off guard. The Tuscans removed the most valuable cargo, but left the *Carminati* to continue her sorry voyage. Then, on 28 January 1607, 'forty miles off land, an English berton, flying the Flemish flag, bore down on her and signalled to strike sail, which she did. The master, supercargo, crew, and passengers were put in a boat with a few biscuits and the *Carminati* was taken away westward. The berton had a crew of 110 men, including a few Turks, the rest were English. It seems that she is the same ship that plundered the *Rubi*.'

Though he knew enough to conclude that the *Carminati* and the *Rubi* were taken by the same English captain, the governor of Zante still did not know his identity. To discover this, we must rely upon the stories of others. It is the records of the High Court of Admiralty, the body charged with regulating English activities on the high seas, that reveal Ward's role at this time, through cases brought against men who had sailed with him.

In the spring of 1608 two men appeared in the Admiralty courts and made a series of sworn depositions that are directly contradictory. At this point we cannot know whether John Keye of Limehouse, mariner, or Geoffrey Wiseman of Southwark, mariner, was telling the truth. Neither is it possible to decipher the exact role either played in John Ward's capture of two prizes in the warm waters of the Ionian Sea during the early winter of 1606. This is because neither Keye nor Wiseman was primarily interested in furnishing an accurate account of their service under Captain Ward. Instead, Keye was obsessed with destroying Wiseman and attempting to clear his own name, while Wiseman was more than ready to return the favour. Nonetheless, the sea tales that these men told broaden our understanding of how Ward managed ships and men, in battle and out. Almost incidentally, the testimony of the two men also identifies the English captain who captured the richly freighted *Rubi*.

The tale starts with John Keye in Sicily, at Messina, in the autumn of 1606, without work. Casting about for a new appointment, he landed himself a position as master of the *John Baptist*, a small English merchantman of 90 tons with a crew of seventeen Greek, French and English seamen. In late October he set sail from Messina for Chios by way of Crete, carrying luxurious damask cloth belonging to two English merchants valued at £500. The ship was roughly halfway through its journey when, off Sapientza on the western Greek coast, it was set upon by Captain John Ward, at about 8 o'clock at night. Keye, who shortly would have ample opportunity to inspect Ward's ships, states that Ward had under his command 'a Flemish flyboat of two hundred tons, called the *Gift*' and a pinnace of 50 tons' burden. The *Gift* – one of Ward's prizes, renamed with sardonic humour – was armed with thirty cannon and crewed by sixty-seven English, Dutch and Spanish sailors in addition to twenty-eight men that Keye calls 'Turks', a very loose term that could include any Ottoman Muslim, either Anatolian janissary or North African seaman. The pinnace was crewed by an additional nineteen men who apparently were English. It was a fairly standard practice among privateers and pirates to sail two ships under one command, the smaller a satellite to the larger.

There could be little shame for Keye in surrendering the *John Baptist* to Captain Ward, given the odds. Keye was in a small ship with seventeen crew while Ward had command of two vessels with a combined crew of 114 seamen and soldiers and some thirty pieces of ordnance. Though fighting was out of the question, Keye fulfilled the responsibilities of his command by fleeing as best he could. Ward brought Keye's flight to an end almost five hours later, at 1 o'clock in the morning, just outside of the Ottoman-held port of Koroni. Not daring to put up resistance, Keye struck sail and surrendered.

Ward had Keye and his five top officers brought on board the *Gift*, while thirteen of Ward's men were stationed on the *John Baptist* to prevent any attempts at revolt among the remaining eleven members of Keye's crew. Keye then alleged that the nineteen men on Ward's pinnace – among whose number was a common seaman named Geoffrey Wiseman – colluded with the thirteen men assigned to guard the *John Baptist*. Transferring the damask cloth from the *John Baptist* to the pinnace, these men fled into the night. This, according to Keye's testimony, was a double piracy, for Wiseman and the others had stolen from Ward that which Ward had only just stolen from Keye.

Ward seems to have taken in his stride the defection of these men, if it actually were a defection. Now in command of the *Gift* and the *John Baptist*, Ward continued his tour of the Ionian Sea. According to Keye, Ward pressed the men of the *John Baptist*, including Keye, into his service. Like the merchant tailor Richard Parker, whom

Ward had met at Salé in 1605, and many other seamen brought before the Admiralty courts, Keye claims that he was given no choice but to sail with the captain. This does not square with what we know of Ward's methods of recruitment, which at all times relied on the enticements of wealth rather than threats or compulsion. When a ship surrendered without fighting, as the *John Baptist* had, Ward demonstrated time and again a willingness to release in one of the ship's boats those who did not want to enter his service, or even to leave them in the plundered ship itself.

But this is hardly the most unlikely element in Keye's testimony. Keye's claim that the men in the pinnace stole from Ward the cargo of the *John Baptist* defies credibility. How quickly and how stealthily could they have emptied the *John Baptist*? And how fast could an over-manned pinnace, moving ponderously beneath the cargo of a ninety-ton merchantman, dash out of sight of the *Gift*? Keye tells us that the *John Baptist* did not surrender to Ward until 1 a.m. If the men were transferred between ships and all was made secure over another hour or so, a conservative estimate, this would mean that Ward would have posted his night watch and allowed his men to turn in around 2 o'clock or 2.30. Perhaps Wiseman and his conspirators waited until 3 a.m. to begin to tranship the damask cloth, accomplishing the task over the next two or three hours, somehow escaping the notice of the night watch on the *Gift*. They then fled into the dawn, when they surely would have been observed by the men of the *Gift*. Had Ward wanted to, it would have been a simple matter for the *Gift* to run down the pinnace and recapture his prize. Reading between the lines, it seems that Wiseman and the others were allowed to take the cargo of the *John Baptist* and depart in the pinnace, presumably in lieu of prize shares.

Instead of making haste to recapture the pinnace, Ward continued sailing amidst the Greek islands. Before long he encountered the *Mary Ann*, another English ship. Ward did not attempt to take the *Mary Ann*, out of either friendship or a desire for richer prizes. Keye, however, paints a moving picture of himself pleading with Ward for permission to tranship, which permission Captain Ward denied. This is another of the ploys that rogue seamen used before the High Court of Admiralty, alleging that they attempted to leave Ward's command but were compelled to stay on.

Shortly after parting with the *Mary Ann* and two weeks after the capture of the *John Baptist*, on 16 November Captain Ward fell into pursuit of 'an argosy of Venice' named the *Rubi* – or the *Ruby*, as the Admiralty court scribe would have it. Ward's men made a hostile boarding of the ship and found themselves in possession of a merchantman of 300 tons' burden, heavily laden with pepper, indigo, flax and other luxury goods purchased in Alexandria and intended for Venice. It was a tremendous coup.

Ward's crew were now spread across three ships – the *Gift* (200 tons), the *John Baptist* (90 tons) and the *Rubi* (300 tons) – and turned home without delay. At Tunis Ward transformed the *Rubi* into a square-rigged man-of-war, adding cannon and recruiting about 140 men, 'all English for the most part'. Keye, however, testified that as soon as he reached Tunis he escaped from the outlaws and reported to Hugh Changett, the French consul who by treaty also served English needs. Here ends Keye's testimony, without word of what role he played in the taking of the *Rubi*, or whether he took his prize shares, or how he was able to afford passage to London from Tunis. It is a straightforward story, of a kind encountered time and again in Admiralty records: a seaman is compelled to sail with the dread Captain Ward, but flees at the first opportunity, refusing to partake in any ill-gotten goods. Even in the unlikely event that this tale should seem believable when first encountered, it wears thin with repetition.

Keye made his deposition on 1 March 1608. The next day Geoffrey Wiseman appeared before the court and offered his testimony. Wiseman had just been painted black by Keye, who had first established that Wiseman had sailed in confederacy with John Ward and then played pirate to the privateer by betraying Ward and stealing off with the damask cloth from the *John Baptist*. Refusing to act the innocent, Wiseman made no attempt to refute these accusations. Instead, he sought to drag Keye down with him.

Wiseman confirmed that he and the others in the pinnace fled west from the Greek islands, taking the damask cloth back past Sicily, where it had been laded shortly before, and into the western Mediterranean. The flight of the pinnace ended when it was wrecked by a storm off Formentera, the tiny sister-island to Ibiza, near the Spanish coast. Wiseman and other survivors were rescued by a Dutch merchantman and taken to Tunis. This is the last place for which they should have made had they just betrayed Ward, as Keye alleged, but a logical destination for a once more impoverished and unemployed former shipmate still on good terms with the captain.

Wiseman was in Tunis to witness the triumphant return of Captain Ward in command of the *Gift*, the *John Baptist* and the *Rubi*. Meeting with his old mates, Wiseman heard tales of what had transpired after the departure of the pinnace. He offered these stories as part of his testimony before the High Court of Admiralty in 1608. Wiseman states the *Rubi* was travelling in convoy with another vessel when Ward encountered her. Since the *Rubi* was larger than the *Gift* she would have made formidable prey on her own; given that she was travelling in company, she should have, by rights, been immune to attack by pirates or privateers. Ward had other ideas.

Ward behaved as he had prior to his assault upon the war galley of the Knights of Malta in 1605 and before daring to attack the French merchantman off the Cornish coast in 1603 – both encounters which, like the putative battle now at hand, pitted him against a more powerful foe. Calling his men on to the deck, Ward laid out the situation and called for a vote on whether or not to attack the magnificent *Rubi* and her escort. 'Masters', Wiseman quotes Ward as saying, 'what should we do? Should we fight with these argosies? We are greatly weakened in that thirty of our best men are run away with the pinnace.' Wiseman averred that it was none other than John Keye who carried the motion to attack the *Rubi*, boldly declaring that 'if he were in a barque but of fifty tons he would take one of them, and that if they lost that opportunity they should never meet with the like again'.

Wiseman further testified that Keye followed strong words with strong actions. Once Ward had run down the *Rubi*, whose escort fled during the chase, Keye was the first of Ward's men to board the Venetian vessel. Fluent in Italian, Keye falsely declared himself to be the captain of the *Gift* and demanded that the Venetian crew yield up any 'gold, jewels or matters of worth'. Gathering up 3,000 pieces of gold in addition to items of jewellery, Keye secreted these about his person and neglected to dump them with the general plunder at the mast of the *Gift*. In short, Wiseman levelled the same charge at Keye that Keye had brought against Wiseman, each claiming that the other had willingly participated in piracy under Captain Ward, and then had double-damned himself by stealing plunder from a thief.

Wiseman continued to unfold his story, describing how, en route to Tunis, one of Ward's men – William Graves, the captain's closest friend and most trusted lieutenant – informed him of Keye's subterfuge during the capture of the *Rubi*. When Ward confronted him with the theft Keye acted the penitent and surrendered the jewels and 2,500 pieces of gold, cunningly keeping 500 back for himself. Ward, so often generous with his spoils, surprised Keye by rewarding his treachery with 500 more gold pieces, presumably in tribute to Keye's chutzpah. Keye, considerably enriched, was permitted to leave Ward's service, taking his prize shares and bonus with him. Wiseman rounded off his testimony by pointing out that shortly after Keye's return to England he moved from his modest dwelling in Limehouse to a greater one in London.

Fortunately, we are not in the position of having to decide who was telling the truth. Wiseman and Keye had tarred each other with the same brush, but Keye, it turned out, had better allies. Calling upon a London merchant who had been resident in Tunis during 1606 and 1607, the court heard testimony that Keye 'would not suffer . . . to frequent the company of Ward or Bishop', the latter being the most notorious of Ward's confederates. Keye himself swore that he 'would rather die then live amongst that lewd company in that wicked manner'. Of course, both of these statements could be true and still not absolve Keye of either charge levelled by Wiseman: that Keye had been an active participant in John Ward's activities in the Ionian Sea during 1606, and that Keye had pillaged the *Rubi* to his own benefit, in contravention of the laws of nations and privateering convention. In the event, the court charged Wiseman (among others, including Ward) with the boarding and plunder of the *John Baptist*, and the 'assault' of 'John Keye, master, and others'. If an English indictment ever were issued for the taking of the *Rubi* it has since been lost.

While it is not possible now to compile a comprehensive list of ships captured by Ward between 1605 and 1610, his most active period among the Barbary Corsairs, there are several short lists, included in news pamphlets of 1609, that offer a selection of Ward's assaults and those of his lieutenants. These lists offer an idea of the more pedestrian cargoes that formed the bulk of Ward's, or any privateer's, prizes: 'A small barque of Falmouth, laden with pilchards'; 'The *Elizabeth* of London, laden with oil from Toulon in France, Tho. Hilles, Master'. To strike upon something so rich as a cargo of spices, such as that on the *Rubi*, or of luxurious textiles, as on the *John Baptist*, was a rare occurrence. Among the captures made by Ward's subordinates are two startlingly lopsided victories: 'A French man-of-war, who had in her ninety-five men and fourteen pieces of ordnance, yet surrendered without any one shot shooting: there were three Cavalieros of Malta in her' and 'a small ship of Ward's . . . of sixty-five tons took a Holland ship of 500, worth four and twenty thousand pounds'. One capture in particular was notorious in its day, though forgotten now: 'The *Trojan* of London, she was taken, and all her men made slaves but for shooting off one shot in their own defence.'

The taking of another two ships, the *Charity* and the *Pearl*, temporarily halted English trade into the Mediterranean. This was not because of the high value of the cargoes of these vessels – indeed, the *Charity* carried only corn – but rather because their fate revealed the devastating effectiveness of the Barbary Corsairs in the years following John Ward's arrival in Tunis. 'The merchants [of London] are all in confusion on this account', wrote one observer, describing the impact of the tale's circulation in London. 'No ships venture to put out, nor is there anyone who will insure except at excessive rates.'

The published report of the incident is taken from a letter written by an eyewitness, a factor on the *Charity*, the man responsible for overseeing the trading of goods during the ship's numerous stops in the Mediterranean. The letter was written to the merchants who chartered the *Charity* and who hired the factor, officers and seamen to, in the factor's own words, 'offer our bodies and our lives to enlarge our own fortunes, as to increase your possessions'. But instead of mooring in the Thames and presenting a fat ledger of accounts to the merchants in London, the factor describes how 'from Lisbon we are now enforced to write, and we must entreat you with patience to read, of nothing but of the world's Period makers, Death and Destiny: of sorrow instead of prosperous success, of our lamentation at sea instead of bringing profit to shore.'

The factor's letter begins with the penultimate stop of the *Charity* at Ancona, Italy, where unnamed goods were exchanged for a heavy cargo of wheat. From Ancona the *Charity* was intended for Malaga, Spain, to sell the wheat, lade a new cargo and return to London. Heading south, coasting the eastern shore of the Italian boot, the *Charity* fell in with the *Pearl*, another ship of London bound for home directly and shortly out of Venice. Each rejoicing in the company of the other, the two vessels emerged from the Adriatic Sea into the Mediterranean and turned west on a 'flattering wind' that carried them from Sicily to Spain in fifteen days: a voyage 'by all and the best mariners accounted very rare and wonderful'.

Just off the Spanish coast their luck died with the wind. The ships attempted to head south, the *Charity* for Malaga and the *Pearl* for Gibraltar, but 'the wind presently began to be more duller and calm, and shortly after to chop up westerly (which was against us).' As the ships laboured against the wind a cluster of sails broke the horizon: three round ships, flying upon the wind, coming towards them. 'Having no cause to mistrust them', it was several hours before the seamen realized that the destination of the strange ships was the *Charity* and the *Pearl* themselves. Panicking, Master Lewis of the *Pearl* and Master Bannister of the *Charity* ordered a reversal of course, the ships fleeing upon the wind as best they could: but the lumbering merchantmen, their hulls crammed with heavy cargo and fouled with seaweed and barnacles, were no match for their pursuers, 'they being clean vessels, by which it appeared they were newly come out of harbour, and which helped them to be of better speed'. It was not long before the strangers had overtaken the *Pearl*, the slower of the pair. The *Charity*'s crew looked on as the *Pearl* was brought to surrender, striking sail in submission.

'We being of better swiftness, and having seen what they had offered, it was no boot to bid us make haste, so that we gave our vessel all the sail we could, but to a bootless purpose. For after long chase, they came up also to us, and . . . they called aloud to us, and bade us "Amain for the Great Turk".' Though the *Charity*'s men could see Ottoman soldiers lining the decks, yet 'the sailors and seafaring men within these three ships . . . were all of them Englishmen, and all or most of them known to our master, Master Daniel Bannister, or to diverse [members] of our company.' The factor then names the commanders of the three ships, now referred to as admiral, vice-admiral and rear-admiral to distinguish their places and roles within the small fleet: 'Linckes, master of the admiral . . . Powell, of the vice-admiral and . . . Foxeley, an ancient man, of the rear-admiral.' It was now apparent to the *Charity*'s crew that these were not just any Ottoman corsairs, but were 'confederates of Ward's'. What's more, they were much more powerful than the *Charity*: 'the admiral carrying thirty pieces of ordnance, and the other two . . . having twenty eight a piece, besides six hundred Turks with small shot, who are held to be the best shot in the world'. The *Charity* had 'but eleven pieces of ordnance' and twenty men.

Nonetheless, Bannister responded to the privateers' threats with defiance, refusing to strike sail 'to any pagan breathing'. As the privateers made ready to 'lay us directly aboard with their ships', Bannister made the only threat that he could realistically deliver, declaring his intention 'to burn ourselves and them together' by exploding his gunpowder as soon as Ward's men grappled alongside. The factor describes the furore as the crew of the *Charity* (henceforth 'the Charities') prepared their ship for battle and their souls for death: 'some of us managing all things fitly below, whilst others manned all things readily above; every man of us having made his soul fit for heaven and consenting his body to a watery grave . . . we [now] fitted our netting, hung out drabblers . . . [and made] ready for a sea-fight, we having little but faithfulness and courage to withstand them, and they like a violent sea ready to beat against an unfortified shore.'

'They were ready to call upon us in fire, and we as furnished to make answer in flame', notes the factor. But Linckes, Powell and Foxeley knew more of their craft than to spend ball and powder only to watch a prize slip below the waves. In a move worthy of their mentor, John Ward, one of the ships crowded in close and staged a pageant for the edification of the Charities. The janissaries, who had been making a show of power at the rails, gave way, allowing a group of Englishmen in chains to be led forth. Shouting across the waters, the slaves declared that if the Charities

> had a desire to see our Country again; if we had parents to mourn for their sons, wives to lament for their husbands, or children to cry out for their fathers, not to shoot so much as the voice of one small shot against [Ward's men] . . . We [i.e. the English slaves] have withstood them, as you may do, which hath brought us into slavery as you shall be. . . . [If] your resolution be such, to prefer an honourable death before a dishonourable peace, then fight it out bravely . . . since that death is easiest to take, the which you now have in hand.

Was this mere theatre? Were these actual slaves, or were they simply English seamen who had entered Ward's service and were now playing a role? We know that Ward fully exploited his janissaries first for their psychological effect, preferring to persuade a surrender rather than fight a famous battle. Although Master Bannister and the Charities had refused to surrender even as the janissaries had made their war calls and clashed their swords, and the privateers' gunners had rolled out all their cannon in an impressive show, Linckes, Powell and Foxeley remained unwilling to escalate into open combat. Whether or not the English slaves were genuine, they had the desired effect: the Charities' resolve crumbled, and Bannister began to negotiate the surrender of his ship.

An hour later the lead privateer prepared to grapple on to the *Charity*. Even before the boarding could begin in earnest, the English crew of the privateer began to call out low and urgently to the Charities, warning them of 'these Turks, whom I doubt not but you have heard to be cruel enough'. The seamen of the privateer warned that the janissaries 'have as much command or more than ourselves', and that even though 'it was in no way [our] intents, neither was it . . . Captain Ward's pleasure, that any private seafaring man's venture should be anyways hindered by him or his confederates': the terrible janissaries could not be controlled. These sometime friends and acquaintances offered to take into safekeeping the personal effects of the Charities, the better to avoid them falling into the hands of the allegedly tyrannical janissaries.

The *Charity*'s men, and especially Bannister, who had many years experience at sea, were not sufficiently naïve to believe this whole-heartedly, yet still, 'partly for fear not to dare to mistrust them, and partly with hope to reserve somewhat', the Charities made a pact with the privateersmen. With great stealth 'every man distributed unto them what we had, namely our needful shift of apparel, to wit, linen and woollen, and our master, Master Bannister, who was to go aboard of them, even his whole provision, to the silver whistle and chain about his neck . . . still hoping that thieves might prove to be men of their words, and that there might be found some conscience in them because they were our countrymen.' The factor notes, ruefully, that 'with this, pitiful poor birds, were we caught.' Thieves did not prove to be men of their words, none of the Charities would see their goods again, and each, 'for want of shift [i.e. change of clothes], he knew he should be lousy before he got home'.

The sky was already dark by the time the privateer had grappled on to the *Charity*. Bannister and eleven others were removed from the vessel, and a contingent of janissaries crossed over. 'We were for that night guarded, and every man having his sentinel to watch him. . . . [We had] little mind to sleep, who were in doubt every minute to have our throats cut.' Meanwhile, Bannister was having a reunion of sorts on board the privateer. He had already picked out some former acquaintances among the privateers' seamen. What he had not expected was to be warmly welcomed by the janissaries themselves.

It fortunately fell out that our master, having in former voyages, much used the trade of transporting passengers from Algiers and Tunis to Alexandria and Constantinople, he seemed well to be remembered by many of these pirates . . . [who] informed their captain what service heretofore our master had done to their nation, as also what courtesy hath themselves and diverse [others] of their friends had received at his hands. . . . Our ship was not a stranger unto them, for our master had brought in her last voyage the great pasha of Tunis from Constantinople to Tunis.

Friendly reunions notwithstanding, business was business: with morning the looting began in earnest. Although Bannister had characterized his cargo as naught but corn, 'which they utterly neglected, as a commodity unworthy of them', hardened privateers could only be true empiricists, scorning all but the evidence of their own eyes. Heading below decks, the janissaries 'fell violently to ransack, pillaging our traffic, cutting down our cabins and staving our chests to pieces.' They 'did such rummage in every corner' that they quickly found the more valuable merchandise which the Charities had hidden 'deep amongst the corn'.

Next, they carried off the *Charity*'s war supplies. 'Leaving us with nothing to call our own but what we had on our backs, they took away all the [gun] powder we had, saving what our ordnance was laden withal, leaving us not so much besides as would prime one piece. They bereft us of our great shot [i.e. cannonballs], all our muskets, all our small shot [i.e. musket balls], of our match, pikes, ladles and sponges [used in the working of ordnance], rapiers, swords, daggers.' By the time this second wave of looting was over the Charities were deprived 'of all necessary munition for defence . . . leaving nothing with us, what necessity should so ever succeed, but the vast sea and the unconstant winds to defend us.'

Still the *Charity* was not picked clean. The janissaries headed below decks once more and snatched 'our beef, pork . . . all our butter and cheese, rice and oil' while the English privateersmen swarmed into the riggings and pilfered 'part of our sails and tacklings', as much cable as could be liberated with ease, and any other ship's supplies that the *Charity* had stowed against wear, storms and other disasters. 'In brief, we were left [with] nothing to defend us, little or nothing to feed us, [but with] misery enough to torment us.'

The factor notes that, though the privateers' seamen and soldiers alike had only goodwill towards the Charities personally, nothing could prevent them from fully exploiting a prize that they had captured. 'Although they gave us liberty, they would not leave us without languishment. Although they could find in their hearts to bid us farewell, yet they would do the best in them . . . to famish us ere we could come home.'

The misery that Ward's men left in their wake stands in contrast with the joyfulness of the privateers in their looting. Partakers of a fraternity forged through joint enterprise, this new brotherhood superseded even the ties of friendship that Ward's men had known among the community of English seamen. 'They were overlookers of all and . . . whatever they liked and laid hands on, being all sharers, they cried to one another, "this is for us!" . . . Their will is a law. They are free men of the sea, and their liberty must have no resistance.' Is it so difficult to see how John Ward could draw recruits even from among his victims?

On account of Master Daniel Bannister's past good services, the Charities were allowed their ship and their liberty even as the *Pearl* was manned with a prize crew and dispatched to Tunis. This was not the end of their trials, however. The next day the *Charity* saw a French merchantman being pursued by Ward's ships. A furious battle followed, and then 'our eyes were made witness that they took the merchant and the master and hanged them up at their yard arms, and as before they had sent away one of ours [i.e. the *Pearl*] so they commanded away his ship to Tunis and made slaves of the rest of the company, being four score and four men'. When the factor's tale was later taken up by an enterprising publisher and made into a hot-selling news pamphlet, this became the emblematic image stamped on to the pamphlet's title page: the French merchantman, masts now sporting Ottoman crescents, cannon blazing away at an English ship, two turbaned janissaries on deck brandishing cutlasses, two dead Christians dangling from the yards like macabre pennants (see plate 2).

Before the *Charity* reached safe harbour, it was pursued twice more by pirates: first, by a French pirate, from which it sought shelter with a convoy of four English ships and a Fleming; and secondly, under attack by a man-of-war and pinnace, under the command of the infamous Captain Simon Danziker, whose operations from Algiers rivalled those of Ward at Tunis. On discovering how little plunder there was to be had of the *Charity*, however, Danziker 'scorned to rob an hospital, to afflict where misery was before, or' – more to the point, perhaps – 'to make prey of them who had nothing left' and let them go.

SEVEN

'Princely and Magnificent'

The riches he hath gained,
And by bloodshed obtained,
Well may suffice to maintain a king;
His fellows all were valiant wights,
Fit to be made prince's knights,
But that their lives do base dishonours bring.

This wicked-gotten treasure
Doth him but little pleasure;
The land consumes what they have got by sea,
In drunkenness and lechery,
Filthy sins of sodomy,
Their evil-gotten goods do waste away.

from 'The Seaman's Song of Captain Ward'

The contrast could not be more stark between the pitiful state of the captain's victims and the riotous life and prosperity of Ward and his men ashore. But it was not all drunkenness and sodomy, as alleged in 'The Seaman's Song of Captain Ward': like any successful entrepreneur, Ward recognized the need to channel a good portion of his earnings back into his business, using it to convert merchantmen into privateers, as well as to purchase ordnance and ships' supplies, and to attract and retain the hundreds of mariners needed to work his fleet. Ward's life on shore was divided between Tunis and its port, La Goulette.

Tunis, in the early 1600s as today, is about 10 kilometres inland from the Mediterranean Sea. La Goulette – French for 'the gullet', but really just a generic term for any narrows or bottleneck at sea – is the name given to the seaport that opens into Lake Tunis, which stretches from La Goulette to Tunis itself. Much later, during the nineteenth century, when Tunisia was a French colony, the western end of Lake Tunis was drained and elevated to make way for the Ville Nouvelle, a new city for the colonial authorities. Near the end of the century the French also built a causeway through the middle of the Lake to accommodate a roadway and a rail line from La Goulette to Tunis. With the exception of these substantial alterations, the situation of the port and the city is much the same today as in the seventeenth century.

La Goulette, for much of its history, has been a grim little town of seafarers and port workers, its spectacular beaches much appreciated by the corsairs who hauled their ships on to the gently sloping sands to scrape and clean their hulls between tours. The activity of the corsairs in La Goulette, from routine careening to the kind of refitting that allowed Ward to convert merchant ships like the *John Baptist* and *Rubi* into privateers, was watched over by Ottoman soldiers looking out from the thick, unadorned walls of Borj el-Karrak. This massive fortification, only recently completed when Ward began to sail with the Tunisian corsairs, served as the garrison for the local detachment of janissaries. It also included quarters for the slaves who rowed on the galleys that were the vessel of choice for most corsair captains. Beyond the Borj el-Karrak, La Goulette consisted of the shacks of the port workers and little else. Ward, like many deeply salted seamen, was often known to spend nights in port on board his ship, and there was not much in La Goulette to tempt him away from his captain's cabin.

More prestigious accommodations, and more lavish entertainments, were afforded within Tunis, and it was here that Ward made his official residence. Modern Tunis has largely sprung up around the ancient walled district called the Medina. As a result, the Medina still retains something of the flavour of the city of John Ward and

Uthman Dey. Tunis's principal mosque, the Zitouna, built in 698 and rebuilt in the ninth century, still rises majestically at the physical and spiritual centre of the Medina. During Ward's day the mosque included a theological faculty that was an important centre of learning within the Islamic world. The wealth that maintained the mosque and its associated institutions was generated in the series of souks, or markets, that radiate out from it. The Souk el-Trouk, known as the Turkish Sailor's Souk, is suggestive of the sale of looted cargoes, while the Souk el-Berka was the site of the slave market, where, among others, the Christian crew of ships that resisted John Ward's assaults were brought in chains and sold.

These souks lay west of the Zitouna Mosque and led into the square that contains the Mosque of Yusef Dey, the first Ottoman-style mosque built in Tunis. Named for Uthman Dey's son and heir, the mosque was built in the early seventeenth century at the very time when John Ward's ships were raiding the length and breadth of the Mediterranean Sea. Just west of this mosque lies the Place of the Kasbah. Today this is an open plaza, but, prior to being razed by the French in the nineteenth century, it was the site of the most important military fortress in Tunis and the seat of its government. In earlier days the kasbah loomed over the twisting alleys and boisterous markets where corsair *raïs* like John Ward sold off prizes and slaves, bought supplies and hired crews.

South of the Zitouna Mosque lay the homes of some of the wealthiest residents of Ottoman Tunis, including Uthman Dey. Uthman's primary residence, Dar Othman, still stands, its beautifully metrical architecture and glorious tile-work testifying to the wealth of its owner, but also to his desire to use Ottoman architecture to express his views on aesthetics and power: a significant architectural choice for the leader of the bloodiest janissary revolt in Ottoman North Africa. Like the Mosque of Yusef Dey, Dar Othman dates from the building boom of the early seventeenth century, by which time Uthman and his family had established their authority and were consolidating their wealth. Uthman's wealth came in no small part from the activities of the corsair *raïs*, and especially from those, like Ward, in whose expeditions Uthman was a private investor.

Concurrent with Uthman's tremendous building projects was a more minor one overseen by Captain John Ward. At some point, probably after 1607, Uthman, delighted with the riches that Ward had rendered to him personally as well as to the state, 'gave [Ward] a large piece of ground, that sometimes before was an old castle, and all the stone that belonged unto it: upon which it is reported he hath built a very stately house, far more fit for a prince, than a pirate.' Though we do not know the exact location of Ward's mansion, it was deemed sumptuous. A traveller who visited Ward in 1615 described it as 'a fair palace, beautified with rich marble and alabaster stones'.

Many commented on the incongruence between Ward's life in Tunis and his humble origins. That a low-born commoner should rise to such heights was unseemly, at least according to the literate English elite whose opinions have survived, and the means of his rise, Ottoman privateering, was appalling. For his part, Ward revelled in the luxuries he could now afford and replicated in Tunis select features of English social exclusion. Andrew Barker wrote that Ward 'lives there in Tunis in a most princely and magnificent state. His apparel is both curious and costly, his diet sumptuous, and his followers seriously observing and obeying his will.' Like kings and lords, Ward 'hath two cooks that dress and prepare his diet for him, and his taster before he eats'.

By the time of Barker's captivity in Tunis, late 1607 or 1608, Ward had made his residence into a sort of alternative court. 'I do not know any Peer in England that bears up his port in more dignity, nor hath his attendants more obsequious unto him,' Barker wrote. 'There is no admittance of a suitor on any business, but their business is first made known to one of his followers that is near him, which if [Ward] list not to regard, [the suitors] have their answer from this man: "that his greatness is not at leisure, neither will he be spoke withal."' Should he deign to entertain one of these suitors, like his social superiors back in England, Ward demonstrated his power by making the man wait. Barker commented that he did not know 'of any affairs that were dispatched by [Ward], in the time of my imprisonment there, at their first coming, but with long attendance, much suit, yea and (by your leave) some bribes. . . . His success hath made him desperate and resolute, his riches have made him proud.'

Ward may have become puffed with pride, but his reputation for being able to influence official affairs in Tunis was well founded. One suitor whom Ward entertained was the then-famous Scottish traveller William Lithgow, who found himself caught on the horns of Ottoman bureaucracy in his attempts to procure a passport – today it would be called a visa – to travel overland through Ottoman North Africa. Lithgow, who struck up a warm friendship with 'old Waird' and spent several days in his company, does not comment on whether Ward made him gratuitously wait attendance or bribe underlings before their initial meeting, but the traveller does state that his visa was obtained thanks to Ward's interventions. Another observer recorded that Ward was deeply involved in the intimate circle of men around Uthman Dey: '[Uthman] has two ministers, Amurat, the Genoese [renegade] and Hasan, [another] Genoese [renegade]. In Hasan's house in Tunis Ward [sometimes] lodges, and while Hasan is away [Ward] looks after money on [Uthman's] account.'

Ward had become part of Uthman's retinue, but he also developed a select retinue of his own from among his crewmen. At the core of this group were a number of hand-picked seafarers often described as Ward's bodyguard. These men formed a glowering circle around their captain, their presence, initially, an affectation of authority rather than a necessity. Lithgow writes that their 'lives and countenances were both alike, even as desperate as disdainful'. Another writer refers to them as Ward's 'court guard'.

Ward did not need to have men on his payroll in order to have a crowd about him. As news of his success at sea spread, adventurers and rogues made for Tunis in hopes of sailing with him. Among their number was at least one English gentleman, Sir Francis Verney. Verney's story of mistreatment by the English state is, in its way, almost as pathetic as that of John Ward and the other low-born seamen left without work in 1603.

Sir Francis was the eldest son of a rich and ancient line of English gentlemen. In the normal course of events Verney could have expected to benefit from the English system of primogeniture, which necessitated that the bulk of noble or gentle estates passed to the eldest male of the line. Verney's mother died while he was a boy, however, and when his father remarried his stepmother quickly deprived Sir Francis of his inheritance. Having coerced the young Sir Francis into an arranged marriage, she leaned on friends and political connections in order to secure passage of a private member's bill in the House of Commons. Enacted into law, this authorized a departure from primogeniture and settled the Verney estate upon her son from a previous marriage. Friends later testified that Sir Francis's father acquiesced to these machinations, but we have no records to indicate why he allowed the brutal, but legal, dispossession of his first-born son.

Until he attained majority Sir Francis had no legal recourse. In 1603, when he was nineteen years old, he began a quixotic quest for justice. Many were sympathetic but there was nothing to be done. A few stray parcels of land were broken off the vast Verney holdings and tossed to him. The intention was to placate him, but this only fuelled his rage. During 1607 and 1608 Verney, deeply in debt on account of his extravagant lifestyle and his legal struggles, sold that to which he could lay title and fled England, determined to make his own name and fortune. In addition to dismayed creditors, Verney left behind his unlooked-for and unwanted wife, just one more casualty in an already tragic story.

Verney made for North Africa, perhaps drawn by stories of John Ward and others who had arrived destitute but whose riches were now legendary. He briefly served as a mercenary in the civil wars that gripped Morocco upon the death of Sultan Ahmad al-Mansur. It was not long, however, before Verney was known to be sailing with Captain John Ward from Tunis. This made for wonderful gossip back in England. The Verney family feud had long been the subject of poisonous whispers among the nobility and gentry, and Sir Francis's outlandish adventures had occasioned great interest. Ward's name, already frequently heard on English docks and in the Admiralty law courts, now became infamous at the royal court and in the great halls and palaces of the English elite.

Verney's arrival in Tunis, closely followed by his request to sail with Ward, must have fuelled the captain's pride and confirmed to other Englishmen that Ward was the rising star of the Barbary Corsairs. That a true English gentleman should sue for his favour was a mark of how far Ward had risen since the dark days of 1603. Verney could offer Ward no more than the distinction conferred by his presence, however, for his minimal experience in battle and complete ignorance of life at sea suited him for no role but that of ornament. His life ended badly. A dissolute spendthrift in Tunis as in England, Verney soon fell into 'great poverty and [became] deeply in debt to the Turks'. In 1610 he converted to Islam at the side of his master. This afforded him no special treatment. Five years later, in August 1615, impoverished and plague-ridden, Verney was abandoned by his shipmates on the coast of Sicily where he died within weeks.

More qualified men also made their way to Tunis. The name most commonly associated with Ward's was Captain Richard Bishop, who, like Ward, had had considerable experience at sea among the Elizabethan privateers. Bishop sailed in alliance with Ward from the latter's earliest days in North Africa, even back as far as Ward's stint as a Barbary pirate. Writing in 1609 one commentator stated that '[Ward's] chief of trust in [all] his practices' was Bishop, 'whom [Ward] employed to go forth and bring in prizes at his pleasure.' Like Ward, Bishop took an active interest in the fortunes of other ex-privateers, and there are several accounts of his efforts to help redeem English seamen enslaved in North Africa.

One of the men that Bishop redeemed was Captain James Harris, the son of a moderately wealthy merchant of Bristol, who became famous during the Anglo-Spanish wars for the good returns that his privateering tours brought to his investors. In the dusk of Queen Elizabeth's reign Harris was captured by the Barbary Corsairs of Tunis and enslaved. Having by chance received word that Harris was one of the thousands of galley slaves in the bagnio at La Goulette, Bishop willingly paid out 300 ducats for his liberty, and then informed him of the sad state of affairs for seamen in England. Harris willingly joined the enterprise of Ward and Bishop and paid for it on the Admiralty gallows at Wapping.

111

Another seaman executed at Wapping was Captain William Longcastle, a longstanding member of Ward's band who eventually cashed in his shares and returned to England, where he thought to 'live privately' in the village of Cawsand, near Plymouth. Perhaps it indicates something of Ward's fame among the common folk of England that Longcastle found it impossible to live anonymously, 'his name infamous for a Rover, notorious for a Pirate, and known for certain to be a confederate with Ward.' Once arrested, tried and convicted, Longcastle turned penitent so convincingly that one observer described him 'making [his] way to the gate of salvation by confessing [his] sins, knocking thereat for entrance, with sorrowful sighs' and a repenting heart. Not that it helped him: Longcastle hanged with the rest. John Ward, had he heard of this, might have arched an eyebrow and smiled a cynical smile: Longcastle had a reputation as a Bible-kisser, even during his years of fleecing Christians as a Barbary Corsair.

Verney, Harris and Longcastle all served as commanders under Ward, and Bishop was Ward's business partner and proxy, but it was William Graves who was the captain's closest friend. When Ward went to sea Graves inevitably was one of his officers. Graves also sailed independent of Ward, though in the latter's name, often in the *Mamatrice*, a ship owned by Uthman Dey. Graves captured the *York Bonaventure*, the *Amitie* of London and other English ships. Graves's most remarkable conquest was of 'four great ships of Holland, of three and four hundred tons apiece . . . taken in one day'. Like Harris and Longcastle, Graves, too, ended his days in a noose, but at Marseilles rather than Wapping. Taken by the French, he was executed and his men, described as 'about an hundred Infidels', were 'all made slaves'.

Among Ward's men Graves was called his lieutenant, reputed to be 'very inward with him, and one among the rest [that] might do most with him'. If we think of Ward's castle in Tunis as a mock-court, we can think of Graves as Ward's counsellor and fool, the only man who could slander him without consequences. 'At their feastings and bacchanals [he] would often revile Ward, calling him Boore, and Oyster-catcher, and upbraid him with the mean baseness of his beginning, and would often tell him that if it should one day be his fortune to kill him (as he thought it would) he doubted not but God would presently send an angel from heaven to carry him immediately thither for depriving the earth of such a villainous creature.'

It is not surprising that we know little of John Ward's daily life. He excited public and official interest because of his activities at sea, and most commentators describe his actions in disabling and looting prizes. Few were concerned with Ward's more peaceful pastimes, and fewer yet with his interior life.

Those descriptions of Ward's life ashore that we do have are embroidered with the most lurid details imaginable. Even Andrew Barker, often enough furnishing a sober view, succumbed to sensationalism when describing shore leave for Ward and his men. Noting that 'goods ill-gotten are most commonly worse spent', Barker states that 'with this treasure, which thus unjustly they had enriched themselves withal, they accustom their lives to all disorder'. So debauched were they that 'their habit and carriage ashore' became 'far more detestable, and uncomely to be talked of, [and] by Christianity to be condemned and abhorred' than their previous crimes. 'Their thieving at sea, swearing, drinking, dicing . . . are the least of their vices. Unlawfully are their goods got, and more ungodly are they consumed.'

'Like brute beasts', Barker declares, 'they mix themselves . . . with the enemies of their Saviour: so that he that was a Christian in the morning, is bedfellow to a Jew at night.' Either Barker's better nature or the cold eyes of the English censors prevented further details, and so he decided to 'leave their Sodomy, and the rest of their crying sins (which I fear their Atheism hath led them into) to the Judgement of the Just Revenger, and not give them to be talked of further by my pen'.

Atheism and sodomy: these are among the most common charges levelled against Ward and his crew in the surviving anecdotes and accounts of his affairs. Accusations of sodomy can be read as a short-hand for moral depravity – sodomy was forbidden in the seventeenth century – rather than, necessarily, as a literal description of Ward's activities. Mediterranean seafarers were never very far from port, and a vast infrastructure of brothels had developed to serve their generally heterosexual needs. Ward was married and he appeared to love the wife he had abandoned in Plymouth, at least to the extent that he periodically sent cash and gifts to her; but this is hardly a sure sign of exclusively heterosexual desire. Ward does not appear to have considered transporting his wife from Plymouth to Tunis. Nor do visitors to his mansion in Tunis make mention of women, although William Lithgow describes the men – 'fifteen circumcised runnagates' – that Ward kept as domestic servants. Whether he personally surveyed the penises of Ward's men (perhaps during a gay orgy?) or simply inferred that they were circumcised by their conversion to Islam, he does not state.

As with Ward's sexuality, we are on uncertain ground when we turn to the allegations of atheism made against him. The term was used so loosely as to lack any meaning beyond identifying those outside the national faith community. One famous Elizabethan accused of atheism was the playwright Christopher Marlowe. Marlowe's writings reveal a man obsessed with the spiritual limitations of conventional Christian morality. Disgusted with the hypocrisy he perceived to be rampant within Christendom, Marlowe indulged in heterodox theological speculation that shares much with the philosophies of late medieval Christian reformers such as John Wyclif or Martin Luther, and little with Friedrich Nietzsche, the great atheist of the modern age. As an indication of the vagueness of the term we can note that, in addition to Marlowe, many others were identified as 'atheists': all Jews and Muslims, most Asians and Africans, and all North and South Americans.

Turning to the 'atheism' of John Ward, we can discover instances of outrageous, scandalous behaviour, but no positive indication that he had ceased to believe in God. There is one tale of a privateering cruise during which 'there fell a great storm of lightning and thunder, by which foul weather [Ward's ship] was put from

Turks taking the English
Selling slaves in Algers
Execution with A batoone.
Turks burning of A Frier &c.
Mayork
Divers Cruelties
Makeing the boat & their Escape to Mayork

1. This narrative cartoon recounts the capture by Algerian corsairs of an English crew in the 1640s. The first frame illustrates the continuing use of round ships by Ottoman privateers following their introduction by John Ward.

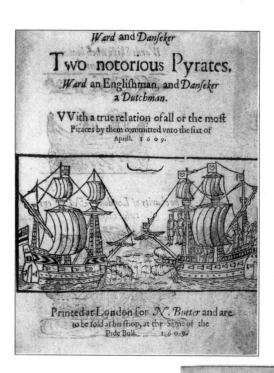

2. *Ward and Danseker* is the second edition of *Newes from Sea*, the earliest news pamphlet to recount Ward's exploits. The narrative was stitched together from various sources, including gaol-cell interviews with those of Ward's men who had been arrested in England and were awaiting execution.

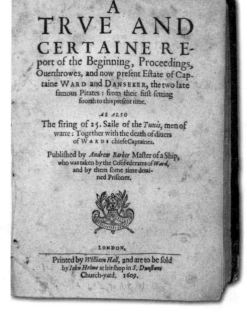

3. Published shortly after *Newes from Sea*, this pamphlet offers eyewitness testimony of Ward's operations in Tunis. It was written by Andrew Barker, the commander of a merchantman captured by William Graves, Ward's close friend and lieutenant.

The Ianissarie going to the warres,

4. A janissary, one of the highly trained and much-feared infantrymen of the Ottoman Empire, shown here in a sixteenth-century illustration. When Ward sailed as an Ottoman corsair, janissaries served on his ships as the soldiers who would conduct the first boarding and subduing of a prize.

Calender aReligious Turke.

5. Englishmen of Ward's day fixated on circumcision as a defining feature of Islam, often misunderstanding it as a ritual mutilation of the male genitals. This engraving shows 'a religious Turk', with a convenient cut-away to expose his circumcised and pierced penis.

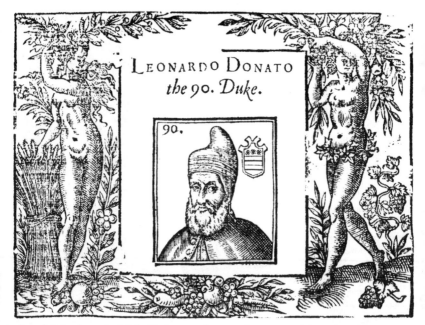

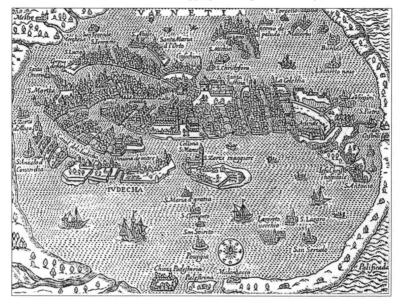

6. and 7. In the early 1600s Venice was the seat of a commercial empire with outposts throughout the eastern Mediterranean. Leonardo Donato sat as doge from 1606 to 1612, when Ward wreaked havoc on Venetian shipping. The map shows the city in 1612.

8. Before arriving in Tunis, and again when a series of crises forced him to relocate from Tunis to southern Ireland, Ward conducted operations along Europe's North Atlantic seaboard, as shown on this sixteenth-century map.

Cap.ᵗ SMITH led Captiue to the BASHAW of NALBRITS in TARTARIA. Chap. 12.

Drub. man

Smith

Bashaw

9. Captain John Smith was briefly enslaved by the Ottomans in eastern Europe. Smith later described how 'Ward, a poor English sailor' arrived in North Africa and 'taught the Moors to [sail] men-of-war'.

10. The eastern Mediterranean, as shown on this contemporary map, was Ward's hunting ground during the years of his greatest fame.

11. William Lithgow, a famous Scottish traveller, visited John Ward in Tunis in 1615. When he published his account of his travels he prefaced it with this image of himself dressed in his 'Turkish suite'.

12. Thanks to Ward's interventions with the Ottoman authorities, Lithgow was able to secure a visa that allowed him to travel overland to Fez where he is shown here.

13. 'and so there hanging till from that ebb two tides had overwhelmed their bodies. . . .' The watery gallows at Wapping, reserved for felons convicted by the High Court of Admiralty.

all cables and anchors but one'. Despite the worsening situation, Ward occupied himself 'deeply drinking in his accustomed manner'. William Longcastle, the greatest puritan ever to wax fat by robbing, murdering and enslaving his fellow Christians, 'perceived they were in imminent danger' and led the crew in prayer 'as the necessity of the time required'. Longcastle called their captain to join them, 'but such were his distempered passions, and the frantic errors of his own will' that Ward 'bade them pray that would, but for his own part he neither feared God nor devil'.

Taking this incident at face value, what is striking is not Ward's godlessness, but the strength of will behind his refusal to indulge in the anguished prayers of Longcastle. Ward and his men had prospered by theft and murder in the name of Islam; this sudden appeal to a Christian God smacks of hypocrisy born of desperation.

Extensive reading of the incomplete and often hostile sources on Captain John Ward does not provide any clear evidence that he was an atheist, but a sense that his very life could only foster cynicism towards all religions. During his youth he likely worked as a smuggler, exchanging the wool of Protestant sheep for wine made of French Catholic grapes. With the revival of English fishing, Ward's sore back and callused hands brought fish to Catholic tables, allowing them to fulfil their religious obligations of fasting. During the Anglo-Spanish wars John Ward fleeced Spanish Catholics in the name of English Protestantism – until King James made this a crime. It is hardly surprising that when Ward turned first to piracy and then to Ottoman privateering he willingly abandoned any pretence of religious justification for his actions.

More than any other profession in the seventeenth century seafaring necessitated Protestants mixing with Catholics and Muslims. As a pirate and, later, a Barbary Corsair, Ward would also have had contact with North African Jews in Morocco, Tunis and Algiers. Extensive interfaith contact, occasioned by activities condemned by Christianity, Islam and Judaism alike but greedily embraced by individual Christians, Muslims and Jews, seems to have left Ward theologically rootless. His refusal to pray with Longcastle during the tempest need not have been a repudiation of God, but it could well have been a reasoned rejection of the efficacy of prayer. Ward's scorn for prayer could only have been strengthened if he had heard word of Longcastle's ostentatious piety prior to being hanged in England.

Ward might reject the efficacy of prayer but he did not reject the efficacy of the bottle. It is worth noting that while Longcastle urged him to pray Ward preferred to drink. Virtually all of the sources mention his prodigious appetite for alcohol. Excessive drinking was hardly a distinguishing characteristic among seamen of the day, but Ward seems to have been in a class of his own. Was this an attempt to drown his theological doubts or was it routine alcoholism? We will never know.

One of the most interesting sources from this period paints a picture of John Ward between cruises. The deponent was an English sailor, recently out of Tunis. The sailor evidently had spent time among Ward's men and probably sailed with them, given his detailed knowledge of Ward's operations. In his deposition the sailor sketches a deft portrait of Ward, providing a glimpse of the man behind the legend:

John Ward, commonly called Captain Ward, is about fifty-five years of age. Very short, with little hair, and that quite white; bald in front; swarthy face and beard. Speaks little, and almost always swearing. Drunk from morn till night. Most prodigal and plucky. Sleeps a great deal, and often on board when in port. The habits of a thorough salt. A fool and an idiot out of his trade.

EIGHT

The Reniera e Soderina

Ward used riches won during the extraordinarily successful winter season of 1606/7 to transform the *Rubi* into a square-rigged man-of-war and to extend his operations at sea. This expansion signalled his growing ambitions. When Ward captured the *John Baptist* he had been in command of one ship, the *Gift*, and had used the *Gift*'s pinnace (a ship's boat, not generally counted as a ship in its own right) as an auxiliary craft. When Wiseman and the others took the pinnace and headed west, Ward made his assault upon the *Rubi* while in command of two vessels: the *Gift* and the *John Baptist*.

In the spring of 1607, Ward left Tunis harbour and headed east with four ships under his command. William Graves, who had commanded the vessel that captured Barker's merchantman, the *York Bonaventure*, identified only two of these for Barker: the transformed *Rubi* and Ward's flyboat, the *Gift*.* It is likely that the third was the *Little John* (possibly the *John Baptist*, now rigged out for war), and the fourth was probably either the refitted *Carminati* or the

---

* It is not clear if Ward used one flyboat, named the *Gift*, over several years, or if he favoured the flyboat design, owned several and named each one the *Gift* in turn. The same can be said of the *Little John*, a small merchantman that Ward used like a pinnace. Whether the name *Little John* was an ironic tip of the hat to Robin Hood or a tribute to John Ward himself we do not know.

Mattalena, the latter being a French merchantman that, according to Barker, Ward brought back to Tunis sometime after the taking of the *Rubi* (perhaps captured in the same cruise in which Ward had taken the *Carminati*).

Ward's decision to sail four ships under a unified command reflects his confidence as a commander and strategist, and his desire to assault larger ships or ships travelling in convoy. Ward's fleet left La Goulette and made for the Adriatic Sea. 'We were four well-manned and well-appointed ships', stated Graves, 'over whom Captain Ward was our worthy general.' William Graves sailed as Ward's lieutenant. Encountering a storm, the fleet was scattered. When the skies cleared only the *Rubi* and the *Gift* remained in contact, but they decided to proceed on their own. Whether the other two ships made their own cruise or turned back to Tunis, Graves did not say.

Journeying on, still in command of his two largest ships, Ward came upon a behemoth, one of the oversized merchantmen that the Venetians had taken to using to discourage pirate attacks. The ship, making for Venice, could only have been freighted with an important cargo: the Venetians deployed their super-ships on their most valuable trade routes, often using them to shuttle silks, spices and other luxuries from the Middle East. Graves described the ship as 'a great argosie of fourteen or fifteen hundred tonnes, very richly laden with Venetian goods, and who, by computation, was esteemed to be worth two millions at the least'.

The *Rubi* and the *Gift* were moderately large ships, each of about 300 tons' burden. They were dwarfed by the monstrous Venetian vessel before them. Any attempt by the corsairs to board the Venetian would come from below, into a hail of cannon, mortar and small-arms fire. Undaunted, Ward deployed his two ships and prepared for hostile action. Graves described what followed as 'a merciless and incredible fight, as a man may compare between those two tyrants, the remorseless winds and the resisting waters. It was long, it was cruel, it was forcible and therefore fearful: but in the end our captain had the sunshine; he boarded her, subdued her, chained her men like slaves and seized on her goods as his lawful prize.'

Barker, knowing Graves's loyalty to John Ward was combined with a seaman's proclivity to make a good story better, believed this 'tale rather a vain-glorious boast from him, to raise his captain's fame, and the more to amaze us, that were his prisoners, than any discourse of truth that was worthy of credit'. Barker therefore approached another of his minders, a man 'in discontent and dislike with his master [i.e. Captain Ward]' on a day when Graves was nowhere to be seen. Instead of maligning Ward, the malcontented mariner, as if against his will, began to heap praise upon his captain as extravagantly as had Graves, and not just for the capture of the vast Venetian merchantman, but for Ward's conduct generally during 'these last three years' since their arrival in Tunis. The mariner maintained that Ward 'is grown the most absolute, the most resolute, and the most undauntedest man in a fight, that ever any heart did accompany at sea'. The man cited 'the aforesaid fight' with the Venetian to illustrate his point. Reckoning that the Venetians outnumbered them by three to one, the seaman maintained that Ward 'did in the deadly conflict so undauntedly bear himself, as if he had courage to out-brave Turks'. In the rush to board the massive merchantman the seaman stated that Ward went so far as to be 'pricking others on even with the point of his poniard'. In the end, the seaman held that he 'could impartially say' that Ward's resolution alone 'was cause of the victory. . . . His forwardness made cowards venturous.'

The ship that Ward seized that day – 26 April 1607 – was the *Reniera e Soderina*, and its capture caused a sensation throughout the Venetian territories. The value of the cargo that the *Soderina* was carrying, on her way home from Syria and Cyprus, was only part of the reason that her loss to the corsairs caught the imagination of the people and government of Venice. More significant was the capture of the magnificent ship herself, one of the largest sailing vessels used by the Serene Republic of Venice in its Mediterranean commerce. Ships built on the scale of the *Soderina* were supposed to be the solution to the piracy that had become so widespread that it had begun, during the later sixteenth century, to cripple the movement of Venetian shipping in the Mediterranean. Oversized vessels like the

Soderina were intended to dissuade raiders and encourage them to turn their attention to smaller, easier prizes.

The loss of the *Soderina* renewed old nightmares among the Venetians, who, for a brief time, had dared to imagine that they had solved the pirate problem. The *Rubi* had been a valuable prize, and its loss had caused the governor of Zante to send spies into Ottoman ports and to begin to track the activities of the unknown corsair who had assaulted her. When news of the loss of the *Soderina* reached Venice, once again through Zante, preparations began for an official inquiry. The report of this inquiry describes how the battle unfolded, and why, despite the size of the *Soderina*, John Ward was able, in Graves's nice turn of phrase, to have the sunshine.

As Graves had stated, the battle began with thunderous gunfire. Ward's ships came upon the *Soderina* as she was becalmed in the Gulf of Settelia. Though insufficient to push the massive timbers of the *Soderina* through the waters, there was wind enough to move Ward's smaller ships. The corsair lost no time in exploiting this advantage to the fullest. As Ward's expert gunners pummelled the *Soderina* with all that they had, his skilled seamen moved the *Gift* and the *Rubi* in and out of range of the guns of the *Soderina*, offering the Venetian gunners only the narrow profile of stem and stern before veering off to deliver broadside after broadside into the hull, decks and sails of the *Soderina*. The calm gulf would have quickly filled with the acrid smoke of exploded powder, the seamen of both sides rendered half-deaf by roaring cannon fire and the screeching recoil of the gun carriages. After three hours of this punishment, Venetian sources record that the *Soderina* had five leaks in her hull and small fires had broken out at various points amidst the sacks of cotton that the Venetians had used to protect them from the English shot.

Seeing the effect of the cannon, Ward made the decision to board. As the *Rubi* and the *Gift* came into range, the captain of the *Soderina* did his best to muster a defence. And now the Venetian documentation reveals the shameful secret behind the grand façade of the magnificent *Reniera e Soderina*: she was undermanned. Instead of travelling with a full complement of professional soldiers the captain had taken on paying passengers in order to realize greater profits.

Greed and presumptuousness had allowed the vessel's great size to become her only, rather than her first, defence.

As Ward's ships approached, the Venetian captain consulted with his passengers and crew on whether they should sacrifice their honour and surrender without a fight, or muster what defence they could. 'After deciding on the advice of everybody to fight, [the captain] divided up all his crew and passengers, and stationed some on the quarterdeck, others on the main deck and poop, and thus they all seemed to be very gallant soldiers with weapons in their hands.'

Given that the corsairs had not been frightened off by the size and gunnery of the *Soderina*, this last attempt at illusion seems more foolish than brave. Ward, at any rate, was undeterred: 'The two ships that came to attack, even though two or three shots were fired at them, strove without further ado to lay themselves alongside, and on coming within range fired off twelve shots, six each, always aiming at the crew and sails, without firing once into the water.'

This final display of precise gunnery had a psychological as well as physical effect upon the untrained defenders. 'Their plans, designed to terrify, succeeded excellently, because two of those who were defending the quarterdeck were hit by one of the shots, and when they were wounded, indeed torn to pieces, all the rest fled, leaving their weapons lying on the quarterdeck and all of them running to their own property, even while the two vessels were coming alongside.' In the ensuing panic, cowardice turned to mutiny. 'For all his efforts, the captain was not only quite unable to force the crew to return to the quarterdeck, he could not even make them emerge from below decks or from the forecastle. Indeed, the ship's carpenter and some others confronted him with weapons in their hands and told him that he should no longer command the ship.'

This final image, the prelude to surrender, provides a nice contrast to the description of Captain Ward goading his men on to attack. While Ward drove his men forward 'even with the point of his poniard', demanding nothing less than the capture of a seemingly impossible prize, the Venetians turned their weapons against their captain, forcing him to surrender to an enemy that should have been repelled.

121

The capture of the *Reniera e Soderina* speaks to the reasons why John Ward was an extraordinarily successful corsair. Like his decision to attack the armed galley of the Knights of Malta, his determination to take the *Soderina* reflected an ambitious spirit that could not be satisfied with safe prizes such as storm-scattered convoys and floundering merchantmen. But for all of the pride and daring that lay behind his initial decision to proceed, the attack itself was carried out patiently and methodically, taking great care to minimize the risk to his men. As in the encounter with the Knights of Malta, Ward once again relied upon his gunners to do most of the work. While the guns grew hot from repeated firing, Ward remained cool, putting off boarding the *Soderina* for three hours – long enough that his cannon had destroyed the defences and unnerved the Venetians. They were not defeated by brute force but by careful tactics.

The Venetian investigation illuminated many of the reasons behind the capture of the *Soderina*, including the poor decisions that were made by the captain and his crew in manning and defending their ship, and the smart tactics that the English raider used to expose and exploit the vessel's weaknesses. However, the Venetian investigators proved unable to put a name to the English captain who had led the assault.

Back in Tunis there was no mystery: the arrival of the *Rubi*, the *Gift* and the *Reniera e Soderina* at La Goulette – and Ward's subsequent activities as he began the work of converting her from a merchantman into a man-of-war – caused a sensation. One look at the prize, a Goliath in chains, and all connected with Ward's enterprise, however slenderly, knew that they would receive handsome returns. For Captain Ward and the men who sailed with him, the mooring of the *Soderina* under the shadow of the Borj el-Karrak meant a substantial change in fortunes. As they cashed out their shares, some of Ward's English crew began to think of returning home. At some point during the following year, at least a dozen of these men – the wily John Keye and that pious pirate William Longcastle among them – chartered a voyage back to England on board the *Unicorn* of Bristol.

It is thanks to the trial of several of these men that we can quantify what the capture of the *Soderina* meant for regular crewmembers.

Thomas Mitton and Walter Hancock, both common seamen, testified before the High Court of Admiralty in May 1608 that they each held five and a half shares when they sailed with Ward in the spring of 1607. Shares cashed out at £15 for a total yield of about £83 for each man. To put this in perspective, an English family could subsist on about £11 to £14 per year at this time – meaning that Mitton and Hancock could support themselves and their families for about six years by living solely off the proceeds of this one prize. It remains entirely possible that these men may also have had savings from the capture of the *Rubi*, the *John Baptist*, the *Carminati*, the *Mattelena*, or any number of prizes lost to historical record.

The money did them little good. We only know of the good fortune of Mitton and Hancock because they were apprehended and tried in the Admiralty courts as pirates. Given the habitual superstitions of seamen, the arrest and trial of these individuals, within a year of their arrival in England, could only be a dark omen for the rest of Ward's men. Even as his shipwrights, carpenters and gun founders toiled at La Goulette to convert the *Soderina* into a mighty man-of-war, Captain John Ward, having been drawn to a giddy height on fortune's wheel, was about to experience the inevitable downstroke.

'After the capture of the ship *Soderina* by the English bertons', Zorzi Giustinian, official representative of the Serene Republic of Venice to the Court of King James I, wrote to his political masters on 25 July 1607, 'I set to work to find out who the pirate was. It turns out it was a certain Ward, a famous [corsair], proclaimed and banished from this kingdom. His usual haunt is Tunis and other places in Barbary. I can discover no more. If I do, I will not fail to communicate it.'

Giustinian took his duties very seriously, and over the coming years he would faithfully write back to Venice with much news about this 'certain Ward'. In the 1600s foreign ambassadors had two roles: to represent their national interests, and to collect and report foreign intelligence. Giustinian issued letters and diplomatic dispatches like a paper mill, most of them formally addressed to the doge and senate of Venice, a torrent of paper, ink and sealing wax. A highly respected member of the king's court, he was routinely invited to major feasts and events and was often to be found in the private quarters of the royal family.

Official relations between Catholic Venice and Protestant England had been severed decades earlier, but then re-established at the very end of Elizabeth's reign, primarily with a view to increasing trade between the two nations. To Elizabeth diplomatic relations with Venice were desirable but hardly essential. Under the new king the restoration of full diplomatic and commercial relations with Venice was a primary foreign policy objective, almost as important as the termination of the Anglo-Spanish conflict. This was because, to James, relations with Venice were far more important for symbolic reasons than for economic benefit.

King James, who affected *Rex Pacificus* as his motto, was determined to be the Great Peacemaker, a new King Solomon. James was possessed of the bizarre and self-aggrandizing notion that he, personally, would bring about the end of religious wars within western and central Europe, healing the schism caused by the Protestant Reformation. Peace with Spain was only the start: the king sought alliances with other Catholic powers, and especially with the Serene Republic of Venice. And for once James's personal aspirations chimed with those of his nation.

In the early 1600s Venice occupied a central place in the English imagination, a fact well attested by the numerous plays of the period, by Shakespeare and others, set in Venice or with some Venetian connection. Venice was powerful, rich and cosmopolitan – a place where the money bags of Shylock the Jew could grow fat and Othello the Moor could become a general on the front lines of the wars to contain the Ottomans. Though its power was on the wane by 1600, the republic nonetheless controlled territories throughout the eastern Medi-terranean, welding them into an empire of commerce that still supplied much of Europe with the luxuries of the Orient and the Middle East, despite inroads made by English, French and Dutch interlopers.

Even more than its wealth, Venice was famous for creating what was widely held to be the most sophisticated, just and balanced political system of the day. Venice was the only major European power that was a republic rather than a monarchy, and was touted as heir to the spirit of Athenian democracy – no small compliment during the era of ancient and classical revival known as the Renaissance. But this was not democracy as we know it. In Venice, as in classical Athens, the franchise was carefully restricted to a narrow social and economic elite.

The state was overseen by a duke, or doge, who was appointed for life, but who was a mere figurehead, existing only as an embodiment of the collective will of the great council and its various subsets. Membership of the great council was the key to all political power and influence, for it was the great council who elected men, selected from their own ranks, to serve on the senate (the legislative branch of government) and the *collegio* or cabinet (the executive branch). Who could sit in the great council was determined with reference to a set of gentle bloodlines that had been identified in 1297, but the system, in practice, was not as restrictive as it seems. Families who had become wealthy thereafter married into the bloodlines of 1297, thus bringing new blood and new money into the halls of power, even as the traditional ruling elite was propped up by an illusion of longstanding tradition.

During the early sixteenth century it was commonly believed that the Serene Republic was ruled by the best government that human reason could devise, and the abundant wealth that pooled and flowed through the city-state seemed proof of the blessings of a benevolent deity. King James so craved the approval of the Venetian state that the various ambassadors dispatched to London by the doge and senate found themselves welcomed into the very heart of his court. In addition, between 1607 and 1612 James and his principal advisors made a series of extraordinary, and embarrassingly obvious, attempts to insinuate the king's second son, Charles, Duke of York, into some sort of pseudo-official capacity in Venice. At one interview James himself baldly asserted, 'my Lord Ambassador, you must make my son a patrician of Venice', stating on another occasion that he hoped Charles would 'be seen walking in the Piazza of St Mark'. The ambassadors were aware that such comments were 'not put out by mere chance', and they also knew that recognition of the prepubescent prince as a 'patrician of Venice', that near-mythic land of rational, virtuous government, would have been a personal triumph for the king.

Being posted to England, however, was hardly a coup for Zorzi Giustinian. The Giustinian family was wealthy and famous for its devotion to state service. It was expected that Giustinians would serve the state in high-profile foreign postings, but an appointment to the court of King James was not a plum. Viewed from the sun-drenched piazzi of imperial Venice, England was a cold, dimly lit and barbarous island at the European periphery, its language as obscure and guttural as its arts and industry were rudimentary.

Arriving in England early in 1607, Giustinian accepted his posting with good grace even as his grateful predecessor departed for beloved Venice. Whatever his feelings for the English climate – not to mention the English diet – Giustinian, from the start, embraced his dual role as Venice's official representative and chief spy in this remote backwater, and he applied himself to local intrigue with gusto.

Of particular interest to Giustinian, and to his political masters in the senate, was the real talent that common Englishmen had demon-strated for the unsubtle art of piracy, and that more refined English-men exhibited for the giving and taking of graft. During the summer of 1607 Giustinian reported on both of these characteristics. In coded missives, more frank than the ambassador's plain Italian letters, Giustinian declared his belief that all English seamen either were pirates or strove to become so, and that all English officials, from the lowest Admiralty quill-pusher to the highest courtier, desired nothing so much as personally to profit from the ill-gotten gains of the commoners who rode the waves.

Giustinian probably learned the fate of the *Soderina* from another foreigner in the English capital, a man named Mustapha who had arrived in London in July 1607 bearing letters of introduction from Murat Raïs, a commander of the galleys at Algiers. Following in Mustapha's train were a dozen 'Turks' (in the careless sense of the word, a synonym for Muslims), 'whereof three only are decently apparelled, the rest looking like the ambassadors that came to Joshua with old shoes and threadbare apparel'.

Mustapha himself 'hath many changes of garments very rich, and several turbants'. He claimed to be on an embassy from Ottoman Sultan Achment, but it was an embassy of a curious, non-urgent fashion. He had already spent over a year in North Africa on undisclosed business, followed by seven fruitless months in France, cooling his heels and waiting for an interview with King Henri IV. In France, his goal had been to negotiate the release 'of 150 Turks chained to the great galleys at Marseilles'. According to Mustapha, he brought eighty French-born Ottoman galley slaves with him into France 'whereof four were circumcised' (suggesting that they had converted to Islam). These eighty he magnanimously freed upon arrival at Marseilles, evidently hoping to receive in return the freedom of the enslaved Ottomans. This proved an imprudent bargaining strategy, and after seven months, during which 'he could not get one Turk released', he decamped for England.

During banquets and feasts Mustapha delighted his English hosts with tales from his travels, including his encounters with the famous English captain of the Barbary Corsairs, John Ward. At the time that he met Ward, his travelling companion had been the French ambassador, Monsieur François Savary, Comte de Brèves. De Brèves had asked that Ward take pity upon French merchants and mariners. 'I, favourable to the French?' Ward had exclaimed, incredulous. 'I tell you, if I should meet my own father at sea, I would rob him and sell him when I had done.' Mustapha then asked Ward if he wished to send a message into England 'for the procuring of his pardon', but Ward answered that 'he would never see England again but would be buried in the sea'.

Besides gadding from court to feast to fête, it is hard to see what exactly Mustapha hoped to accomplish in London. Over the next few months it emerged that the envoy's allegedly official mission was to complain of English seamen who were assaulting Ottoman shipping while working as Florentine privateers or pirates, and of the English shipwrights and gun founders who had set up shop in Livorno and were outfitting them. Mustapha's hosts could be forgiven for finding this a bit rich, considering that the Ottomans themselves had profited from the flight of English mariners, carpenters and gun-casters after 1603. Mustapha demanded a private audience with King James, whose abhorrence of Islam generally and the Ottomans in particular was well known. The result was that, as in France, he was granted lodgings and a small stipend and deliberately, resolutely ignored by the king. This may have been exactly to Mustapha's tastes, for, as in France, he seemed little inclined to transact any business at all: he was content to await his royal audience and live the life of a peripheral courtier. Eventually the audience was granted, Mustapha presented his complaint, a vague reply was offered, and in November 1608 he was sent packing. Not, however, before a new word had entered the English language: 'to chauss or chouse, meaning to cozen' or cheat. The word stems from the Turkish *ciaus*, the title that Mustapha had claimed as ambassador.

Whatever the true nature of Mustapha's mission, the *ciaus* had unwittingly become the pawn of a more subtle player. John Ward had relied upon this garrulous charlatan to spread word of his publicly declared intention to live out his days in Tunis and be 'buried in the sea'. In secret, however, Ward had matured a plan to negotiate the purchase of a royal pardon from James, to allow himself and the majority of his followers to return to England. In October 1607 representatives of Captain Ward arrived in London and began making the rounds of English officials and courtiers. It did not require any sophisticated spying for Giustinian to learn of this: he himself was visited by one of Ward's envoys. Giustinian received, delivered into his lap, a summary of his obsessions: an ex-pirate turned Ottoman privateer who had enriched himself by raiding Venetian shipping, and who now sought to exploit the venality of English officials to allow a triumphant return to English shores. And this was not just any ex-pirate, but the very man who had humiliated Venetian pride through the capture of the mighty *Reniera e Soderina*.

Giustinian dipped his quill and began to write. 'I am in duty bound in the interests of the owners of the ship *Soderina*, which was captured by the pirate Ward who has his headquarters in Tunis, to inform your Serenity of representations made to me by an English merchant who, on leaving Venice, touched at Tunis this last August and is now arrived here.' So begins Giustinian's first substantial letter on the issue of Ward's pardon, addressed to the doge and senate and dated 24 October 1607. He continues:

> This person tells me, in the name of Ward, that he and all his [English] followers, who number about 300, offer to give up their piratical career and to return to England, if they can obtain the king's pardon. They know that this they can never obtain without the consent of your Serenity [i.e. the doge] because of the many injuries they have inflicted upon your subjects; he therefore offers to restore all that these subjects have a right to and that he now holds, namely, three ships with their guns and armament and goods to the value of thirty or forty thousand crowns in silk, indigo and other merchandize.

Ward, of course, could not return goods that had already been sold or otherwise distributed, and so the Venetians would have to content themselves with what was on offer. Giustinian nonetheless understood that a better settlement might be reached through negotiation, stating that 'my informant declares that he himself has seen these people, and that Ward would give even more'.

Financial incentives were not the only enticement, and perhaps were not even the primary one, that Ward's man laid out before the Venetian ambassador. Using language more suited to Giustinian's perspective than John Ward's, the captain's emissary stressed 'how important it was to remove from his nest a pirate with so large a following'. The removal of Ward and his followers from Tunis, it was alleged, 'as far as England was concerned . . . would mean the cessation of piracy in those waters'. Failure to seize this opportunity would drive Ward deeper into his alliance with the Ottoman authorities 'who draw great profit from these depredations'. Having discharged 'the commission he held from Ward', the man concluded his interview with Giustinian by stressing the need 'to keep this offer secret, for if the Turks come to hear of it, it is likely they would hinder the design on account of the profits they now draw'.

The presence of Mustapha at court – and he would be there for several weeks yet – even as Ward's men approached Giustinian and various Admiralty officials, lent the affair a particularly secretive air. Ward's emissary 'begged for an early answer so that long delay might not imperil the plan', but Giustinian coolly deferred, reporting to the doge and senate that he 'left the question in such a position that your Serenity may handle it as seems to you best.'

The Venetian ambassador, however, had overestimated his own importance and underestimated Ward's determination. The next battle in Ward's campaign to win a pardon would not happen in England, but in the council chambers of Venice.

'An ambassador is an honest man sent to lie abroad for the good of his country': this according to Sir Henry Wotton, the official ambassador of King James to the Serene Republic of Venice. Much to Wotton's chagrin, this private jest, scribbled in the autograph book of a friend in 1604, would eventually become so well known that it nearly cost him his king's favour and his prestigious appointment to Venice. In the autumn of 1607, however, these troubles lay years in the future. For our purposes, Wotton's indiscreet pun on the word 'lie' can serve as a concise expression of how he viewed his duties.

On 5 November 1607 Wotton appeared before the Venetian cabinet to address the doge and selected senators on the question of an English pardon for Captain John Ward. Wotton would never broach such a question openly, for it would compromise the dignity of King James to have his personally appointed representative publicly address the exchange of looted gold for a royal pardon. Instead, Wotton offered such a wealth of hints, hedges and general- ities that, though they could never hold him or James to any particular proposal, the senators could have little doubt that plans and discussions were proceeding in London.

'That famous pirate, Ward, so well-known in this port for the damage he has done, is beyond a doubt the greatest scoundrel that ever sailed from England', stated Wotton. 'About him, I have two accounts which are at variance with each other, yet both may be true.' Wotton possessed correspondence from Tunis, dating from September, that described how Ward had converted the *Soderina* into a raiding vessel and was prepared to sally forth, heading once more for the Adriatic Sea, turning the Venetians' own magnificent vessel against them. Or they could choose to believe another report of which the English ambassador had heard, that Ward was prepared to defect from the Ottoman corsairs and sprint across the Mediterranean to enter the service of 'certain Italian princes' – a veiled reference to the grand duke of Florence, who, notoriously, was willing to blur privateering into piracy so long as the gain was his. Or, Wotton continued, they could believe the third report, that Ward was seeking to return to favour with King James. And yet a fourth proposal, this one originating from Wotton himself: perhaps all three reports were true. Ward's pursuit of an English pardon, suggested Wotton, 'seems to be in contradiction with the former news, and yet it is possible that he is preparing for a career of piracy abroad should he fail to obtain a pardon'. Wotton concluded his oration:

> I think that his Majesty will do all that is for the public good. But while he may pardon Ward for his crimes he will never free him from the responsibility for the goods he has robbed from private individuals. Ward wants to return home and also to keep his plunder, but the King will never assent to that. But if your Serenity could see a way by which he could, in part, give satisfaction to the gentlemen and citizens who are owners of the booty he has plundered, I do not think the return to the King's favour would be so difficult a matter. And that would be a public benefit.

Wotton now turned to other matters, and shortly afterwards the doge completed the interview with a few non-committal comments. Stating that Ward would 'meet with a warm reception if he comes into these waters', he promised to canvass the senate and make a reply to Wotton on the issue of Ward's pardon shortly.

Five days later, on 10 November, Wotton was summoned to hear the outcome of the cabinet's deliberations. The comments were brief: 'the Republic trusts his Majesty to grant no pardon until those who have suffered are fully indemnified.' Full indemnity: an impossible demand, for it was now six months since Ward had taken the *Soderina* and her cargo was already long parcelled off, sold to the highest bidder in cut-rate lots, the proceeds divided among Ward's crew, financial backers and the Ottoman authorities. A request for full indemnity was a contemptuous rejection of the sordid business.

Nonetheless, a mere two days after this Wotton made the extraordinarily undiplomatic decision to revisit the topic during his next interview with the cabinet. On 12 November he opened the question of Ward's pardon once again, despite the cabinet's hostility to the proposal. First, Wotton attempted to resolve the awkward issue that he appeared to be negotiating on behalf of a declared criminal by pretending that he was merely passing the time by indulging in court gossip. Remarking, as though offhandedly, that 'as to Ward, I am not sure that he has actually applied to the King [for a pardon]. It may be all a court intrigue', Wotton embarked on a new round of proposals for the cabinet to consider. In other words, while taking the astonishing measure of returning to a topic of debate that had been absolutely quashed by the doge and senate, Wotton smoothly denied that his actions had any significance whatsoever. He then ploughed on, repeating his previous point that James would willingly pardon Ward, but not at the cost of the friendship of the Venetians. The king, however, remained mindful of the benefits of pardoning Ward and so removing him from the Mediterranean. As a sop to Venetian pride, Wotton then insinuated that there could be a further inducement to allow Ward's pardon: Ward would be assassinated upon his return to England. Or, in the ambassador's own words, 'it has sometimes happened that men have been condemned to death, pardoned by the king and yet their confederates have pursued them and they have had to die'.

We do not know why Wotton was willing to risk the displeasure of the doge and senate by reopening the topic, but an accomplished diplomat would not commit such an indiscretion without good cause. It is reasonable to conclude that he was acting on orders from London to press the case as far as he could. And so the tale returns to London, where Wotton's equivalent, Zorzi Giustinian, was becoming increasingly incensed at the dark machinations of courtiers who he was positive were being bribed – and what is more, being bribed with choice extracts from the luxurious cargo that Ward had looted from the *Soderina*.

Zorzi Giustinian had taken up his post early in 1607, and we are very fortunate to have the notes that his predecessor prepared to introduce the new ambassador to the major personalities at the English court. This account was not meant to be public reading, and it is far from uniformly complimentary. Starting with the royal family, the outgoing ambassador described Queen Anne ('very gracious and moderately good looking. She is a Lutheran') and touched upon her four children, but he focused his attention on the power brokers at court. Like many observers of the English nation under King James, he remarked upon the preference of the king for the sport of hunting rather than the work of governing: 'The king is so devoted to the chase that he leaves all to his councillors. . . . The power of the [Privy] Council was never greater than now, by reason of the king's carelessness of rule.'

In Venice the power of the Great Council and its various subsidiaries, including the cabinet and senate, whose members were elected from and by the Great Council, was a sign of the health of the empire. But, as an experienced diplomat like Zorzi Giustinian knew, the English Privy Council was a different matter. 'The [Privy] Council dealeth with all things, not only affairs of State, but money and also justice, so that whoso would attain anything he must be protected by one of the lords of the Council, and that by means of presents and gifts.' Bribery had become the chief engine of affairs, steering the English state into danger and discontent:

These gifts they take not only from the subject, but as well from strangers and ambassadors of princes, which breeds a great hatred of these lords. . . .

Of the lords of the Council the greatest is Sir Robert Cecil, Earl of Salisbury, Secretary of State, whose authority is so absolute that he may be called king indeed. He is a man of some forty-four years, little and crookbacked, but with a noble countenance, an admirable speaker, and well-skilled in the French tongue. In all matters of state he is of greatest weight, a bitter foe to his enemies, but a friend to his friends, though more prone to revenge than to affection.

Giustinian, no doubt, carefully read his predecessor's briefing notes, but he did not allow his actions to be guided solely by them. A shrewd diplomat, he recognized that, despite the mounting power of the Privy Council and the Earl of Salisbury, the authority of the king was absolute. While the course of John Ward's pardon negotiations demonstrate the accuracy of the outgoing ambassador's allegations of a corrosive, deep-seated culture of bribery at the English court, Giustinian's approach to the issue reflected his own grasp of the power dynamics that of necessity lay at the heart of the English monarchy.

On 15 November 1607 Zorzi Giustinian was summoned for a personal audience with King James; after this audience he described the experience, in detail, in a series of dispatches to the doge and senate. In these letters, bland, complementary and neutral text is written in plain Italian; sensitive information and analysis is carefully encoded in cipher. Writing plainly, Giustinian describes how in his interview with the king he broached the topic of misbehaving English seamen generally, observing it to be 'desirable that his Majesty should impress upon his subjects the need for a strict observance of the rules laid down, otherwise every day might bring some fresh disorder'. Giustinian further assured James 'that the sole object of your Excellencies [i.e. the doge and senate] was to free the sea trade from the depredations and damages inflicted by privateers'.

While Giustinian and James spoke, the Earl of Salisbury looked on. Before departing the audience chamber, Giustinian asked to be received by the earl. His request was granted, and Giustinian and Salisbury picked up the threads of the conversation that had just drawn to its formal, convention-bound conclusion. The ambassador could now speak less obscurely and more passionately. Following brief preliminaries, Salisbury directly addressed the subject of Ward's pardon, and presented it to the Venetian ambassador as a fait accompli. Arrangements for the pardon were proceeding apace among the relevant English officials, and Salisbury reported that 'he had been assured that the Republic [of Venice] had already assented to this pardon, but that he would never believe it until he heard the fact from me'. The earl subtly warned the ambassador that Venetian intransigence on the subject was causing the republic to be sidelined. If Venice did not begin to make more reasonable demands, recognizing that it would never receive full indemnification of all those injured by Ward, the city would neither profit from the pardon nor halt it. Salisbury was presenting Giustinian with one last opportunity to act in the interests of Venice.

The ambassador cleaved to the original Venetian position. 'I feigned to be extremely annoyed at this information', Giustinian states, and then records his lengthy response to Salisbury's gambit. First, he acerbically observed that 'though under the cloak of pity and religion this plea is advanced, yet this Ward practises piracy in such a fashion that clemency would become injustice if extended to him'. Then, brazenly lying to Salisbury, Giustinian maintained that, far from assenting to Ward's pardon, the doge and senate had not yet even been informed of the movement to secure it, for he had 'not even had the courage to write to the senate on the subject, so far out of place did the proposal appear'. In closing, Giustinian stated that Venice was adamant in its refusal to allow Ward's pardon because the republic wanted him free, so that its war galleys could make an example of him at sea. 'You may imagine, then', he informed Salisbury, 'that the Republic will never consent to Ward's pardon. Nay, I am sure that thanks to the provision that is being made to clear the seas of this pest, Ward too will easily be wiped out.'

Switching to cipher, Giustinian observed to his readers that 'I think I perceive that Ward's attempt may be based upon something more than appears on the surface; for this [corsair] has become extremely rich, thanks to his plunder, and maybe he relies on the power of gold to overcome here all opposition.'

Over the coming weeks, Giustinian began to spend intelligence monies to track the arrival of ships from Tunis, and to make enquiries as to their cargoes. His investment was soon rewarded. On 5 December the *Husband* arrived in England, crammed with goods that still bore the merchants' marks from the *Soderina*. Writing to the doge and senate, he declared his hope to reclaim the goods, and 'by this example to deprive that perfidious pirate of a great incentive to continue his diabolical designs; for if the goods are thus recoverable the others will soon lose the taste for buying stolen goods.' Then, in January 1608 there arrived in Portsmouth the *Seraphim*, again laden with goods bearing marks from the *Soderina*. And within two months another ship arrived at Bristol, laden with yet more goods from the *Soderina*.

Meanwhile, the English were intensifying their efforts to wear down Venetian attempts to block Ward's pardon. The men who lobbied Giustinian were not minor officials, but some of the most powerful lords of the land – including the Earl of Salisbury and Lord Admiral Charles Howard. Giustinian notes that 'here they magnify Ward's preparations, and the High Admiral sent to . . . warn me to take steps to avert the impending peril'. Giustinian reported that he assured the lord admiral that Venice 'was all ready to check him [i.e. Ward], and that if he came out he would perhaps find what he did not look for'. Switching into cipher, Giustinian acknowledged that 'although I fear that the reports of Ward's strength are only too correct, I know that here they are very willingly exaggerated by those who expect to draw large profit from Ward's restoration to this country: for beyond a doubt they will make him pay dear for it.'

Giustinian's inclusion of the lord admiral himself among those who would personally profit from Ward's pardon demonstrates not only the vast sums being dispensed by Ward's agents, but also the magnitude of the problem facing the Venetian ambassador. The lord admiral was the highest Admiralty official in the land, and was the person to whom King James and the Earl of Salisbury deferred on all naval matters.

If Giustinian had been content to follow conventional wisdom, John Ward would have received the pardon that was, despite Venetian resistance, slowly grinding its way through the Admiralty bureaucracy, its path greased by officials right up to the lord admiral and other Privy Council members who had been bribed by Ward's emissaries. Instead of conceding the game, Giustinian decided that the pardon of John Ward would be an intolerable affront to Venice, a further humiliation of the Serene Republic by the most notorious Barbary Corsair since Barbarossa. Giustinian sought to take his case direct to the king.

The ambassador's campaign to bring King James into the matter personally began in Venice. 'I am of the opinion that your Serenity should take special notice of the matter to Ambassador Wotton', Giustinian advised the doge and senate. 'It is quite certain that, as the [Lord] Admiral will be against us, we require the support of the Earl and of the King himself, otherwise it will be impossible to resist the numerous scandalous proceedings which in such cases take place at the Admiralty [courts].'

Acting on this advice, the doge summoned Wotton before the cabinet. The English ambassador was asked to remind James and Salisbury of a recent incident, involving an Irish rebel who had escaped to the continent, in which Venice had assisted England, and to request that the king and the earl return the favour by disrupting the flow into England of goods looted from the *Soderina*. Wotton promised to do what he could, and within a couple of months Giustinian began to feel some relief.

In mid-February 1608 the king broke away from the perpetual hunting party that occupied the majority of his waking hours and, briefly, turned to affairs of state. 'The moment the King gave me the chance by coming to London for two days', Giustinian wrote to the doge and senate, 'I discharged my mission.' Describing the wealth of goods from the *Soderina* that were now quarantined in England awaiting adjudication through the Admiralty courts, Giustinian, scandalized, indicated the likelihood that this merchandise would soon be released to facilitate the pardoning of Captain John Ward. Giustinian knew how badly James craved Venetian approval in order to magnify his stature within Europe, *Rex Pacificus* in name and deed. The ambassador relied upon a subtle appeal to the king's vanity. It worked. Finally Giustinian received the assurance he craved, the plain, irrevocable and public statement of the king's position, a statement that had to be obeyed: 'The King declared he would never pardon Ward without the assent of the Republic, although [i.e. even though] Ward was spending large sums to obtain it. The King promised his support in the whole affair.'

Ward's negotiations for a pardon had fallen into a stalemate. He had done everything possible to advance his case, seeking to intimidate the Venetians through fear of his preparations for a new tour, and to satisfy them partially by offering the return of some of the goods looted from the *Soderina*. As for the English, Ward's massive campaign of bribery had distributed handouts through the admiralty offices and the royal court. Given the ardency with which the Earl of Salisbury and the lord admiral pressed for Ward's pardon, it is evident that at least one treasure ship must have made it through Giustinian's intelligence network, providing sufficient store of graft to start the wheels in motion. The identification and impounding of the cargoes of three others between December 1607 and March 1608, however, halted all lobbying on Ward's behalf. It also apparently exhausted the resources that Ward had allocated for his English pardon for himself and his men. The lord admiral and other officials who hoped to profit from Ward's pardon had been out-flanked by the Venetian ambassador. Ward had gambled a fortune and had lost it all.

NINE

Shipwreck

During the summer and autumn of 1607 Sir Henry Wotton received repeated assurances from the doge that John Ward would have a 'hot reception' if he were to venture against Venetian ships, and that a naval campaign was being prepared against the infamous corsair. Meanwhile, rumours of Ward's refashioning the *Soderina* into a man-of-war had reached London and Venice. Ward's putting to sea in a massive vessel such as the *Soderina* could only mean that he was determined to pursue the largest Mediterranean traffic, including other oversized Venetian galleys and galleons. In his interviews with Wotton the doge maintained an attitude of unconcern for Ward's preparations, but in actual fact the Venetians had good reason to fear. As Wotton noted on 18 January 1608, the *Soderina* was a 'splendid' ship, and Ward 'is very clever at keeping together a crew of all nations, and is a very cool hand'.

Despite the doge's composure there were clear signs that the Venetians were unnerved. On 7 November 1607 orders that named Ward as a principal threat to Venetian commerce were issued by the senate to the commanders of the war galleys that escorted shipping through the eastern Mediterranean. In December news reached Venice that Ward was once again at sea, though he had not yet completed his conversion of the *Soderina*. Ward's ships, described as four heavily armed bertons (i.e. square-rigged round ships), were bold enough to come within range of the Venetian fortress at Zante, fire a few salvos and, much to the shame of the Venetian forces, withdraw without losses. Following this incident, new orders were issued instructing that commercial shipping be halted at the Venetian fortress at Corfu and requiring the commanders of the armed galleys to escort those at Zante and elsewhere back to Corfu. Despite these precautions, in January Ward proved as much a threat as ever, capturing two Venetian vessels, the *Balbi* and the *Spelegato*, in quick succession. In February the same orders were issued again, this time with the proviso that no ships were to proceed beyond Corfu without explicit permission from the senate and an armed escort. Nonetheless, in March Jan Casten, a captain serving under Ward, captured the *Angeli*, yet another Venetian commercial galley, while sailing in the far eastern waters of the Mediterranean Sea.

The suspicion that Ward was actively targeting Venetian interests is supported by a letter that Sir Henry Wotton wrote to the Earl of Salisbury in the spring of 1608. 'The voice here is newly arrived that Ward hath taken another Venetian vessel of good value', wrote Wotton, probably referring to the *Angeli*. 'Hatred of [Ward] increaseth among [the Venetians] and fully as fast as fear of him.' Wotton then tells the story of a seaman named Moore, captain of an English merchantman recently arrived in Venice. While approaching the Strait of Otranto, Moore had been hailed by Ward. On learning that Moore was bound for Venice, Ward's seething anger erupted. 'Tell those flat caps', said he, 'who have been the occasion that I am banished out of my country, that before I have done with them I will make them sue for my pardon.'

This is a remarkable anecdote, not only for what it tells us of Ward's assault on the merchants of Venice, but also for his grasp of the situation in London, where the Venetian 'flat caps' were indeed the reason that his English pardon was refused. Ward's mansion in Tunis, it turns out, imitated a royal court not only in an assembly of rough-speaking, callused courtiers aping court custom, but also in the apparatus of statecraft. Captain John Ward was spying on London and Venice even as London and Venice were spying on John Ward.

From the spring of 1607 through to the spring of 1608 the *Reniera e Soderina* was a fixture at La Goulette. Sea captains and travellers recently arrived in London and Venice from Tunis described the progress of Ward's refitting of the vessel, including the installation of gun decks and the cutting of gun ports, exclaiming upon the dozens of brass cannon that had been hauled into the ship. Ward spared no expense in fitting out what he had apparently come to think of as the flagship of his private fleet.

At the same time the Venetians were making preparations of their own, getting ready to meet Ward's increased threat in one of their massive war galleons, a great ship that, unlike the *Soderina*, was designed to sail as a vessel of war. This is the only explanation for what, otherwise, is a bizarre anomaly in the history of Venice's ongoing war against the pirates. During the late 1580s and 1590s, Venice had tried on several occasions to use its great warships against pirates and privateers, but with very little success. The problem, as described by Wotton in a letter of 1607 written to the Earl of Salisbury, was that a large ship at sea is visible at many miles greater distance than a small ship. Wotton wrote that Ward and others like him 'won't let themselves be caught by the great galleon; they will fly. It does not pay them to fight, they like to plunder in safety.' None knew this lesson better than the Venetian admirals, who had witnessed just this effect when they had deployed their war galleons against the pirates some thirty years previously. Their decision to revisit a failed strategy only makes sense in light of the fact that Ward was busily fitting out another vast ship to use against the republic. Events proved the admirals' preparations unnecessary.

In mid-March 1607 news reached Venice that Ward had put forth in the converted *Soderina*, now a man-of-war with seventy guns and some 400 crew of diverse nationalities, Christian as well as Muslim, with janissaries to serve as soldiers. On 16 March it was reported via the Venetian outpost at Corfu that the *Soderina* had been spotted some days earlier making for Alexandria. Then, in a letter dated 18 March, further news came from Corfu:

Evidence of Mario Logilletti, of Marseilles

At Marseilles there is a report spread by the men of a vessel which put in there, that about one hundred miles off Cerigo they had fallen in with wreckage that had four men and a boy on it, who said they were Turks, part of the crew of a ship that had gone to the bottom because she was rotten. She was a ship taken by the corsairs from Venetians and manned in Tunis by Turks and English. She had two bertons in her company.

Piers and taverns were abuzz with the news, while government agents sought to separate rumour from fact, attempting to distinguish those with knowledge of the event from those who offered mere hearsay.

On 24 March Sir Henry Wotton was summoned before the cabinet to hear the following speech:

We take this occasion to inform your Excellency, if you have not heard it from other quarters, that we have news from Marseilles that the Venetian ship *Soderina*, which was fitted out as a privateer by Ward, appeared off the island of Crete, where she was sunk with her crew, including, it is supposed, Ward himself, for he left the ship at the height of the storm in a small boat with very little freeboard. This news is brought by some Turks who escaped from the wreck on a raft and landed at Marseilles.

The English ambassador, who had so recently puffed up Ward's threat in his attempts to negotiate Venetian permission for the captain's pardon, nonchalantly shrugged off this report as stale and possibly unreliable. 'Would to God the news were true. I have heard the same news from the master of an English ship bound from Toulon to Leghorn. He wrote me the news. If it be true this may free the seas.'

But was it true? During the next several months multiple reports made their way into Europe from the Mediterranean, most of them along the lines of this summary account from 'a sailor in the fleet of Marcantonio Gradenigo': 'Heard that the *Soderina* had gone to the bottom. Her captain was a famous man.' From the sultan's court in Istanbul, the Venetian ambassador wrote to the doge and senate in hopes of confirmation that 'the rumour that Ward has been drowned is true'. The news reached Zorzi Giustinian in London early in April, though by this time he was paranoid that he was being manipulated by information leaked to him by the lord admiral and his associates and so did not know what to make of the report. 'At court this morning', Giustinian wrote, 'I found a rumour that Ward and his ship had been wrecked and lost. Some say that this rumour was set about on purpose by the merchants interested in the goods' – that is to say, the goods looted from the *Soderina* that had turned up in England. Evidently, the hope was that if Ward were dead the sequestered goods would be released.

Gradually, the full story came out. The *Soderina*, crewed by nearly 350 North African and Ottoman Muslims as well as perhaps forty or fifty Englishmen and other Europeans, had set out in the company of two smaller square-rigged round ships. Their tour had started well with the capture, looting and release of two English ships, followed by the capture of a medium-sized French merchantman. Determined to continue the tour, Ward, who had found the *Soderina* to be leaky and slow, took command of the French prize himself. The small fleet was then scattered by one of the savage Mediterranean storms that can arise in the winter and spring, on whose account traditional seafaring halted during the winter months. The *Soderina* was swamped and broke up, partly as a result of her rotten timbers, but largely because of structural damage that Ward himself had caused while cutting gun ports and installing her new gun deck.

Following the storm Ward returned to Tunis where he found that his problems had hardly begun. The death of a soldier or two was to be expected, and the families of the North African seamen whom Ward had trained to sail round ships also lived with the understanding that their husbands, fathers and uncles were engaged in a risky business. But the loss of 350 soldiers and seamen at a single blow, and the survival of their so-called admiral from the same disaster, had stoked outrage. Ward's mansion now became a fortress under siege, the centre of riots demanding that he pay the price that justice required.

Unable to walk the streets of Tunis on account of anger over the shipwreck, Ward also found his official relations with Uthman Dey had cooled. Not only had Ward created a brouhaha in the local population, but Uthman, like other investors in the conversion of the *Soderina*, had lost his money when Ward's men lost their lives. The solution to the captain's problems seems obvious: return to sea, escape popular opprobrium and capture new prizes to satisfy the demands of Uthman Dey and the other investors.

This simple plan proved impracticable. It may have been that Ward was rattled. The commander who prized his carefully trained and loyal crews above all had led several hundreds to their deaths, not in battle, but on account of his own hubristic scheme to make the *Soderina* his flagship. Alternately, rumour held that Ward had lost the trust of his men, and that they would not abide his command without muttering and mutiny. Among Christian seamen it was said that Ward favoured Muslims, while Muslims held that Ward was using them as swabs and cannon-fodder. A story made the rounds that Ward had left the *Soderina* on account of open mutiny by the Ottoman soldiers and North African seamen on the vessel – that Ward survived because he and several of his European officers had been exiled, placed in one of the ship's boats and left under the open sky.

This latter tale was certainly not true, for Ward was unlikely to have survived the blow that broke up and sank the *Soderina* if he had been set adrift in a ship's boat. Moreover, rumours of racial and religious divisions among Ward's men may have been started on account of the captain's shrewd exploitation of European Christian prejudices. In 1608 Ward's men would swindle the seamen on board the *Charity* by pretending to be at odds with the janissaries. Rumours of racial or religious divisions among his men no doubt owed their origins to similar tactics. Nonetheless, the fact remains that Ward was unwilling or unable to put to sea following his disastrous outing in the *Soderina*.

Instead, his ships went out under his subordinate commanders while Ward spent his days ashore, isolated in his mansion. One of these proxies, a Dutch captain named Jan Casten, was at sea with two ships, one mid-sized and one smaller, in March 1608. Lurking amidst the Ionian Islands, Casten hoped to surprise Venetian shipping coming from or going to the Middle East. It was not long before he took the *Angeli*: good fare, but not sufficient to warrant a return to Tunis.

The sinking of the *Soderina* had forestalled the deployment of a war galleon against Ward's forces, but Venice's war galleys, the standard bulwark against the privateers and pirates in the eastern Mediterranean, remained at sea with special orders to guard against Ward and his men. While Casten hovered off the Peloponnesian coast, not far from the Venetian island of Sapienza, he was set upon by three galleys under the command of the Venetian Admiral Giulio Venier. The galleys closed in on Casten's three ships (the two round ships that he had commanded from Tunis and the *Angeli*) and briefly engaged in a hot exchange of cannon fire, allowing Casten to pepper them with several broadsides while the galleys' gunners lobbed ineffective volleys back. Venier and his two captains then turned tail and ran, heading north up the Peloponnesian coast.

Casten, no doubt inspired by memories of Ward's great lopsided encounters, then made a fateful error: he pursued the Venetians. His decision to do so is utterly at odds with the privateer's code, which dictates no pursuit of prizes whose capture would cost more than they were likely to yield. Nonetheless, Casten, perhaps intoxicated by having, like his master, put the Venetian war galleys to flight, thought to press his advantage. In doing so he fell into Venier's trap, placing his round ships at a complete disadvantage relative to the Venetian galleys. With Casten's broadside-mounted cannon pointing at the arid coast and the open sea, Venier brought his powerful stern cannon to bear on the pursuing round ships, unleashing a fearful and furious torrent of great shot as well as quantities of grape and chain that left his pursuers' riggings in tatters, blood streaming from their scuppers. Turning back upon Casten's ships, Venier's oarsmen hauled hard while his soldiers prepared for a hostile boarding. The Venetian flagship matched itself to Casten's vessel; by the time the smoke cleared Casten was dead and his ship captured. Meanwhile, one of Venier's subordinates overpowered Casten's prize crew and recaptured the *Angeli*. The last of Casten's ships made a desperate run for the fortress at Modone, slipping into range of the Ottoman guns. Even as shot from the shore batteries rained upon them the Venetian soldiers and crew pressed their advantage, overpowering Casten's men and taking the round ship. Launching their auxiliary boats, a handful of Ward's men escaped to the Ottoman coast, but victory undeniably belonged to Venier: Ward's forces had been routed. Some fifty Ottoman privateers and Casten were dead, forty-five were taken alive, a prize was recovered and two round ships captured.

Venier's triumph, without any substantial damage to his galleys or loss of men, afforded the admiral a moment of celebrity in Venice. The senate issued a letter of 'warm congratulations' and a prize of 2,000 ducats for the recovery of the *Angeli*. Coming hard on the heels of the *Soderina* disaster, this could only cheer Ward's enemies and strengthen their resolve to see him brought to account. Thirty-six of the men captured by Venier were hanged in a mass execution at Zante, while the rest met the same fate in other Venetian territories to distribute the effects of this very visible form of justice.

Ward's bad luck showed no sign of turning. Negotiations for an English pardon had been confounded by the tireless efforts of Venetian Ambassador Zorzi Giustinian, the goods with which the captain had intended to grease the wheels of English bureaucracy seized by the state and sequestered. Ward and his supporters in Tunis had invested heavily in the conversion and outfitting of the *Soderina* and lost all. And now one of Ward's chief lieutenants had been hunted down and executed, his ships captured and taken to Venice in triumph. John Ward began to weigh his options, options that were severely limited by his dwindling reserves of goodwill among the authorities and investors of Tunis. Though it had been his refuge since 1605, John Ward began to contemplate leaving the city altogether.

In May 1608, John King, finding himself in Algiers, made a good trade: a tun of cheap English beer for a tun of good Alicante wine. The provisional merchant was Captain John Ward, and he willingly gave up the valuable wine for ale from home. And why not? Rolling heavily in the wake of the modest vessel that Ward commanded was a Spanish prize carrying nothing but wine, as well as a fully-laden French merchantman. With his departure from Tunis, Ward's luck was back.

King has little else to say about John Ward, though he does offer further information about the captain's 'vice-admiral', a French settee of 240 tons commanded by an English master named George Blake. Besides Blake, there were another dozen Dutch and English mariners and perhaps 150 Ottoman and North African Muslims. Blake brought two prizes into Algiers in addition to Ward's two.

It is curious to find Captain Ward back in Algiers after the nearly fatal encounter that he and his men had had with the pasha five years previously. Nonetheless, Ward, now counted an Ottoman *raïs* through his arrangements with Uthman Dey, was allowed to do his business in the port without official interference. It may be that the pasha of Algiers, having seen how Ward had enriched Uthman Dey, offered to allow him to sail as a *raïs* in the Algerian *taifa*, for this was not to be Ward's only stop in the city in the coming months. In November 1608 Ward would return, reportedly sailing in ships for which the pasha had 'furnished him with much artillery'. In the meantime, Ward had other destinations in mind. He sold cargoes, slaves and prize ships, purchased victuals and supplies and was off, his two ships making west, away from Tunis.

King's story is corroborated and augmented by an intelligence report compiled by the English ambassador and submitted to the Venetian doge and senate in the summer of 1608. The report provides an account of Wotton's interview with an unnamed English sailor, recently arrived in Venice from a Mediterranean tour that had taken him through Tunis. The sailor had been in the Ottoman port long enough to have several meetings with John Ward and to witnesses the captain's departure.

According to Wotton's source, the losses that Uthman Dey sustained when the *Soderina* sank were offset by the fortune he had made by having first options on her cargo, purchasing it 'for barely a half of what it was worth'. Since the sale of a cargo usually preceded the division of the shares, Uthman profited twice: once by buying low and reselling, and once by reaping his appointed shares as an investor in Ward's enterprise. The sailor also stated that, prior to the *Soderina* disaster, Ward had attained a significant position in Uthman's household and in the Tunisian administration, serving as an advisor to Uthman's cronies and looking to Uthman's domestic affairs when business called for the *dey* to leave Tunis. Nonetheless, the *Soderina* disaster, which made Ward the object of rage among Uthman's subjects, inevitably changed the nature of his relationship with the *dey*. Wotton's source confirmed earlier reports that upon his return Ward 'was nearly torn in pieces by the janissaries, who heard of what had happened from five Turks who were saved on some planks of the *Soderina*'. The sailor went on to say that Ward now owed his very survival to Uthman, who 'pacified the Turks'.

Wotton's seaman was present when Ward next left La Goulette 'about last Easter' in command of a fleet of three ships. Ward's modest vessel was armed with 'twenty-four pieces of artillery and fifty men, English and Flemish, not a single Turk, owing to their suspicion of him'. The second, and larger, ship sailed under the command of a Muslim named Mehemet Raïs, and had 'one hundred Turks and twenty-six cannon on board'. The final vessel was a small pinnace, accounted by the informant as 'very small, not having more than thirty-five Turks on board and from ten to twelve pieces [of artillery].' This diminutive fleet headed west, for Ward's 'notion was to sail out of Gibraltar and try his fortune further off'. How far off, Wotton's man could not say.

Ward's stop at Algiers in May 1608, noted by the Englishman John King, was the first landfall on what was already a successful privateering tour. King's observations reveal a few points, the most important of which is that the small barque or pinnace had been abandoned, its Muslim crew folded into that of the larger of the two other ships. King's statement, that this ship was manned overwhelmingly by Muslims but was under the command of an Englishman named George Blake, is not necessarily out of step with the account that the anonymous sailor made to Sir Henry Wotton: it is likely that Blake was a renegade, one of the many English seamen who had joined the Ottoman privateering effort by converting to Islam. If this supposition is true, then it would appear that Blake took the common name Mehemet upon his conversion, but used his previous Christian name when dealing with Englishmen like John King.

The anonymous sailor's account ends on two very significant points. The first is that the *Soderina* disaster, instead of alienating him from the administration of Uthman Dey, actually drove Ward deeper into Uthman's debt. On account of Uthman's protection of Ward from the family and friends of the Muslims who had perished, the captain now owed his very survival to Uthman. This observation helps to explain the unusual demographics of Ward's little fleet. It would appear that he was once again sailing with janissaries who were, in effect, his gaolers. The 135 'Turks' that are described by the English seaman apparently were deployed by Uthman Dey to protect his material investment in Ward's latest endeavour, and 'certain it is that he has promised Uthman to spare no one whom he can defeat, for he is now completely under the protection of the Turks'. As in 1603, when he sailed with Algerian janissaries in order to purchase the freedom of his men from the pasha of Algiers, Ward was now obliged to play the privateer under the watchful gaze of his master's men. It is certain, then, that portions of the value of the four prizes that Ward brought to Algiers were reserved for Uthman Dey, and that Ward, though still the 'admiral' of his fleet, was not a free agent.

The final point to be noted from Wotton's informer is contained in a seeming non sequitur that he included at the end of his account. Making no reference to Ward whatsoever, the seaman stated that, also in April 1608, another English commander based in Tunis fitted out, too. Captain Richard Bishop 'had forty men with him, chiefly Flemish, who had fled from the ships lately captured by the great galleys of Venice at Modone' – the men who had survived Jan Casten's disastrous battle with the Venetian war galleys. These men, who 'had gone back to Tunis on a Marseilles ship', evidently had immediately signed on to sail with Bishop, a principal confederate of John Ward.

Over the summer of 1608 reports reached Venice and London that Ward and Bishop were once more working in concert. It is a remarkable testament to the loyalty that Ward inspired among his men that Bishop and his crew immediately set out to augment the captain's small fleet at the very moment when Ward's fortunes were at their lowest ebb. What's more, these same reports trace the movement of Ward, Bishop and Mehemet Raïs/George Blake right out of the Mediterranean Sea into the North Atlantic and to the province of Munster in south-west Ireland – an easy cruise from Ward's sometime home in Plymouth. John Ward had returned to his home waters, to the delight of Venice and the horror of England.

TEN

'The War against the Pirates'

The complicated nature of John Ward's reputation in England is demonstrated by reactions to the Venetian success against Jan Casten. Ambassador Giustinian noted that the defeat of Ward's fleet 'has been received, in appearance at least, with much satisfaction by the English, but in reality not without some regret for the large gains that were reaped from the booty, and because they had an idea that their ships and their men were not to be beaten. The King, however, and all who love order and quiet are pleased.' Those English who loved 'order and quiet' were less pleased with the ultimate outcome of the disasters and disappointments that had begun to dog John Ward. Instead of being induced to abandon his dangerous profession, Ward merely relocated from the Mediterranean Sea to the North Atlantic; from North Africa to south-west Ireland; from Tunis to Munster.

Ward found ready welcome in Ireland, but not because 'the whole country is wild and woody, the people easily aroused', as Sir Henry Wotton alleged to the doge and senate of Venice. During the decade after 1603 piracy became a major problem in Munster on account of the perfect combination of a number of factors, none of which had much to do with the Irish themselves.

The end of the Anglo-Spanish conflict had had its greatest impact on English seamen in the West Country. As these men fell away from the straight and narrow path of law-abiding beggary they found a pirate's paradise just across the Celtic Sea. Abounding in bays and coves, the Irish coastline offered small craft limitless opportunities for shelter and fresh water, while deep-water ports at Baltimore, Leamcon and Youghal offered berths for even the largest ships.

The suppression of the Gaelic rebellion between 1601 and 1603, followed by the restoration of English colonization into the Munster plantation, produced a flow of out-of-work and out-of-luck Englishmen into an economically depressed and war-ravaged region. Upon arrival, their dreams of a new life withered amidst the hostility of the local population and a lack of opportunities to practise traditional trades. The combination of state-sponsored migration from England coupled with an utter lack of employment in Ireland left the would-be colonists ripe for recruitment into piracy. In 1618 Sir Henry Mainwaring would dub Ireland 'the nursery and storehouse of pirates'.

Neither the lord lieutenants appointed by the crown nor the various Admiralty officials appointed by the lord admiral had sufficient human or economic resources to police the region. English pirates swaggered down the streets of Baltimore under the gaze of royal and Admiralty officials because in most cases the pirates could call upon more followers than the crown had soldiers. English officials, at any rate, were more interested in using their limited powers to cash in on the spoils of piracy rather than to attempt to halt the trade.

Meanwhile, the Irish themselves were largely indifferent to the progress of piracy in their midst. There would always be some Irish seamen who elected to sail with the pirates, and even a few Irish pirate ships, sailing under Irish commanders. But for the most part the pirates who sailed from Munster in the early 1600s were poor English tradesmen seeking to raise enough money to set up their proper trades in Ireland or return to England, while the captains and shipboard officers were unemployed English seamen seeking to escape destitution. Typically, the Irish did not profit through the buying and selling of booty either. Though the residents of ports sometimes received gifts from pirate captains eager to retain their goodwill, the trade in looted cargoes was mostly the province of English merchants. The one role that consistently fell to the Irish themselves was to sell supplies and victuals to the pirates, and to provide on-shore accommodation and entertainment. This in itself was quite lucrative, given the free hand with which pirate crews spent their shares.

Upon his arrival in Munster, early in the summer of 1608, Ward himself was transformed from privateer to pirate, once again raiding without the sanction of any state. In Munster he found a thriving community of English pirates, including many old friends. He also found opportunity. The Munster pirates lacked structure and organization. Few of the commanders and fewer of the new recruits had become pirates by choice, and most hoped to return to legitimate employment soon; as a result, the voyages chartered out of Munster were one-off affairs, most of the crew hoping that this would be their first and last cruise. John Ward, who had already successfully transferred into North Africa the small-fleet system of privateering practised by the English under Queen Elizabeth, prepared to revolutionize the Munster pirates too, converting green amateurs into an international menace.

Prior to Ward's arrival, a pirate ship would venture on its own or perhaps with one or two companions of opportunity. Standard tactics involved lurking along established sea lanes, and especially at bottleneck points such as the entrance to the Strait of Gibraltar. Potential prizes would be sighted and sized up for their ability to resist attack, with the pirates assaulting only those that they could easily intimidate or overpower. Sailing with companions increased the odds in the pirates' favour, but only slightly. To increase greatly the effectiveness of their operations, the pirates needed to work out a command structure and fleet tactics. A fleet of three ships, operated under one command, was considerably more powerful than three ships that sailed together merely as a convenience, each determined to take a prize, even at the expense of its companions.

By 8 August 1608 the lord admiral had intelligence that 'the pirates Bishop, Sakill and Jennings are now all in consort with the Archpirate Ward'. Once again Ward was playing the evangelist, spreading the good news of increasing your booty through cooperation and preaching the transformative powers of greed. He had found ready converts: Bishop had been among Ward's men for years, but Sakill and Jennings were more recent recruits from the Munster pirate community. These men used Munster as their home base but ranged widely, raiding the Atlantic coast of Spain and even crossing to the New World to prey upon the fishing fleets of the Grand Banks (a ready source of new recruits as well as the dried fish that was an essential part of the shipboard diet) or to raid Spanish shipping in the Caribbean. Unlike in Tunis, Ward had no compelling reason to bring his prizes back to his home port. Once again he began to dump prize cargoes in Morocco's Atlantic ports.

The effectiveness of actions led by 'Archpirate Ward' in Ireland, as in North Africa, induced others to align themselves with his group. These recruits sailed under the command of the captain or his subordinates, but only for a specific cruise. Ward was not jealous of power or influence, and subordinate captains floated in and out of his confederacy as easily as seamen joined, left and rejoined his crews. This fluidity appealed to the out-of-work English planters who made up the reluctant pirate underclass of Munster and those captains from the merchant marine who viewed themselves as temporary pirates. Meanwhile, every captain and seaman who left the confederacy carried with him, besides the gold in his pocket, tales of success, even against armed Spanish fleets. By the end of the summer, the Venetian ambassador to Spain wrote that 'in the ocean, off Lisbon, is an English pirate with fifteen big ships, and every day he is growing stronger, being joined by the Dutch. . . . Recently an English ship left Lisbon with a cargo of sugar to the value of 100,000 crowns. Livorno was her destination, but she discharged in Barbary.' Switching into secret code, the ambassador noted that the Spanish, like the Venetians before them, were so unnerved by Ward that they had begun to 'fear for the safety of the [treasure] fleet [from the New World]', the best protected of all of Spain's shipping.

While Ward harried the Spanish along their Atlantic coast, Captain Simon Danziker, sailing with the Barbary Corsairs of Algiers, hovered in the Mediterranean. An English diplomat in Spain, Sir Charles Cornwallis, commenting on a recent truce between the Spanish and Dutch, reported to his masters in the Privy Council that 'The two famous pirates Ward and Dauncer [i.e. Danziker] (whether by God's providence or man's invention I know not) so behave themselves upon these coasts, as this truce gives us not the advantage and security that by sea we hoped.'

Meanwhile, in London, Ambassador Giustinian had not given up his campaign to have Ward punished and to secure compensation for those who had suffered in the capture of the *Reniera e Soderina*. The removal of Ward from the Mediterranean had given Venice a reprieve, but Giustinian continued to plead with King James for the confiscation of goods known to have been looted from the *Soderina* and the punishment of Ward and other English pirates, whether they were in English waters or Venetian. James, too, was reaching the limit of his patience with the inability of the Admiralty to rein in Ward and other pirates. Royal commissioners began to investigate evidence of collusion between admiralty officials and the pirates, and it was not long before a number of West Country vice-admirals had come under heavy censure.

At the same time, royal ships were sent out to scour the seas around England and Ireland in hopes of encountering vessels from Ward's confederacy. Zorzi Giustinian described two encounters between Ward's fleet and King James's ships during the early autumn of 1608. On 4 September Giustinian wrote that

for some days past there have been reports of frequent piracies committed in these waters near the Isle of Wight. A royal ship was sent out, but without any result. It seems that there are two pirates, followers of Ward, who have their headquarters in Ireland and are endeavouring to get ships with which to return to Tunis and carry on their depredations in the Mediterranean. They have already captured some French bertons and they profess that they will not damage the English. One is called Captain Lusip [i.e. Bishop], the other Gianins [i.e. Jennings].

A couple of weeks later Giustinian reported that 'the pirate followers of Ward about whom I wrote are growing stronger every day. A rumour is spreading today that they have sunk a royal ship that went out against them.' It seems that Ward's men did not in fact sink a royal ship in the autumn of 1608, but it is true that English efforts were stepped up to bring the pirates to justice at that time. Captain James Harris, who had been ransomed from Ottoman slavery by Bishop, followed Ward and Bishop from North Africa to Munster. As Harris put out from Baltimore for a cruise he was surprised by a royal man-of-war under the command of Sir William Saint John, captured and taken into custody.

Zorzi Giustinian had succeeded in thwarting Ward's pardon and had goaded James into action against the pirates and against corruption within the Admiralty, but these activities could never satisfy Venetian lust for vengeance against John Ward personally. In London and Venice assassination plots began to brew.

On 2 October 1608 Sir Henry Wotton, the English ambassador in Venice, appeared before the doge and senate with an unusual offer made on behalf of an English seaman who had informed Wotton of Ward's operations earlier that summer. 'This man [is] now in England', stated Wotton, 'and on the strength of his knowledge of Ward and even of a certain friendship for him, [is] prepared to kill him and burn his ships. To carry out this design he required a ship of his own maintained at the charges of the Republic.' Wotton himself endorsed the scheme, stating that 'in view of the importance of this offer' he himself 'presents it and recommends it', all the more so because he knew the anonymous seaman to be 'capable and brave'.

This was not the only conspiracy against John Ward. Shuffled among the English state papers relating to Ireland is a letter sent to the Earl of Salisbury from Dublin, written by an English spy named Henry Pepwell. The letter is dated August 1609 and relates Pepwell's efforts over some eighteen months to arrange the assassination of Captain John Ward. Originally a secret agent residing in Livorno, from whence he informed Salisbury 'of diverse wrongs done by the late duke of Florence', Pepwell, 'according to directions from the

Lord Admiral', decamped to Tunis in the spring of 1608. There he bent all of his efforts 'to persuade Ward and his confederates to forsake their wicked course of life' or 'to destroy them and their proceedings'.

Pepwell arrived in Tunis shortly after the *Soderina* disaster, when Ward was barricaded into his mansion. Despite this low ebb in Ward's fortunes, Pepwell nonetheless was outmanoeuvred. 'What with gifts and further hope of spoils' Ward and his cronies so charmed Pepwell's crew 'that they became pirates with him': not the first time that Ward exploited greed to transform a deadly enemy into an ally. Unable to approach John Ward himself, Pepwell insinuated himself among the captain's men, associating with the leading English corsairs: Bishop, Anthony Johnson, William Graves and Samson Denball, as well as various Dutch pirates including Danziker and Jan Casten (identified by Pepwell as 'John Kerson of Flushing'). Of these, Pepwell learned that Casten 'hated Ward extremely' and would willingly 'take or destroy Ward, his ship, and company' if Pepwell could 'procure [Casten's] protection in England', and if the traitor was to be allowed to keep a generous share of Ward's booty. Pepwell, confident of the goodwill of Salisbury and the lord admiral, swore that Casten would be rewarded amply. It will never be known whether Casten was really discontented, or whether this was a ruse to draw out and frustrate Pepwell's mission, for shortly after Pepwell and Casten made their compact Ward sent Casten into the eastern Mediterranean on the mission that would see Casten's fleet shattered by Venetian war galleys and Casten himself killed in battle.

Pepwell sold off his pinnace 'at an under rate to the Turks' in order to finance his return to England. Unable to secure an audience with his patron, the Earl of Salisbury, Pepwell was advised by one of Salisbury's secretaries to complete his assignment and so return to favour with the earl. Pepwell now made his way to Ireland and renewed his acquaintance with Bishop, to whom he 'propounded' the terms offered to Casten. Like Casten before him, Bishop declared himself Pepwell's man, 'complaining of the wrongs Ward had done him, especially detesting his associating with Turks at sea, his taking of Christians and selling them, with diverse other outrages'. It is unlikely that one of Ward's most trusted and longest-serving lieutenants would choose to unburden himself to an Englishman of no stated profession who just 'happened' to be in the area looking for an assassin to kill John Ward. Bishop played Pepwell for a time, continuing to make promises that he would never keep. Pepwell found Bishop – in reality one of the most powerful of Ward's inner circle and ultimately the inheritor of the captain's operations in Munster – to be 'of small strength' and 'unable to put in execution that which they had determined'.

Whatever Pepwell's previous services to Salisbury and the lord admiral, it is evident that he was singularly unsuited to the kind of insinuating espionage required to infiltrate Ward's entourage and eliminate the man that the lord admiral now regularly referred to as the 'Archpirate'. The would-be assassin ended up stranded in Ireland, writing to the Earl of Salisbury from Dublin, a forlorn failure.

During the summer and autumn of 1608 the English and Spanish informants remained vigilant, watching the movements of Ward and his confederates. Their reports sketch out an enterprise that quickly expanded, so that while Ward remained the archpirate of Munster, Bishop and Jennings began to command small fleets of their own. As in Tunis, Ward sought to decrease his own time at sea, and by autumn Bishop had assumed the greater profile in Munster, while Ward prepared for a return to the Mediterranean.

Meanwhile, in England, the Earl of Salisbury had received his own promotion, consolidating and extending his control of English affairs as the newly appointed lord treasurer. Things were changing at the Venetian Embassy, too: late in the summer of 1608 Giustinian's successor, Marcantonio Correr, had arrived. Giustinian introduced his successor to the personalities at the English court and prepared to return to his beloved Venice. For a brief time the dispatches to Venice were signed by both men.

Late in October, Giustinian and Correr advanced to the doge the transcript of the examination of an English seaman named Thomas Butler, recently arrived from the Mediterranean. He reported that, though the Spanish had dispatched five war galleons to capture or kill Ward and Danziker they had not met with any success. Danziker, reputed to have captured an incredible twenty-nine prizes in one month, was still at Algiers, where it was rumoured that Ward had newly established himself. The Venetian ambassador to Spain soon confirmed that Ward had entered the Straits of Gibraltar, and shortly after that 'the English corsair who recently passed the Straits is reported at Algiers, putting together three great ships. The king [i.e. pasha] of that country has furnished him with much artillery.'

It is not clear why Ward returned to North Africa after his Irish summer, but rumours quickly spread that this was to be his last season in the Mediterranean. Though it might not have the climate of Tunisia, Munster appeared to offer him the opportunity to retire from sea and live in peace. Ward evidently believed that he could rely on the goodwill of the local population – a marked improvement over his status in Tunis, where he could not walk the streets without fear of popular justice. In addition, the proximity of Munster to England's West Country, and the presence in Munster of many of Ward's friends from the old days, meant that he could begin to put together the pieces of the life he had had before he became an outlaw.

Ward had underestimated the strength of the reaction that was brewing against him. On 28 November 1608 King James ordered a sweep of the pirate haunts of Munster, and on 4 December three commissions were issued. Egged on by Zorzi Giustinian and Marcantonio Correr, James took pains to ensure that Ward would not be able to retire anywhere in his dominions, including Ireland. In January 1609 the king issued a remarkable proclamation that definitively crushed any hopes the captain might have held out for an English pardon, and marked a decisive shift in royal policy. Between 1603 and 1609 English piracy had flourished, unchecked. From 1609 James took a personal interest in the problem, at least partly on account of his close relations with Giustinian. The result was a series of initiatives that systematically undermined the legal and social norms which had allowed piracy to flourish among the king's subjects. By 1621 James could stand up in the House of Commons and declare, with some measure of truth, that he had won his 'war against the pirates'.

The king's war had actually started in the autumn of 1608 with a general inquiry into the state of corruption among Admiralty officials. In September 1608 Henry, Lord Danvers, President of Munster, was summoned to London and placed under arrest. Danvers was compelled to account for his possession of twenty chests of North African sugar, which seemed to London to be 'a token of too much familiarity' with the pirates. It was also demanded why he had 'given shelter to Ward the pirate'. Lord Danvers could only reply that 'the pirate was far stronger than himself' – Ward's combined seamen and soldiers greatly outnumbered the 300 troops that Danvers had been allowed. Marcantonio Correr remarked ominously that 'it is thought that he will end ill'. The king's campaign against corruption in the Admiralty peaked in the summer of 1609 when Lord Admiral Nottingham himself was called upon to explain his 'too great lenity to offenders', with particular reference to 'the pirates Bishop, Sakell and Jennings, the Archpirate Ward, and the flyboat they took near Spain'. Nottingham later groused to the Earl of Salisbury that he hoped he 'shall not have cause to wish he had been put in his grave when his old mistress [i.e. Queen Elizabeth] was'.

The lord admiral's starchy panic and the Venetian ambassador's gleeful hope for appropriate punishments were both misplaced. Whatever his animosity towards piracy, James was not in the habit of chastising his officials, even those who behaved in a grievously and demonstrably corrupt fashion. The entire royal service was built on the principle that office holders should do what they could to make their posts profitable, for the official stipends that were allowed them were rarely sufficiently generous to meet even basic expenses. Lord Danvers no doubt believed that his acceptance of pirate booty was not corruption but remuneration. Nonetheless, in the autumn of 1608 James had decided that things had gone too far, and in his proclamation of January 1609 he had served warning to his own officials, particularly those who had encouraged and hoped to profit from John Ward's desire for a pardon.

For months the king had been grumbling to Salisbury, the Venetian ambassadors and many others that he was tired of English merchants and officials profiting from the spoils of piracy, and that a change of affairs was in order. In November 1608, Zorzi Giustinian and Marcantonio Correr had reported a conversation in which James had candidly stated that he 'suspects that the officials of the admiralty support the pirates', noting that 'there is great disorder at the admiralty'. The king had also stated his intention to make a blanket prohibition of all English trade into North Africa.

The proclamation that was made from Whitehall Palace on 8 January 1609 did not go quite so far, reflecting, perhaps, the palliations of Salisbury and others of the Privy Council. But the document does lay out, in no uncertain terms, that the King had had enough, and that things would henceforth change. And most remarkable of all, it singles out one particular pirate as the object of James's wrath: Captain John Ward.

The opening sentence of the proclamation states that those 'lewd and ill-disposed' English subjects who engaged in piracy were 'insensible and desperate of the peril that they draw upon themselves, and the imputation they cast upon the honour of their Sovereign, so precious to him'. James then turns his wrath from the pirates to the officials who were supposed to check these faults. Making an oblique reference to the interrogation of Lord Danvers and the general inquiry into Admiralty corruption, the king continued that he had 'lately found by many pregnant circumstances, that most of these great faults are continued by the connivance, or corruption in many of the subordinate [royal and Admiralty] officers, especially such as are resident in and near the ports and marine counties'.

The king identified the provincial vice-admirals as being especially at fault. To avoid confusion James laid out the circumstances in which the vice-admirals should be considered culpable; these extended beyond openly aiding and abetting the pirates to more subtle offences, including errors of omission in not halting the progress of suspicious crafts 'such as apparently shall be furnished for the wars, and not for merchandizing or fishing'. If the active or passive behaviour of any vice-admiral or other Admiralty official was found to allow the flourishing of piracy, the king directed that these officials 'shall suffer imprisonment until the offenders [i.e. the pirates] may be apprehended, and [the officials] shall be answerable to the parties aggrieved, for their contempt and offence in this behalf committed'.

Having laid out the consequences for Admiralty and royally appointed officials who were negligent in the suppression of piracy, James turned on the merchants who trafficked in merchandise that was looted by 'Captain John Ward and his adherents, and other English pirates'. Any English subject who would 'dare to buy, barter, exchange, or receive directly or indirectly any goods taken at the Seas' by 'the said Ward or his adherents, or any other pirate or pirates whatsoever' would suffer 'under pain of death as accessories in cases of piracy'. The king viewed Ward as a test case. From this point forward he would suffer none of his subjects to have any dealings with the captain or 'his adherents'. James had personalized piracy by giving it the face of John Ward.

After the proclamation came action: a concerted attempt to locate and arrest men who had sailed with Ward. Captain Harris was taken at sea, and another of Ward's Munster captains, Jennings, soon joined him, arrested in a sting as he tried to purchase his own pardon. Marcantonio Correr reported that Jennings, who 'is very rich', was arrested at 'the hands of the very people who had tried to secure a safe conduct for him'.

Shortly thereafter William Longcastle and William Taverner, men who had participated in the capture of the *Soderina*, were rounded up by the vice-admiral at Plymouth. The vice-admiral sent the men to London for trial but not before he relieved them of 600 pounds of tobacco, in the process proving that arresting pirates could be almost as profitable as sheltering them.

Amidst this round-up yet another would-be assassin stepped forward, this one far more credible than the hapless Henry Pepwell.

A fortnight after the king's proclamation against Ward, Marcantonio Correr was visited by a gentlemanly sea captain. Correr's guest stated that he had 'the intention and means to capture the pirate Ward', having previously held a command of ships in one of Ward's fleets. Given the ongoing arrest of the captain's men, it is obvious why this individual refused to disclose his identity. The catch was that he was now destitute, without a ship, and would require a sizeable investment from the Venetian and Spanish ambassadors in order to sail to Tunis. Correr declared himself in favour of 'so laudable a design', but informed the man that he could not advance any large sums without express permission from the doge. Nonetheless, Correr 'praised his intention and assured him that if he succeeded he would reap great glory and adequate recompense'.

Over the next three months the mysterious captain repeatedly called on Correr, who advocated on the man's behalf to Venice. 'I should think any sum well spent if the capture were effected', he wrote to the doge. In the end, the man raised funds on his own by allowing individual merchants to purchase shares in the voyage against rewards offered upon Ward's death or capture. The last time the captain visited Correr was on 19 March 1609 when he declared that 'he would be content with a suitable reward after the deed is done'. The man then departed on his mission, never to be heard from again. Correr's final advice to the doge on the matter was to 'Pray God that if he does not succeed [in killing Ward] that he take not himself to piracy.' We know that he failed to kill John Ward; we do not know whether Ward seduced him back into the ranks.

With the king's proclamation of 8 January, followed by sweeping arrests of his former companions, John Ward was forced to accept that he could never live peaceably in Munster. Once again he began to cast about for other options. In the spring of 1609 he left Algiers for unknown reasons; but instead of heading for Munster he shifted east, returning to Tunis and resuming his previous arrangement under the direct protection of Uthman Dey. Ward's Irish summer, though it failed to lay the groundwork for a permanent move out of the Mediterranean region, at least revived his devastated finances, presumably also allowing him to settle accounts with Uthman Dey and the other *Soderina* investors. By July he was reported to be acting as admiral to a fleet of twenty-three vessels.

Life in Tunis remained uncomfortable, however. Previously Ward had walked the streets with an entourage of friends and hard men as a show of power. In the summer of 1609 these companions were no longer just for show, for Ward continued to be the focus of popular hostility among Muslims. He remained hopeful of escape and even while working and living under the protection of Uthman Dey he opened another set of secret negotiations, now with the grand duke of Florence.

Our information on these negotiations, as on Ward's discussions with London, comes primarily through the archives of Venice. On 18 July 1609 Giacomo Vendramin, the Venetian Resident in Florence, reported to the doge that 'the famous pirates Ward and Danziker, desiring to enjoy their ill-gotten gains in peace, give out that they would like to settle in Italy, but they require guarantees that they shall not be molested'. Vendramin also observed that Danziker's negotiations had stalled at the preliminaries, having 'no one to speak for him', but that Ward's representatives were close to a deal. The arrangement would see Ward settle in Tuscany and 'bring with him 150,000 crowns of plunder'.

Two weeks later Vendramin continued the tale. 'The question of a safe conduct for the pirate Ward was reopened in Council the other day.' The Venetian noted that the proposed pardon 'met with some opposition' because Ward's 'crimes were so great and he had offended so many sovereigns'. Those in the Great Council who supported the scheme responded that since his crimes were so great, 'every sovereign would be glad to see him withdrawn from his present calling' – the exact same argument employed by those who had favoured Ward's pardon in London. In Florence, however, this argument carried the day, 'and so the resolution was taken to open negotiations with him. They intend to see him live in Livorno, if he will come here and to employ him against the Turk. There are some who urge that it is rash to trust a man who has been in such close relations with infidels and who might quite well play some trick on those who least expect it.'

Even as Ward's representatives haggled in Florence, word spread that the corsair had endured yet another setback. Late in July, a Spanish fleet commanded by Don Luis Fijardo conducted a daring strike into La Goulette. 'Under cover of the night', the Venetian ambassador to Spain subsequently recounted, Don Luis 'sent in all the ships' boats with artificial fire, and burned [the corsair fleet] in less than four hours without suffering any damage to himself.'

As with the multiple and various accounts of the *Soderina* disaster, over the next several months reports circulated throughout the Mediterranean world that differed as to how hard Ward had been hit and by whom – several of the later accounts erroneously state that it was a French fleet, not a Spanish one, that glided into La Goulette – but there can be no doubt that Ward was hit, and hit hard. The best account is from the governor of Zante, the Venetian outpost closest to Tunis. In mid-August he forwarded to the doge the deposition of 'Captain Walter, captain of the English ship the *Gionato*'. According to Walter, Ward's entire enterprise was devastated, to which news the governor simply replied, 'I hope it is true.' Two weeks later, the governor confirmed that Ward had indeed lost twenty-three ships in the action.

The loss of so many vessels was a terrible setback, but at least they were moored and not at sea, fully provisioned and crammed with crew and soldiers, as the *Soderina* had been. Ward was in danger of acquiring a reputation for the kind of ill luck that sailors do their best to avoid. It was becoming increasingly important for him to find a way out of the game altogether – which makes it all the more surprising that he turned down the terms offered him by the grand duke of Florence.

On the face of it, Ward's decision is astounding. Why would he reject a seemingly providential offer of escape, a secret door that would allow him to disappear from Tunis at the very moment that his prospects were at their bleakest? Why would he stay on to face, again, the wrath of Uthman Dey and his other financial backers? The problem was that in exchange for allowing Ward to settle in Livorno, and to allow the grand duke to retain some shred of dignity after selling his pardon to such a notorious malefactor, the captain would have had to lead an expedition, like that under Fijardo, against the Barbary Corsairs.

To Ward, this was simply not acceptable. No doubt part of his reticence stemmed from the fact that this would involve making war on friends; but his reasons were not entirely sentimental. To understand fully why this condition made the pardon unacceptable we must consider the tragedy of Captain Simon Danziker.

Danziker, a Dutch captain who took to piracy at about the same time as Ward, is often credited with bringing to Algiers a variation of Ward's arrangements at Tunis. Ward and Danziker periodically sailed together, though, as was common with men who joined Ward's fleets, Danziker was in no way tied to Ward and they spent more time working independently than together. Stories often circulated that the two had had a falling out, supposedly on account of the division of spoils, but this does not seem to have been true. As late as the winter of 1608 and spring of 1609, when Ward was working from Algiers with munitions supplied by the pasha, he was reported to have sailed in company with Danziker. More tellingly, the first reports from Florence stated that Ward and Danziker were interested in retiring to Livorno together.

Danziker soon dropped out of the negotiations at Florence. It turned out that there was something of a bidding war for the right to pardon him. In the spring and summer of 1609 reports came to London from Spain that an English rogue, the Catholic sea captain Sir Anthony Sherley, had received support from the Spanish crown for his scheme to relieve Danziker's ravages on Spanish shipping by buying the corsair's friendship. Sir Charles Cornwallis, an English diplomat in Spain, reported that Sherley, 'with allowance or rather procurement of the Council' had been ordered 'to promise (besides pardon and protection) unto Dauncer [i.e. Danziker] whatsoever conditions within any limits of reason he can require' such that Danziker would 'serve the king of Spain by sea'. The royal council had gone so far as to prepare a list of temporizing tactics to be employed should Sherley's secret mission be discovered.

By July hopes had faded that Sherley would be able to bring Danziker over to the Spanish – though Cornwallis still reported the opinion that 'were there a right course taken with him, [he] might (as is thought) without any great difficulty be either withdrawn from his occupation, or be destroyed for using it'. Shortly thereafter, however, Marcantonio Correr reported from London the startling news that, without any previous notice whatsoever, Danziker had successfully negotiated a pardon from the king of France. In hindsight it should have been obvious that Danziker would be drawn to France, for he had lived in Marseilles at one time and was reported to have married a daughter of the then mayor of the port.

Correr reported this news to the doge on 6 August 1609, but Danziker remained at Algiers, still working as an Ottoman privateer for another three months. Given this lag, it would be understandable if the doge and senate of Venice thought that Correr must have been mistaken. In fact, Danziker was merely waiting for one final score. He achieved this, spectacularly, early in October. 'As the [Spanish] fleet was entering the Seville canal', wrote the Venetian ambassador to Spain in his report to the doge on 12 October, 'Simon Danziker, with eight galleons and two galeottes, hung upon their rear' – here the ambassador switched from plain Italian into code – 'and *captured a great galleon and two ships; half a million of gold in booty* was taken and that, one may say, in the very harbour of Seville.' It was a stunning coup for Danziker, and a terrible humiliation for the Spanish.

Danziker waited another few weeks before double-crossing the pasha of Algiers. On 31 October the Venetian resident in Florence picked up the story. 'Danziker has revolted against the Algerians', he declared, describing how the corsair fled Algiers with 'booty to the value of 400,000 crowns' as well as 300 enslaved Christians. The Algerians, alerted to Danziker's intentions, had tried to stop him and this resulted in the death of some 100 Ottoman citizens. 'There will be trouble', concluded the resident darkly.

Danziker's arrival in France was marked with celebrations and a triumphal progress from Marseilles to Paris. The Venetian ambassador to France reported that Simon Danziker 'has taken refuge in Marseilles with four great ships very well armed. He was welcomed by the duke of Guise. Danziker made the duke a present of some Turks, who were at once sent to the galleys.' Soon stories were circulating around Europe of how Danziker received his pardon from the king's own hand. When the Spanish demanded the restitution of the goods recently looted from Seville canal, King Henri IV offered the standard retort in such circumstances, stating that 'he had rendered a service to Spain and other nations by clearing the sea of such a famous pirate'.

A happy ending? Not quite. Like John Ward, Simon Danziker did not begin to search out a pardon until he had sufficient riches to retire from sea. Nonetheless, men as highly skilled as Danziker and Ward were not common, and any ruler willing to accept the opprobrium of pardoning such notorious international criminals also sought to exploit their talents. Even better, if he could bend their skills against the Ottomans themselves – the very men who had sheltered and supported Ward and Danziker for years – it would give the ruler who pardoned them a claim not only to have, as the king of France said, 'cleared the sea of such a notorious pirate', but also to have rehabilitated them and brought them back into the Christian fold.

As early as January 1610 Danziker was given his first task: escorting a French expedition into Tunis. Once there, two of the men from Danziker's ships were so foolish as to let it be known that Danziker himself was sitting in La Goulette. The pasha paid a visit, meeting Danziker on the ship and spending some hours in 'good cheer, great quaffing'. When the two were in 'deep cups' the pasha invited Danziker to come to the kasbah the next evening for dinner.

Danziker duly made his way from La Goulette to Tunis and then across the city, heading for the kasbah surrounded by a bodyguard of twelve companions from the ship. No sooner were they past the outer fortifications, however, than the gates were shut and Danziker was arrested, brought before the pasha and made to listen to a litany of his crimes against the Ottomans. 'Whereupon he was straight beheaded, and his body thrown over the walls in a ditch.' Danziker's men were released so that word of the traitor's fate would spread throughout the Mediterranean world, a grim lesson for John Ward and all others who might be tempted to betray their Ottoman masters.

When offered a pardon by the grand duke of Florence that included service against the Ottomans in North Africa, Ward could only view this as a proposal that, literally, he could not live with. As 1609 drew to a close he was once again holed up in his mansion in Tunis, surrounded by a hostile population. The year – Ward's worst since the accession of King James in 1603 – ended with a macabre spectacle, not in Tunis but in England. As if to make amends for his former laxity, Lord Admiral Nottingham combined a demonstration of his loyalty to James with a stoking of the king's avowed hatred of Ward. On 22 December 1609 a total of nineteen convicted pirates were hanged in a mass execution on the Wapping gallows. Among those who died were captains Jennings, Harris and Longcastle, as well as the seaman William Taverner – all known accomplices of Captain John Ward.

In February 1610 King James held a dinner party to honour the visit of a special ambassador from Venice, Francesco Contarini. Contarini had spent the previous several months travelling overland from Venice, and had in fact been present in Lyons to witness the passage of Simon Danziker and the duke of Guise as they made their way north from Marseilles to Paris in December 1609.

'The dinner was served in full state', wrote Marcantonio Correr to the doge. 'The prince was present, and his Majesty was waited on by the great lords of the kingdom with an attitude of adoration almost, not merely of reverence and respect, for in bringing the water, the drink and the meat they sank upon their knees. The entertainment was royal.' In addition to Correr, Venetian Ambassador Ordinary, and Contarini, Venetian Ambassador Extraordinary, arrangements were made to ensure the presence of Monsieur de la Boderie, French Ambassador Extraordinary.

Throughout the dinner his Majesty indulged in pleasant talk. He told us how his ships had captured some pirates, and how he hoped to extirpate them. He dwelt at length on his hatred of such folk, many of whom he had put to death. He said he would never pardon them, and declared that one pirate had offered him 40,000 pounds sterling, equal to 160,000 crowns, to recover his favour, but he would not even consider the proposal.

The only possible person to whom James could have been referring is John Ward. The sum named is staggering.

The king's very public rejection of Ward's negotiations reassured the Venetians that they remained in good favour with him as much as it served warning to the French, whose king had 'lately given his assurances to the famous pirate Danziker, perhaps not without valuable consideration to someone'.

John Ward himself was left with fewer and fewer options. His English pardon was thwarted; Ireland was closed to him; the Florentines asked that he make a fool's bargain. His alternatives exhausted, he turned to the man who had offered him shelter and community when he had been a mere pirate: Uthman Dey, warlord of Tunis.

ELEVEN

'A Christian Turn'd Turk'

 In 1609 Captain John Ward moved from being merely the concern of Admiralty, court and diplomacy to become the infamous pirate of popular culture. Nathaniel Butter, a shrewd London book-seller with a keen sense for the tastes of the news-buying public, had long focused his energies on producing news pamphlets; in the 1620s he would collaborate with another London bookseller in the production of the first English newspaper. In spring 1609 he issued an anonymous 45-page pamphlet titled *Newes from Sea of two notorious Pyrats, Ward the Englishman and Danseker the Dutchman*. He addressed his audience in the preface:

> To the Reader, which is as much to say, I care not what he be, so he be not a Turk:
>
> Thou hast heard much talk of one Captain Ward, and I know thou desirest to understand what he is. Then, not to belie him (since 'tis a sin to belie the devil) he is a notable thief. He has undone many of your countrymen, by which he gives you warning to have care of yourselves. He has made slaves of many poor Christians, and I hold him no good Christian that will bless him for it.
>
> To content thee, I have here (in white & black ink) hung him out to thee at sea, who could better have wished to have seen him hang'd to death (in hemp) ashore. If thou hast a mind to hear

more of him, spend thy time on a few foul papers following, and thou shalt know as much as I know.

Newes from Sea is divided into two sections. In the first half the reader is offered a heavily anecdotal account of Ward's activities from 1603, through his successful installation at Tunis to the sinking of the *Reniera e Soderina* and the other disasters of 1608 and early 1609. Butter seems to have cobbled this section together from a number of sources, including men who had visited Ward in Tunis and some who had sailed under him. There is little question that one of Butter's major informants was that sanctimonious sea-thief, William Longcastle, whom the bookseller must have interviewed as Longcastle awaited execution on the Admiralty gallows. The second half of the pamphlet, based on the factor's letter, tells the woeful tale of the *Charity* and *Pearl*.

Butter's publication was so successful that before the year was out he brought out a second edition, now lending even greater prominence to Ward's name in the title: *Ward and Danseker, Two Notorious Pirates*. Predictably, Butter's success attracted competition, even as it stoked popular interest in Ward. The most substantial follow-up to Butter's pamphlet was that written by Andrew Barker, formerly master of the *York Bonaventure* and sometime captive of Captain John Ward, entitled *A True and Certaine Report of the Beginning, Proceedings, Overthrowes and now present Estate of Captaine Ward and Danseker* (1609). It is the longest and most detailed description of Ward's activities extant.

Like Butter, Barker cites the endless gossiping and rumours that were circulating about the captain as the reason for his pamphlet. In his preface, Barker highlights the injustice that a brute such as John Ward should become famous merely for being a thief, and promises, drawing on his personal knowledge, to deliver the true story of the rise of 'this notorious and archpirate Ward' and 'what injury he hath done, daily doth, and still endeavoureth to do'.

Barker had a personal reason for writing his account: to clear his name. Butter's pamphlet had identified one of Ward's many prizes as 'the *York Bonaventure* of Hull, of the burthen of 180 tuns of whom

Andrew Barker was Master: this ship had fifteen pieces of ordnance.' Given the size and armament of the *York Bonaventure*, it might have been expected that Barker should have beaten off or fled from Ward. In his own pamphlet, Barker states that 'whereas it was reported in a former book that the *York Bonaventure* (of which I was master) carried fifteen cast pieces at the time of her taking, she had scarce five which she could use or were fit for service'.

Barker's depiction of John Ward stresses the captain's skilfulness at sea, but also his inspirational leadership. Ward is described as a true leader of men, a visionary who could rouse a roomful of drunken sailors to cast off the shackles of the paying work of the Royal Navy in favour of an uncertain future of piracy and plunder. In battle, Barker stresses that it was often Ward's 'forwardness' that saved the day, even more than his knowledge of strategy and tactics. Nonetheless, Barker, like Butter, believed that Ward's 'melancholy disposition' was the result of a tormented conscience. Ward might try to lose himself in drunkenness and sexual perversions, but 'his endless infamy' would eventually bring his 'deserved confusion'. And indeed, both Butter and Barker end their accounts with news of the burning of Ward's fleet in Tunis by Don Luis Fijardo.

These news pamphlets spread Ward's fame among those with sufficient education to read; but his story was also exploited by the ballad-mongers who sold their wares to literate and illiterate alike. Two ballads about Ward were issued in 1609, and in their content and even particular turns of phrase they echo the Butter and Barker news pamphlets. 'The Seaman's Song of Captain Ward, the Famous Pirate of the World, and an Englishman Born' was published first, but a 'second part' quickly followed, entitled 'The Song of Danseker the Dutchman'. Like other English sources on Danziker, including the earlier news pamphlets, this ballad is, in fact, mostly about John Ward.

The ballads share with the news pamphlets a conflicted view of Ward. The balladeers offer open admiration for Ward's skills, and especially for his meteoric rise from obscurity to fame and wealth. Equally, however, the unseemly gathering of a lord's fortune into the hands of a commoner – not to mention the means by which the fortune was gathered – could only be condemned as a perversion of laws human and divine:

> Gallants you must understand
> Captain Ward of England
> A pirate and a rover on the sea,
> Of late a simple fisherman
> In the merry town of Faversham
> Grows famous in the world now every day . . .
>
> Such as live by thieving
> Have seldom-times good ending,
> As by the deeds of Captain Ward is shown.
> Being drunk among his drabs,
> His nearest friend he sometimes stabs,
> Such wickedness within his heart is grown.
>
> When stormy tempest riseth
> The Causer he dispiseth,
> Still denies to pray unto the Lord.
> He feareth neither God nor Devil,
> His deeds are bad, his thoughts are evil,
> His only trust is still upon his sword . . .
>
> His name and state so mounteth
> These country-men accounteth
> Him equal to the nobles of that land.
> But these his honours we shall find
> Shortly blown up with the wind
> Or prove like letters written in the sand.

The appeal of Ward's story lay in his rapid and direct rise from poor fisherman to rich pirate. Balladeers and pamphleteers emphasized his ability, like the trickster in a folk tale, to cheat fate, defy the king and dodge the hangman. Nonetheless, as much as he might be admired, there was an overwhelming need to see him punished, eventually. John Ward, notorious archpirate and violator of the social code, must be served his just deserts:

Such wicked courses cannot stand
The Devil thus puts in his hand
And God will give them soon an overthrow.

This was wishful thinking. The trickster would cheat fate again: John Ward was about to transform himself one more time, rejecting the laws and morality of Christendom and submitting himself to Islam.

'There is confirmation of the news that the pirate Ward and Sir Francis Verney, also an Englishman [but] of the nobelest blood, have become Turks, to the great indignation of the whole nation.' So wrote Ambassador Marcantonio Correr to the doge and senate on 23 December 1610. The announcement of Ward's conversion is jumbled in among other intelligence, halfway through a very long letter, undifferentiated from the rest of the text, clearly no great matter for the diplomat or his political masters. To those who had witnessed Ward's manoeuvres over the previous three years, his attempts to return to England, to settle in Ireland, to purchase an Italian pardon – to men such as the Earl of Salisbury, Lord Admiral Nottingham, King James, Marcantonio Correr and the Venetian doge – this latest development in the John Ward saga could hardly have come as a surprise. Like a ship in the aftermath of a terrible squall, Ward had been buffeted on all sides and now, becalmed, found himself back where he had started. The captain, apparently, had accepted that it might not be such a terrible fate to live out his declining years as a wealthy man amidst sumptuous accommodations in Tunis.

Viewed dispassionately, this seems the inevitable conclusion to Ward's repeatedly thwarted attempts to return to Christendom. Nonetheless, the conversion of Ward and Sir Francis Verney did, as Correr states, excite 'the great indignation of the whole nation'. The short poem by popular poet and satirist Samuel Rowlands, 'To a Reprobate Pirate that hath Renounced Christ and is Turn'd Turk', gives us an idea of the execrations that were heaped on Ward for crossing this line:

> Thou wicked lump of only sin and shame
> (Renouncing Christian faith & Christian name).
> A villain, worse than he that Christ betrayed,
> His master, for God's son, he never denied
> But did confess him just and innocent
> When with his bribe back to the Priests he went.
> Thou that art worse than devils, they confessed
> Christ was the Son of God, thou Hellish Beast
> That hast lived cursed Thief upon the Seas,
> And now a Turk, on shore dost take thine ease,
> Like a devouring monster in a den,
> All that thou hast being spoils of other men.
> Thou that dost serve both Turk and Devil so well,
> Thou seekest to draw (as they do) souls to Hell,
> Having a garment ready in thy hall
> For him that next from Christian faith doth fall.
> Receive this warning from thy native land:
> God's fearful judgements (villain) are at hand.
> Devils attend, hellfire is prepar'd
> Perpetual flames is reprobates re-Ward.

Rowlands seethes with indignation and self-righteous fury, little knowing that Ward's conversion was not driven by wickedness, sin and shame but was the by-product of continent-straddling international politics.

A second glimpse of popular feelings for John Ward can be had from a play by Thomas Dekker titled *If this be not a good play, the Divell is in it*, a jolly comedy about eternal damnation. The play was first published in 1612, the same year as Rowlands' poem, two years after Ward's conversion. One scene has the Dark Lord and his minions gathered in hell when a sub-devil announces that Danziker, recently deceased, has not yet entered hell because 'Charon has bound him for a thousand years, to tug at [his] oar'. He who had made galley slaves of so many during his life has been given the Sisyphean task of ferrying the dead into the Underworld.

The Lord of the Underworld next demands 'Where's Ward?' Another demon replies that Ward's work on earth is not yet done:

> The merchants are not pill'd nor pull'd enough.
> They are but shaven, when they are fleeced he'll come
> And bring to hell fat boats of rich thieves,
> A crew of swearers and drinkers the best that lives.

At which point the residents of hell chant, 'Ward is not ripe for damning yet.'

The minions of Satan might not have been convinced that the captain was ripe for damnation, but the subjects of King James had already made up their minds. John Ward was about to undergo his popular culture apotheosis, a full-on biographical treatment in a stage play. The playwright who undertook the task, and whose playwriting career was to be ruined by the controversy that followed, was named Robert Daborne. The play was a tragedy and it was entitled *A Christian Turn'd Turk*.

Robert Daborne was one man who attempted to understand what might have made Captain John Ward defect to Islam. Lacking access to secret state papers or a network of far-flung covert agents, he had no inkling of Ward's time-and-again attempts to re-enter Christendom over the preceding three years. Nonetheless, Daborne earnestly gathered all of the information that was publicly available. His play betrays strong echoes of the news pamphlets and ballads of 1609 and of other news pamphlets and travel narratives, and he appears to have gone to mariners and merchants with questions about John Ward, life in Tunis and other North African cities, and Christian converts to Islam in North Africa. Daborne evidently spoke with seamen and reflected upon the twists of fortune that had beset the profession since the accession of King James, and his play repeatedly expresses sympathy for the plight of men without work who are too proud to beg. Daborne was well schooled in Christian theology – in later years he would become a minister – and utterly horrified by his perceptions of the personal and eschatological consequences for those abjuring Christianity, but he was also cognizant of the twisting paths of individual circumstances that can lead any man towards vile deeds.

The result is a play that is liberal in its understanding of the social and economic forces that create pirates and, to Daborne's eventual cost, all too persuasive in depicting a slippery slope from poverty-induced piracy to the denial of Christianity. Daborne clearly had no understanding of Islam, and it is one of the play's enduring failures that Ward's new faith is never shown as anything but the obstinate, hostile rejection of Christianity – as though the world's Muslims did not practise a religion but engaged in a vast conspiracy to harass and confound the lives of Christians on earth and then spend eternity in hell. In Daborne's defence he was hardly unique in holding to this view of Islam; rather, this was how many Christians in the 1600s viewed the entire non-Christian world.

Daborne's play opens with John Ward's ship off Ireland, riding at anchor while he entertains a number of merchants in a game of dice called, appropriately, hazard. Daborne uses the game of hazard to draw a line between the positive, legitimate enterprise of the merchants and the thievery of pirates. The merchants risk their fortunes with every toss of the dice, knowing and accepting that they might bankrupt themselves. Ward, however, risks nothing and simply takes all. He is not really playing at hazard; he has only used the game to lure his prey on board the ship. Any loss that he endures in the game he will take back afterward with cannon and sword.

This game sets the moral tone for the play that follows. Daborne will allow that Ward is a very skilled seaman, a great commander and a true friend to the men under his command, but the playwright is resolute in his depiction of piracy as an ignominious activity. The tension between Ward's better and worse qualities is, in large part, what makes his image of John Ward so interesting. Daborne believed that Ward had the potential to be a truly great man, but that he had perverted this potential long before he converted to Islam. For Daborne, Ward's fall from grace occurred when he elected to leave off legitimate seafaring and turn to piracy. Therefore when Ward is made to see the error of his ways, at the end of the play, he does not wish merely to undo his conversion, but longs for 'that content this poor soul did know / When a poor fisherman possessed it'.

The game of hazard that opens the play ends when Ward springs his trap, his ship slipping its moorings and heading to sea, the merchants made captives. The play's audience is then treated to three hours of adventure by sea – swashbuckling sword fights over the hatches of pirate ships, fortunes made and lost with the shifting of a wind – and adventure by land, amidst the slave markets and opulent mansions of a Tunis populated by converted Christians, treacherous Jews and dangerous Turks.

The action is fast paced, the dialogue crisp and pointed, the characters quickly but well sketched. Daborne introduces us to three pirates, each of them potentially heroic, all of them ultimately revealed as self-serving and degraded. Simon Danziker, made to be a resident of Tunis for the purpose of Daborne's play, makes lofty speeches about redeeming his soul and reputation by burning Tunis's corsair fleet and fleeing to Marseilles (Daborne here conflates Danziker's flight from Algiers with Don Luis Fijardo's burning of the Tunis fleet) – but it is soon revealed that Danziker's flight from Tunis is hastened to cheat payment of his massive personal debts. Francisco, a pirate whom John Ward meets and combines forces with at sea, is described as an honourable gentleman, and clearly is based upon the real-life English pirate Sir Francis Verney. Francisco does not convert to Islam in Daborne's play, but his noble hands are stained as he and Ward sell into Ottoman slavery the crew and passengers of an English prize. And finally, John Ward appears as a passionate anti-hero, a man who could have been heroic but for the terrible twists of fate.

Daborne demonstrates Ward's relative goodness, and his sadly perverted capacity for absolute goodness, by contrasting his behaviour with that of yet another pirate captain, a crude, uncouth and unprincipled opportunist named Gallop. True to life, Daborne identified Ward's loyalty to his men as the most obvious fingerpost pointing to the good, honourable man Ward might have become, had he had more legitimate opportunities. Ward's open grieving for a shipmate killed in battle, and his proposal that they make a blood sacrifice to consecrate a captured prize in the memory of their fallen comrades, contrasts with Gallop's shameless cheating of the men under his own command. Making the comparison even plainer is the contrast between Ward's assertion (bewildering, given that he calls himself a pirate in the play) that 'I scorn to take from others to [achieve] my rising' with Gallop's statement, delivered a mere seventeen lines later, that 'So that I rise, let the world sink, and heaven fall.'

A man such as this John Ward could never be driven to conversion by mere opportunism, as a man like Gallop would. When Crossman (Daborne's representation of Kara Osman, properly known as Uthman Dey) and the Governor of Tunis (Daborne's representation of the pasha), together with the rich Jew Benwash, try to draw Ward into conversion, they use many arguments and stratagems including logic, flattery and promises of political and material advancement, but Ward steadfastly rejects them all. It is only when the sultry Muslim temptress Voada enters the play that Ward begins his tragic slide. In the end it is still not opportunism that drives Ward's conversion but despair, combined with faint, contradictory hope in the redemptive power of love:

> with what brain can I think
> Heaven would be glad of a friend such as I am?
> A pirate? A murderer? Let those can hope a pardon care
> To atone with heaven. I cannot; I despair . . .
> The way that leads to love is no black way.

The centrepiece of *A Christian Turn'd Turk* is John Ward's conversion. Daborne, with no understanding of Islam whatsoever, offers pure spectacle to his English, Christian audience: gaudy costumes and fabulous props, including what Daborne calls a 'Mahomet's head', an object of derision trotted out during exotic plays, versions of which could be seen swinging in front of taverns named 'The Saracen's Head' or some such. In the dumb-show of Ward's conversion, the captain enters dressed 'in his Christian habit' and riding a mule, preceded on to the stage by a 'Mufti' and his train of lesser priests, who bear various tokens that Ward will either swear by or abjure. Removed from his mule and forced to the ground, grovelling on his belly, Ward is made to review and then subscribe to 'the laws of their damned Prophet'. Next, his 'Christian' clothing is removed and Ward is dressed in the fantastic costume of a stage Turk: a vast, flowing robe and a large 'turban with a half-moon in it'. Outlandishly clad, he is now led before the Mufti and enacts the final token of his conversion, swearing upon the so-called 'Mahomet's head' that preceded him on to the stage. In token of his circumcision/castration, the Mufti ungirds and removes Ward's sword, which will only be returned 'In wars 'gainst Christians'. Now that he is a complete 'Turk', two cowering Christians are brought on to the stage to offer him a cup of wine. 'He spurns them, and throws away the cup, is mounted on the ass, who is richly clad, and with a shout, they exit.'

Daborne is swift to punish Ward for abjuring Christianity. Over a few short scenes Ward loses all. First to go is his manhood, literally and euphemistically. Like other English writers of the day, Daborne portrays circumcision as something akin to castration, but the playwright goes further, suggesting that Ward was anally raped by his new co-religionists shortly after his circumcision ('Poor fellow, how he looks since Mahomet had the handling of him! He hath had a sore night at "Who's that knocks at the backdoor?"'). This rape, combined with Ward's circumcision/castration, leaves him unable to consummate his passion for Voada, his new wife. Voada, for her part, now scorns Ward, proclaiming that 'our just Prophet hates false renegades' and telling him 'I condemn thee / As a most abject slave and hate thee more / Than all thy wealth could make me love before.' Instead, Voada woos Ward's young page who, in a plot twist made familiar by Shakespeare, is actually a cross-dressing girl.

Now the corpses accumulate and the tragedy grinds to its inevitable conclusion. Ward is stripped of his position in Tunis, his fabulous mansion, his wealth, his friends and his dignity. Finally, he gives a fine gallows speech to the Muslims who had betrayed him:

> O may I be the last of my country
> That trust unto your treacheries, seducing treacheries.
> All you that live by theft and piracies,
> That sell your lives and souls to purchase graves,
> That die to hell, and live far worse than slaves,
> Let dying Ward tell you that heaven is just
> And that despair attends on blood and lust.

As the play closes, the playwright symbolically enacts Ward's damnation by having him ripped into pieces and thrown into the raging sea.

Daborne wrote *A Christian Turn'd Turk* in hopes of exploding on to London's theatrical scene in the manner of Christopher Marlowe twenty-five years earlier. Like Marlowe's *Tamburlaine the Great*, Daborne's play was intended to generate controversy through the shocking amorality and audacity of its lead character – a strategy almost as time-honoured then as today. Although Daborne's writing cannot hold a candle to Marlowe's, *A Christian Turn'd Turk* is hardly the worst play of a drama-besotted era in which new pieces were churned out by the dozen every season. Indeed, the first half of Daborne's work is gripping still, presenting spectacle after spectacle, cutting from pirate ships to sumptuous palaces to slave markets to harems, and the dialogue is snappy throughout. At first brush it is mystifying that Daborne's play was a career-ruining disaster that left him impoverished and spattered in obloquy.

The work still has the power to shock, but none of the features that jolt the modern reader caused Daborne's misery in 1611. It was not his toxic portrayal of sexually voracious women ('Do a woman to death, and she will be satisfied – nothing else will') that resulted in his reduction from playwright to hack-for-hire, whose only work, in years to come, would be to revise plays written by others. Nor was it his sympathy for pirates ('Want of employment, not of virtue, forced / Our former act of spoil and rapine'), nor his views on the social order ('Why, your thief is a gentleman: he scorns to do anything, and he lives upon his comings in'), nor even the scandalous opinions of religion that are expressed by Ward and other characters ('The slavery of man, how this religion rides us! / Deprives us of our freedom from our cradles, / Ties us in superstitious bondage'). Daborne's downfall was caused by his sympathetic portrayal of John Ward.

What little is known about the controversy surrounding *A Christian Turn'd Turk* must be gleaned from the work's preface, which Daborne himself wrote. Until now, interpretations of the incident have been constructed by literary scholars, drawing largely upon literary sources and related documents, and the preface has remained opaque. New insights may be found, however, by reading the preface in light of Captain John Ward's secret negotiations with the English government, his massive bribery of Admiralty officials, and the king's personal rejection of his suit.

The preface lashes out against the play's critics, bitterly defending Daborne's 'oppressed and much martyred tragedy'. The playwright states that he did not seek to have his play published on account of any 'affect to see my name in print', but rather to clear himself and the actors who performed in *A Christian Turn'd Turk* of allegations of wrongdoing. The 'much-suffering actors' had welcomed the play, and from them Daborne had 'received so much worthy respect' that he still felt a debt of gratitude. Nor were audiences disdainful. Daborne states his 'fear [that] the reader should call in question their judgements, that give applause in the action [i.e. on the stage]'. In other words, Daborne's play was sufficiently well received that, being a modest man, he had rather to fear the diminution of this acclaim when people had a chance to read his words, divorced from the excitement of the theatre and the skills of the actors.

Daborne's troubles arose not because his play was a failure, but on account of its success. He swore that he in no way sought to minimize Ward's crimes by making the pirate seem human, for Ward's crimes were so all-encompassing that nothing could mitigate or magnify them ('no man can feign any ill of a parricide'). Secondly, Daborne declares that the actors should be cleared of all taint for 'no man can entitle another to his crimes'. Despite acting out Ward's enormities on the stage, the actors should not be held liable, for 'oratory' is 'an unseparable branch of poesy'. Daborne's defence, then, was that poetic licence justified him in imagining how Ward was drawn to deny Christianity and embrace Islam; poetic licence also justified the vile words that the actors uttered in depicting John Ward's life, and the evil deeds that they performed while on the stage. And should anyone therefore be drawn to disparage poetry as granting too much licence, Daborne maintained that 'no argument more proveth the excellency of poesy than the contempt [that] is thrown upon it by silken gulls and ignorant citizens'.

The nub of the dispute lies with these 'silken gulls' – the courtiers who, bending to the will of King James, and unknown to Robert Daborne, had left John Ward without options. These men – and perhaps, behind the scenes, their royal master, too – could not tolerate any attempt to cast a positive light upon the captain's life and actions. The declaration of guilt uttered by Daborne's Ward at the end of the play, even the symbolic damnation that follows, was not sufficient. Daborne's Ward arrives at conversion by first living through poverty and despair, turning pirate and slowly corrupting his soul. Little did Daborne know that there were specific people, the king among them, who must bear the blame for Ward being left with no option but conversion. To these men, the only acceptable version of Ward's life was that he was an inveterate villain, a ne'er-do-well who, from birth, was a bad seed, a delinquent, a remorseless criminal who deserved only death and scorn, not sympathy and understanding.

Daborne had unwittingly spoken truth to power, and was devastated to feel a wrath whose depth he could not fathom. Having no knowledge of Ward's attempts to purchase the favour of Lord Admiral Nottingham and various of the king's courtiers, Daborne could hardly know the minefield into which he was wandering as he penned *A Christian Turn'd Turk*. The result: a play that had barely opened before it was forcibly closed, and the utter impoverishment of a would-be playwright. That Daborne survived at all is on account of the generosity of actors and theatrical managers who hired him for bit-work projects, mostly doctoring scripts written by others, until he gave up on theatre and entered the ministry in 1618 or thereabouts.

John Ward lived in happy ignorance of Daborne's misfortunes. Far from being torn apart by bloodthirsty Turks, as in the conclusion to *A Christian Turn'd Turk*, he was actually living quite a pleasant life in Tunis. It is a crowning irony to Daborne's story that at the very moment the playwright hit rock bottom, imprisoned for debt and reduced to wheedling friends for spare shillings, John Ward lived free at his ease, amiably enjoying his ill-gotten gains in peace.

When Captain John Ward submitted to Islam and became a Muslim he was about fifty-seven years old. He would spend the last decade of his life in Tunis. We have no sources for the terms of his permanent integration into the Tunis of Uthman Dey. We know that on conversion the name he took – Yusuf – was the same as that of Uthman's son-in-law and heir, suggesting that, despite his occasionally rocky relationship with Uthman, the corsair remained closely associated with the ruling family. Despite this change of name, Ward continued to be known by his pre-conversion name, or by an Arabized version of it such as Captain Wardiyya.

After 1610 Ward returned to sea only rarely, usually when he was under orders to join with the Ottoman fleet. An Ottoman history of the 1600s, written after Ward's death, states that under Yusuf Dey 'Captain Samson and Captain Wardiyya' were 'the greatest corsair captains.' Since Yusuf did not succeed Uthman until 1612, this serves to underline Ward's continuing contribution among the Barbary Corsairs, even into his sixties. His conversion seems to have signalled his willingness to commit himself wholeheartedly and personally to Ottoman Tunis. The deys recognized his merits and promoted him accordingly. Had Ward succeeded in purchasing his English pardon, it is not possible that he would have received such respect in his retirement. If Sir Henry Wotton is to be believed, it is unlikely that he would have lived out a year in England before being quietly assassinated.

In England, Ward's conversion to Islam seems to have provoked no official response; at least none is recorded in the memoranda, speeches and ambassadors' dispatches of the official state papers. King James's dinner party, in which he smugly boasted to the Venetian and French ambassadors that *his* pardon, unlike that of the king of France, could not be purchased, is the last major reference to Ward in official English documentation. And James was wrong, at any rate. In 1611 Ward's long-time crony Captain Richard Bishop, who in 1609 had taken Ward's place as the 'Archpirate' of Munster, secured the king's pardon with little fuss. Bishop settled in Ireland, in Schull, his home watched by the authorities as a known haunt for wanted pirates and other suspicious characters.

Ward's pardon was rejected to appease Venice, not out of justice and certainly not out of expediency. Indeed, it would appear that if the Admiralty and the Privy Council learned anything from the affair it was that no good was served by denying pirates their pardon: it left villains at large to sin another day, it dissuaded not a single sailor from turning pirate, and it cheated loyal bureaucrats and officials of a chance to supplement their meagre remuneration at no cost to the royal treasury. So gravely did the king's advisors repent of their denial of John Ward that in 1612, two years after his conversion, a general pardon was proclaimed from London in hopes of ridding the seas of some of the most effective English pirates by bringing them back within the ambit of English law. Though many took up this offer, the policy was a failure, for it did not address the underlying social and economic conditions that gave rise to piracy. Many of those who took up the general pardon found themselves unable to eke out a living on shore and soon returned to their former ways.

Reviewing Ward's story, it is difficult not to perceive his conversion as opportunistic. In light of his repeated attempts to return to Christendom – first England, then Ireland, then Tuscany – conversion seems to have been a last resort. Nonetheless, we know that Ward took religion seriously enough to eschew the hypocrisy practised by 'holy' pirates such as William Longcastle. As he finally found acceptance and respect among the Muslims of

Tunis, did Yusuf Raïs also find spiritual peace? We cannot know. But the portrait of the ancient corsair painted by one particular British traveller, the Scotsman William Lithgow, offers us a glimpse of a contented, satisfied old age.

'From London must I begin this my second peregrination', wrote William Lithgow, Scotsman, inveterate traveller and, though a commoner, royal favourite. The year was 1615. 'Leaving court, the country and Dover, I courted Calais and so to Gravelines, Dunkirk and Ostend. I measured all Netherlands with my feet in two months' space.' Moving on foot, his preferred mode of transit, he made his way south, into Italy and down the leg of the Italian boot. Set upon by bandits in the Calabrian mountains, Lithgow, famous for subtle wit rather than brute strength, reasoned with the men so well that the bandits were not satisfied merely to release him: instead, their leader volunteered to be his guide through the mountains, and to protect him from other ruffians. Hopping on to a boat to cover the 2 miles from Italy's toe to Sicily, Lithgow continued his walk south, pacing the length of the island before catching sail for Tunis.

Here, Lithgow 'met with our English captain, General Ward, once a great commander at sea, who, in despite of his denied acceptance in England, turned Turk'. Lithgow spent a total of ten days in Tunis waiting for a visa that would allow him to continue his travels throughout Ottoman North Africa and into Morocco. During this wait, Lithgow states that 'divers times . . . I dined and supped' with John Ward, even while visiting Ward's 'fair palace', served at table by 'some fifteen circumcised English runnagates, whose lives and countenances were both alike, even as desperate and disdainful.'

Lithgow characterized Ward as 'placable'. What's more, the old privateer proved a true friend to the Scotsman. We have already seen that Ward, acting on Lithgow's behalf, was able to secure an elusive visa from the Ottoman authorities. Nonetheless, even so intrepid and experienced a traveller as Lithgow was sufficiently disconcerted by Ward's strange life that he refused all offers of accommodation, preferring to spend his nights 'aboard in the French ship' that had brought him from Sicily to Tunis.

Lithgow then set off on what, by the lights of the day, must have been counted an insane voyage through North Africa. He made a large loop, visiting Algiers and then the great Moroccan city of Fez, returning to Tunis by way of the Sahara desert. This last was far the most arduous leg of the journey. He and his personal servant, his sole remaining companion, having run out of supplies, were forced to survive 'upon tobacco, and to drink our own waning piss.' Lithgow nonetheless intended to press yet further into the desert until, finally, his servant 'did threaten me with death to make me seek back for our nearest refuge.' Making their way north and east, they emerged from the desert and made for Tunis, where Lithgow had this account of his travels sworn and confirmed by 'English Ward'.

Lithgow spent several more days at Tunis, recovering from his ordeals in the desert and once more partaking of Ward's generous hospitality. His final observations of Tunis have nothing to do with the thriving city's construction boom, the bustling port or the crowded slave markets. Instead, Lithgow's visit ends on a homely note:

> Captain Ward sent twice one of his servants with me to see two sundry ovens drawn, being full of young chickens which are not hatched by their mothers but in the furnace, being thus: the oven is first spread over with warm camels' dung and upon it the eggs, closing the oven; then behind the oven there is a daily conveyance of heat, venting through a passage beneath the dung, just answerable to the natural warmness of the hen's belly; upon which moderation, within twenty days they come to natural perfection, the oven producing at one time three or four hundred living chickens.

And so Lithgow departed Tunis, offering posterity one last, long glance at Captain Ward in his retirement. His household peopled with old English shipmates who, like their aged captain, had converted to Islam, Ward and his men were now content to plunder the gold found within a chicken's egg rather than that of the high seas.

As the ship carrying William Lithgow dwindled into the horizon John Ward receded into history. Reports of his piracies became less frequent, no doubt to the relief of the merchants of both London and Venice. It has been suggested that a more distinguished Briton visited Ward after Lithgow: Captain John Smith, sometime governor of the Virginia Colony and perhaps the best-known English travel writer of the day. Smith undoubtedly spent time in North Africa between 1602 and 1604, during some of his earliest wanderings, and it is possible that he met Ward at this time. After this, however, Smith's interests overwhelmingly were associated with the New World, and especially with the Caribbean and New England. Though he would write of John Ward in his magnum opus, a sweeping summary of his life and travels titled *The True Travels, Adventures, and Observations of Captaine John Smith*, first published in 1630, by this point Ward was known to Smith solely through second-hand conversations and accounts written by others.

At any rate, by 1630 John Ward's life had already drawn to a surprisingly quiet conclusion. In 1622 the report reached first Venice, then London: John Ward was dead. In the end it was neither a turncoat accomplice nor an assassin's blade that did him in, but that scourge of seventeenth-century life, the plague. Ward's importance in the history of the region was such that when Christian and Muslim historians first wrote of him – shortly after his life had ended, when it would still have been possible to talk with shipmates and other contemporaries – they generally focussed on how Ward had transformed the operations of the Barbary Corsairs rather than on how he had lived his life. English, French, Dutch and Ottoman historians each put their own colour on the captain's accomplishments, but none expressed interest in Ward the man. Today, we know neither the date of Ward's death nor the location of his grave.

After Ward

For nearly four centuries the life of John Ward has excited controversy. He was the most notorious renegade of the age, an overly ambitious and prodigiously gifted seaman who was sufficiently theologically and socially rootless to abandon Plymouth for Tunis and Christianity for Islam. He wreaked havoc upon the shipping of Europe's richest and strongest nations, and the threat he posed caused both the English and Venetians briefly to halt their shipping through the region. He provoked a king's proclamation, and, alongside his friend and rival, Simon Danziker, held sway over the Mediterranean for nearly a decade.

After Ward's death there emerged two traditions in the retelling of his life, one spawned by the penny press and one in history books. Early histories depict Ward as a scoundrel who deserted his nation and betrayed her greatest naval secrets to the North African Moors. The popular view – the mythology of John Ward – is more complicated, offering up a compromised folk hero and thrilling to dark descriptions of life-or-death exploits in a desperate rise from obscure poverty to infamy and riches.

Judged by his contemporaries, John Ward's most remarkable act, even more than his exploits as pirate or privateer, was his decision to offer to Ottoman Muslims tutelage in sailing, gunning and fighting from square-rigged round ships, thus allowing them to prey upon the shipping of north-western Europe. Captain John Smith, writing his *True Travels* of 1630, was among the first historians to level the charge that prior to the arrival of Ward and Danziker, 'the Moors knew scarce how to sail a ship', and that it was these men who 'taught the Moors to be men-of-war.' But Smith's claim merely reiterates, and likely was derived from, the eyewitness testimony of seaman Andrew Barker in his *True and Certain Report* of 1609. It was Barker who laid out the nature of the training that Ward offered to the Muslims of Tunis:

> without the help of which English [i.e. Ward and his men], the Turks by no means could have governed and conducted [round ships], through their unskilfulness and insufficiency in the art of Navigation. Yet of late, to my woeful experience, I can witness they have been so readied by the instruction of our apostate countrymen (I mean of Ward and others, who have been their commanders) to tackle their ships [and] to man and manage a fight.

Barker was also the first to describe this transmission of knowledge from Ward to the Barbary Corsairs in starkly ideological terms, as a looming conflict between Christianity and Islam. Barker warns that Christians must come together and obliterate this threat or 'in succeeding times Christendom must expect no traffic at sea.'

First Barker, then Smith: next, across the Channel a French historian and a Dutch historian also identified Ward as the Judas who betrayed round-ship technology to the corsairs of North Africa. Père Pierre Dan, a French priest who had lived in North Africa while ministering to enslaved Christians, in his *Histoire de Barbarie, et de ses Corsairs* of 1637, erroneously describes Danziker, at Algiers, as first in the field, but once again states that the ability of the North African corsairs to sail square-rigged ships was attributable to Danziker and Ward. Emanuel van Meteren, in his *Histoire des Pays Bas*, writing from Dutch sources, corroborates this view.

Ward's reputation as one half of the duo that betrayed Christendom endured from the 1600s through the 1800s, and received its definitive treatment by the greatest English naval historian of the early twentieth century, Sir Julian Stafford Corbett. *England in the*

Mediterranean: A Study in the Rise and Influence of British Power within the Straits, 1603–1713, published in 1903, examines how the expansion of British sea power in the Mediterranean presaged the British navy's globe-girdling success in succeeding centuries. In Corbett's own words, his book traces 'step by step how the germ planted . . . by Ward, the English mutineer, . . . worked with ever widening effect till it had changed the whole conditions and meaning of Mediterranean power.'

Corbett held that square-rigged round ships were inherently superior to galleys in battle – a position now rejected by most naval historians – and that Ward arrived in the Mediterranean as a wolf in a sheep-pen. Throughout *England in the Mediterranean* Ward is cited as an example of how an experienced English sea captain could exploit the advantages of square-rigged round ships and broadside gunnery to devastate entire galley fleets. In opening *England in the Mediterranean* with Ward's mutiny from the *Lion's Whelp* and making Ward a touchstone throughout the sprawling course of his two-volume history, Corbett obscured the differences between privateering and fleet warfare.

We have already seen that Corbett was wrong: round ships have no natural superiority over galleys. Corbett had co-opted the commentary of contemporary observers of John Ward – Andrew Barker, Père Pierre Dan and the others – in order to advance his own thesis about square-rigged ships and broadside gunnery. And so Corbett inadvertently began the process of rehabilitating Ward. On the one hand, Corbett could not but decry Ward's spoiling of merchant shipping. On the other, he was filled with admiration for how Ward, the archetypal uneducated English sailor, demonstrated the superiority of English technology, tactics and personnel by running riot throughout the Mediterranean. To Corbett, writing in Britain's dying days as a global superpower, this confirmed his own national chauvinism. Lesser nations might vomit forth regional bandits; England spawned a villain who menaced the commerce of three continents.

Corbett would never acknowledge it, but his view of John Ward did not flow entirely from the historical sources; it was, in fact, the product of centuries of mythologizing. We have already seen how the rash of pamphlets and ballads on Ward published in 1608 were torn between admiration for his skills and loathing of the use he made of them. This tension proved fruitful in creating a lively, paradoxical ballad-hero whose appeal endured to the very dawn of the twentieth century, when Ward's reputation died along with the genre.

In addition to the two ballads printed in 1609, 'The Seaman's Song of Captain Ward' and 'The Song of Dansekar the Dutchman', a third dates from the 1620s, and it is to this last that Ward owes his longstanding reputation as a ballad-hero. It is entitled 'The Famous Sea-Fight between Captain Ward and the *Rainbow*'. To the modern reader the name *Rainbow* means nothing; but to people with living memories of the Anglo-Spanish wars of Queen Elizabeth it immediately conjured Drake's famous Cadiz expedition of 1587. Drake sailed into the port and torched a number of Spanish warships, thwarting the invasion of England that the Spanish had planned for that year and delaying it until 1588. The *Rainbow* was one of the principal vessels of Drake's daring raid.

'The Famous Sea-Fight between Captain Ward and the *Rainbow*' takes Ward's attempt to procure an English pardon as its principal subject.

Strike up you lusty gallants, with music and sound of drum:
For we have descry'd a rover upon the sea is come.
His name is Captain Ward, right well it doth appear
There has not been such a rover found out this thousand year.

For he hath sent unto our King, the sixth of January,
Desiring that he might come in, with all his company.
'And if your King will let me come, till I my tale have told,
I will bestow for my ransom full thirty tun of gold.'

In response, the ballad's pusillanimous, pro-Spanish King James exclaims that he could never trust a man who 'hath deceiv'd the

French man, likewise the King of Spain' and fits out the *Rainbow*, 'a ship of worthy fame', with orders to capture Captain Ward. The *Rainbow* engages Ward in battle; her polished, gleaming cannon huff and belch but have no effect on the fearless captain. 'These gallant shooters prevailed not a pin', sings out the ballad, 'For if they were brass on the outside, brave Ward was steel within.' As Ward sails away from the *Rainbow* he calls out to her captain:

> 'I never wrong'd an English ship, but Turk and King of Spain,
> For and the jovial Dutch-man, as I met him on the main.
> If I had known your King but one two years before,
> I would have saved brave Essex life, whose death did grieve
>   me sore.
>
> 'Go, tell the King of England, go tell him thus from me,
> If he reign king of all the land, I will reign king at sea.'

Upon hearing this message, King James responds by mourning the loss of 'jewels three':

> 'The first was Lord Clifford, Earl of Cumberland;
> The second was Lord Mountjoy, as you shall understand;
> The third was brave Essex, from field would never flee;
> Which would 'a gone unto the seas and brought proud Ward
>   to me!'

Cumberland, Mountjoy and Essex were military and naval commanders who, like the good ship *Rainbow*, had won popular acclaim during the Anglo-Spanish wars of Queen Elizabeth.

'The Famous Sea-Fight between Captain Ward and the *Rainbow*', then, is as much about the passing of a great age as it is about Ward. In this original version of the ballad Ward stands for the alienation of the new generation of mariners, men whom King James had left without prospects upon making peace with Spain. The King's hand-wringing over the loss of 'jewels three' merely confirmed that his ineffectual blundering had impoverished the nation.

Later ballads entitled 'Ward the Pirate!' and 'Captain Ward' are descended from 'Captain Ward and the *Rainbow*'. Some stanzas of the older ballad appear, virtually untouched, in the later ballads, and the narrative arc remains intact. Surprisingly, given that the tradition spawned by 'Captain Ward and the *Rainbow*' spans three centuries, the later Ward ballads, like the original, read as though they are reporting current events.

In its nineteenth-century versions the ballad no longer sought to expose the bumblings of King James I. Queen Victoria, though unnamed, clearly rules, and the mention of exact dates in the ballad's text suggests that the events unfold in contemporary time – 'Captain Ward wrote a letter to our Queen on the 14th of February' asserts one version; 'He wrote a letter to our Queen on the third of January' declares another. The focus of these later ballads, moreover, has shifted from the monarch to the pirate. Queen Victoria, unlike King James, plays only a bit-part, and that mostly off-stage.

The descended ballads also differ from the original in characterizing Ward's choice of prey. In the original ballad Ward declared that 'I never wrong'd an English ship, but Turk and King of Spain.' The nineteenth-century versions show Ward preying on English shipping. Many of the ballads identify the sacking of a specific English ship, 'Loaded with silks and satins, a cargo of the best', as the incident that prompts the queen to send forth the *Rainbow*. The charge is repeated when the captain of the *Rainbow* hails Ward, in lines that have no counterpart in the original ballad:

> 'O no,' says gallant *Rainbow*, 'it grieves our Queen full sore,
> That her rich merchant ships can't pass as they have done
>   before.'

The verses that follow offer a shockingly savage portrait of naval warfare. The description retains one of the original ballad's signature lines, describing Ward's steel resolve, but then sheers away from the spirit of the earlier poem. In the original ballad, after exchanging shots Ward and the *Rainbow* part ways, apparently without casualties. Here is how the encounter reads in one nineteenth-century version:

'Come on, come on,' said saucy Ward, 'I value you not a pin,
For if you have got brass for an outward show, I have got
    steel within.'

It was four o'clock next morning the bloody fight begun,
And it did continue to the setting of the sun;
'Fight on, fight on,' said saucy Ward, 'your spirit well pleases
    me,
But if you fight for a month or more, your master I will be.'

The *Rainbow* she fired, till at length she fired in vain,
Till sixty of her bravest men along the decks were slain . . .

The *Rainbow* fired from the morning until that late at night,
Till at length the gallant *Rainbow* began to take great flight;
'Go home, go home,' cried saucy Ward, 'and tell your Queen
    from me,
That if she reigns Queen of England, I'll reign king on the
    seas.'

The quantity of men killed fluctuates among nineteenth-century
versions, but the new tone of the description is consistent. In the
original we read of 'bold Ward' and 'brave Ward'. Now we meet
'saucy Ward'. All versions have the captain declaring his irrepressible
urge to 'master' the queen's ship. And all of the nineteenth-century
ballads end not with a wistful reference to recently departed naval
heroes, but with Ward's boast that he will 'reign king on the seas.'

This boast also appeared in the original ballad, but it takes on new
meaning when divorced from the reign of King James I, when Queen
Elizabeth's once-strong navy suffered enervation through idleness.
In the original, Ward's words are a pledge, a promise to bring order
to a realm in which the king has abdicated his responsibilities. In
subsequent versions, and especially those issued under Victoria,
Ward's declaration sounds as treasonous as his desire to subjugate
the queen's warships.

In an age of empire, and, what's more, an empire that flourished
through a global commercial network connected by sail, Ward's

raiding of British merchant shipping, his desire to master the queen's ship, and his treasonous arrogation of the watery realm are all of a piece. Captain Ward, in being dragged from the seventeenth century to the nineteenth, became a perversion of the national aspirations. Unlike the good merchants of the empire who become rich by making England rich, 'Ward the Pirate' loots and murders to attain wealth. And unlike the true hearts of the Royal Navy, Ward rejects the legitimate chain of command, and even the sovereignty of the queen. His hands stained with the blood of honest merchants and brave seamen alike, John Ward became the enemy of the state and the enemy of the people.

Both the popular culture and the historical traditions of John Ward run cold during the first half of the twentieth century. In the seventeenth century Ward's story had figured in a half-dozen penny ballads and news pamphlets, several popular poems and on the stage. By the end of the nineteenth century his profile had been reduced to that of the bloodstained anti-hero of a single stock ballad. When the ballad tradition died out, Ward vanished from English popular culture entirely. His disappearance from the history books owed something, perhaps, to his decline in the popular culture, but it owed more to the slow overturning of Corbett's thesis in *England in the Mediterranean*. Corbett had made John Ward's success the primary evidence in his argument for the inherent superiority of both English sailors and the round ships that they commanded. As England's imperial and naval fortunes declined, and as naval historians began to reappraise the effectiveness of the Mediterranean galley, John Ward's story shifted from historical evidence to historical anomaly.

Then, in 1942, Ward resurfaced in *For My Great Folly* by Thomas Costain, a first novel by a 57-year-old Canadian newsman turned magazine and literary editor. Costain, who would write a string of bestselling historical romances, notes in his preface that 'there was a John Ward, of course', and promises a novel that 'follows the historical facts closely enough'. Nonetheless, major discrepancies abound. The historical Ward was twenty years older than his fictional counterpart; he was bald while Costain's hero shakes a mane of blond locks; and while the historical Ward changed allegiances but always remained true to the privateers' code – maximize the booty, whatever the cost – the John Ward of *For My Great Folly* is, before all else, an English patriot, faithful always to the interests of his nation. Most surprising of all, the John Ward of the novel despises and often derides Tunis, the Tunisians and their religion. Not only does he fail to convert to Islam, he is a hard-set Christian bigot.

Costain was in pursuit of his own agenda. His Ward is a Christian warrior dedicated to a noble cause: defending Europe from Spanish totalitarianism. Keeping in mind the date of publication – 1942 – the erosion of the division between context and content becomes obvious. Costain's allegory, identifying seventeenth-century Spanish power with the expansion of Nazi Germany, is made plain as Ward and others regularly refer to their foes as 'Jew roasters', doubling a reference to either the Spanish Inquisition or the Nazis' Final Solution. And lest the reader miss Costain's comparison between King James's fawning appeasement of the Spanish and Neville Chamberlain's policy of appeasement of the late 1930s, the author named his chief villain Sir Neville Macherie. Like the Victorian balladeers, Costain dragged Ward through the centuries and made him a contemporary; like Corbett, Costain selected from Ward's story those elements that answered his own needs and ignored the rest.

Costain's book failed to live beyond its moment. Yet still John Ward cannot escape the ideologies of the present. These days, his exploits are not often cited in the histories, strutted on stage, romanticized in novels or trilled out by popular singers. Instead, his conversion to Islam has made him a touchstone among postcolonial literary critics. Robert Daborne's play has found its readership at last, appearing in the syllabuses of English courses and debated at conferences dedicated to 'the Islamic Other' or 'the deconstruction of Orientalism'. At these events Ward's manifold transformations, his services to some states and crimes against others, might be understood and examined, but they will never be valued as heroic.

And yet such a perspective on John Ward is possible. It glimmers between the lines of one final document from the archives. In the 1660s Edward Coxere visited Tunis. Playing the dutiful tourist, the Englishman took note of the site of ancient Carthage, including a hill reputed to contain 'Queen Dido's tomb'. Coxere's guide then pointed out a ruined old hulk, rotting in the harbour at La Goulette, and told him tales of the great man who had once sailed it:

There was the bottom of a ship by the seaside, which was said to be [that of] Captain Ward, the great English pirate, who King James sent some of the royal ships to take; but he, knowing his life lay at stake, had no shelter in any place in Christendom, steers his course for Barbary, where he found entertainment with the barbarians. It is said he was the first that put the Turks in a way to turn pirates at sea like himself. It was said that this Captain Ward, when he turned Turk and had Turk's habit on, and was to drink water and no wine, and little irons under his Turk's shoes like horseshoes, it was said that he gave this report of himself:

> 'I drink water like an ass,
> I am shoed like a horse,
> I have a coat like a fool
> And a head like an owl.'

Coxere's bizarre account of Ward is exactly contemporary with the anonymous Ottoman historian who described him as one of the 'greatest corsair captains'. The contrast could not be more stark: Ward honoured among the Ottomans, abused and disdained by the English.

It was the story of his life.

Notes

ABBREVIATIONS

CSPD = Public Record Office. *Calendar of State Papers, Domestic Series of the Reigns of Edward VI, Mary, Elizabeth and James* I (12 vols, London: the Office, 1856–72).

CSPI = Public Record Office. *Calendar of State Papers Relating to Ireland of the Reign of James I*, C.W. Russell and J.P. Prendergast, eds (5 vols, London: Longman, 1872–80).

CSPV = Public Record Office. *Calendar of State Papers and Manuscripts Relating to English Affairs existing in the Archives and Collections of Venice and in other Libraries of Northern Italy* (37 vols, London: the Office, 1864–1947).

Sals. = Historical Manuscripts Commission. *Calendar of the Manuscripts of the Most Honourable the Marquess of Salisbury . . . Preserved at Hatfield House* (24 vols. in 18, London: Public Record Office, 1883–1971).

EPIGRAPH

Page xiv. 'For whosoever commands the sea . . .' from Sir Walter Raleigh, 'A discourse of the invention of ships, anchors, compasse, &c.' in *Judicious and Select Essayes and Observations* (London, 1650), p. 20.

Notes

1: A FISH DAY FOR SIR WILLIAM CECIL

Pages 2–5. Extracts from Cecil's 'fish day' speech are taken from 'Arguments to prove that it is necessary for the restoring of the Navye of England to have more fish eaten . . .' in *Tudor Economic Documents*, R.H. Tawney and Eileen Power, eds (3 vols, London: Longmans, Green and Co., 1924), vol. 2: *Commerce, Finance and the Poor Law*, pp. 104–10.

Pages 5–6. Extracts from the 'fish day' act are taken from 'An acte towching certayne politique constitutions made for the maintenance of the navye' (5 Elizabeth I, c. 5), 1563' in *Tudor Economic Documents*, vol. 2, pp. 110–17.

Page 8. 'neither so much in quantity . . .' from William Lambarde, *The Perambulation of Kent* (London, 1656), pp. 6–7.

Page 8. Extracts from Defoe's description of Kent are from Daniel Defoe, *A tour thro' Great Britain (1742)*, Samuel Richardson, ed. (4 vols, New York: Garland, 1975).

2: 'THROUGH ALL RANKS OF THE SERVICE'

Page 14. 'rose through all ranks . . .' from CSPV vol. 11, item 268.

Page 16. 'Lawn as white as driven snow . . .' from William Shakespeare, *The Winter's Tale*, Stephen Orgel, ed. (Oxford: Oxford University Press, 1996), Act 4, Scene 4, lines 219–30.

Page 17. 'What hast here? Ballads? . . .' from Shakespeare, *Winter's Tale*, Act 4, Scene 4, lines 257–82.

Page 21. 'had nothing to lose but their lives . . .' from Kenneth R. Andrews, *Elizabethan Privateering: English Privateering during the Spanish War, 1585–1603* (Cambridge: Cambridge University Press, 1964).

Page 22. 'the stay of the West Country' quoted in Gillian T. Cell, 'The fishery: a time of expansion' in *English Enterprise in Newfoundland 1577–1660* (Toronto: University of Toronto Press, 1969), pp. 22–33.

Page 25. 'I served several masters in the wars . . .' from Edward Coxere, *Adventures by Sea*, E.H.W. Meyerstein, ed. (New York: Oxford University Press, 1946), p. 37.

Page 27. 'The greatest scoundrel . . .' from CSPV vol. 11, item 106.

3: THE THIEF'S PATH

Page 29. 'Here lieth Robin Crooktback . . .' quoted in P.M. Handover, *The Second Cecil: The Rise to Power (1563–1604) of Sir Robert Cecil* (London: Eyre and Spottiswoode, 1959), p. 16.

Page 31. 'put her hand to her head . . .' quoted in Leanda de Lisle, *After Elizabeth: How James, King of Scots won the Crown of England in 1603* (London: HarperCollins, 2005), p. 124.

Page 31. 'in the form of a circle' quoted in de Lisle, *After Elizabeth*, p. 124.

Page 32. 'the first wish of the new monarch . . .' from Michael Oppenheim, *A History of the Administration of the Royal Navy and of Merchant Shipping in Relation to the Navy* (London: John Lane, 1896).

Page 33. 'the clash between the Spanish world-empire . . .' from A.L. Rowse, *Eminent Elizabethans* (Athens GA: University of Georgia Press, 1983), p. 46.

Page 35. 'Now of late, since our late Queen's death . . .' Sals. vol. 15, p. 151.

Pages 35–45. Quotations are from Andrew Barker, *A True and Certaine Report of the Beginning, Proceedings, Overthrowes, and now present Estate of Captaine Ward and Danseker* (London, 1609), pp. 1–11. 'All [this] discourse the two poor men who were first taken when Ward took the barque, did after their setting ashore, and return to Portsmouth, relate and constantly affirm to one John Rogers, owner of the barque, in my hearing', interjects the publisher who sought out this report and the longer one of Andrew Barker, Ward's sometime acquaintance and future victim (p. 10). The report of the two seamen is folded into Barker's narrative.

4: BARBARY PIRATE

Page 50. 'herrings of one barrel' and 'offend any of the signors of England' quoted in K.R. Andrews, 'Sir Robert Cecil and

Mediterranean plunder', *English Historical Review* 87 (1972), p. 521.

Page 54. 'Ward, having [got] much money at sea . . .' from *Newes from Sea of two notorious Pyrats, Ward the Englishman and Danseker the Dutchman* (London: 1609), p. B1v.

Pages 60–4. Quotations from Richard Parker's testimony are from Cecil L'Estrange Ewen, *Captain John Ward, 'Arch-Pirate'* (Paignton, 1939), p. 3.

Page 61. 'about as warlike as a coal scuttle' quoted in Clive Senior, *A Nation of Pirates: English Piracy in its Heyday* (Newton Abbot: David & Charles, 1976), p. 27.

5: BARBARY CORSAIR

Pages 66–8. Quotations are from Barker, *True and Certaine Report*, p. 12. This is the historian's best account of Ward's affairs, in large part because Barker carefully distinguished between events that he himself witnessed and those learned through conversation with Ward's men. When describing events, such as Ward's arrival at Tunis, that he himself did not witness, Barker generally notes the name of his source – or, indeed, sources, for Barker would often quiz two or more seamen on the specifics of certain events, the better to determine exactly what had transpired.

Pages 82–6. Quotations describing Ward's assault on the Maltese war galley are from *Newes from Sea*, pp. B2r-B2v.

Page 84. 'yet of late, to my own woeful experience . . .' from Barker, *True and Certaine Report*, p. A2r.

Page 84. "practiseth the casting of ordnance . . .' from *Newes from Sea*, p. F2r.

6: 'THE GREATEST SCOUNDREL THAT EVER SAILED'

Page 89. The deposition of Marco Salamon is from CSPV vol. 10, item 285.

Page 89. 'Such encounters became ever more common. . . .' For a general view of the rising tide of Mediterranean piracy, and the effect of this trend upon the state of Venice, see Alberto Tenenti, *Piracy and the Decline of Venice, 1580–1615*, Janet and Brian Pullan, trans. (Berkeley: University of California Press, 1967).

Page 90. 'I have news that at Sapientza . . .' from CSPV vol. 11, item 634.

Page 90. 'My messenger, sent to get news . . .' from CSPV vol. 11, item 639.

Pages 90–1. The capture of the *Carminati* is related in CSPV vol. 11, item 682.

Pages 91–4. Quotations from John Keye's testimony are from Ewen, *Captain John Ward*, pp. 3–4.

Pages 94–6. Quotations from Geoffrey Wiseman's testimony are from Ewen, *Captain John Ward*, p. 4.

Page 96. 'would not suffer . . . to frequent the company . . .' and 'would rather die then live amongst . . .' quoted in Ewen, *Captain John Ward*, p. 5.

Page 97. The indictment for the plunder of the *John Baptist* is transcribed in Ewen, *Captain John Ward*, p. 5.

Page 97. The three lists of ships captured by Ward and his men are from Barker, *True and Certaine Report*, pp. 22–3 and *Newes from Sea*, p. B²3r.

Pages 97–8. 'The merchants [of London] are all in confusion . . .' from CSPV vol. 11, item 526.

Pages 98–104. Quotations are from the factor's letter, as printed in *Newes from Sea*, pp. D1r-F2v.

7: 'PRINCELY AND MAGNIFICENT'

Page 105. 'The riches he hath gained . . .' from 'The Seaman's Song of Captain Ward, the Famous Pyrate of the World, and an English-man born' in *Naval Songs and Ballads*, C.H. Firth, ed. (London: Navy Records Society, 1908), p. 26.

Page 108. 'gave [Ward] a large piece of ground . . .' from *Newes from Sea*, pp. C4r–C4v.

Page 108. 'a fair palace, beautified with . . .' from William Lithgow, *The Totall Discourse of the Rare Adventures and Painefull*

Peregrinations of long nineteene Yeares Travayles (London, 1632), p. 358.

Page 108. 'lives there in Tunis in a most princely . . .' from Barker, *True and Certaine Report*, p. 16.

Pages 108–9. 'I do not know any Peer in England . . .' from Barker, *True and Certaine Report*, p. 16.

Page 109. 'old Waird' from Lithgow, *The Totall Discourse*, p. 358.

Page 109. '[Uthman] has two ministers . . .' from CSPV vol. 11, item 268.

Page 109. 'lives and countenances were both alike . . .' from Lithgow, *The Totall Discourse*, p. 358.

Page 109. 'court guard' from *Newes from Sea*, p. C4v.

Page 111. 'great poverty and [became] deeply in debt . . .' from CSPV vol. 11, item 894.

Page 111. '[Ward's] chief of trust . . .' from *Newes from Sea*, p. B3r.

Page 112. 'his name infamous for a Rover . . .' from *The Lives, Apprehensions, Arraignments and Executions of the 19. Late Pyrates* (London, 1609), p. E2r.

Page 112. 'making [his] way to the gate . . .' from *19. Late Pyrates*, p. E4v.

Page 112. 'four great ships of Holland . . .' from Barker, *True and Certaine Report*, p. 27.

Page 112. 'about an hundred Infidels' from Barker, *True and Certaine Report*, p. 26.

Pages 112–13. 'very inward with him . . .' from *Newes from Sea*, p. B4v.

Page 113. 'goods ill-gotten are most commonly . . .' from Barker, *True and Certaine Report*, p. 15.

Page 113. 'Like brute beasts . . .' from Barker, *True and Certaine Report*, p. 15.

Pages 114–15. 'there fell a great storm . . .' from *Newes from Sea*, pp. C3v–C4r.

Page 116. 'John Ward, commonly called . . .' from CSPV vol. 11, item 268.

8: THE *RENIERA E SODERINA*

Pages 118–19. Graves's account is from Barker, *True and Certaine Report*, pp. 13–14.

Page 119. 'these last three years . . .' from Barker, *True and Certaine Report*, pp. 14–15.

Page 121. Quotations from the Venetian report on the capture of the *Reniera e Soderina* are from Tenenti, *Piracy and the Decline of Venice*, pp. 77–8.

Page 123. 'After the capture of the ship *Soderina* . . .' from CSPV vol. 11, item 34.

Page 125. 'my Lord Ambassador . . .' from CSPV vol. 11, item 174.

Page 125. 'be seen walking in the Piazza . . .' from CSPV vol. 11, item 362.

Page 126. 'not put out by mere chance' from CSPV vol. 11, item 174.

Page 126. 'patrician of Venice' from CSPV vol. 11, item 174.

Pages 126–8. Quotations on Mustapha's visit to London are from G.B. Harrison, *A Second Jacobean Journal: Being a Record of Those Things Most Talked of during the Years 1607–1610* (Ann Arbor: University of Michigan Press, 1958), pp. 44–63, 147.

Page 127. 'I, favourable to the French . . .' from *Original Letters Illustrative of English History*, Henry Ellis, ed. (London: Harding, Triphook and Lepard, 1825), pp. 83–8.

Pages 128–30. 'I am in duty bound . . . handle it as seems to you best.' Quotations from CSPV vol. 11, item 94.

Page 130. 'An ambassador is an honest man . . .' from Sir Henry Wotton, *The Life and Letters of Sir Henry Wotton*, Logan Pearsall Smith, ed. (2 vols, Oxford: Clarendon, 1907), vol. 1, p. 49.

Pages 131–2. 'That famous pirate, Ward . . .' from CSPV vol. 11, item 106.

Page 132. 'the Republic trusts his Majesty . . .' from CSPV vol. 11, item 110.

Page 132. 'as to Ward, I am not sure . . .' from CSPV vol. 11, item 111.

Pages 133–4. The outgoing Venetian ambassador's notes are from CSPV vol. 10, item 739.

Pages 134–6. Giustinian's interview with King James is from CSPV vol. 11, item 113; his interview with the Earl of Salisbury is from CSPV vol. 11, item 114.

Page 136. 'by this example to deprive . . .' CSPV vol. 11, item 128.

Page 136. 'here they magnify Ward's preparations . . .' CSPV vol. 11, item 129.

Page 137. 'I am of the opinion that your Serenity . . .' CSPV vol. 11, item 135.

Pages 137–8. 'The moment the King gave me the chance . . .' CSPV vol. 11, item 174.

9: SHIPWRECK

Page 139. 'is very clever at keeping together a crew . . .' CSPV vol. 11, item 150.

Page 140. 'The voice here is newly arrived . . .' from Wotton, *Life and Letters*, vol. 1, p. 415.

Page 141. 'won't let themselves be caught . . .' from CSPV vol. 11, item 150.

Page 141. The bewildering decision to launch a war galley to fight the pirates is discussed in Tenenti, *Piracy and the Decline of Venice*, pp. 79–80.

Page 142. 'Evidence of Mario Logilletti . . .' from CSPV vol. 11, item 197.

Page 142. 'We take this occasion to inform . . .' from CSPV vol. 11, item 200.

Pages 142–3. 'Heard that the *Soderina* had gone . . .' from CSPV vol. 11, item 212.

Page 143. 'the rumour that Ward has . . .' from CSPV vol. 11, item 219.

Page 143. 'At court this morning I found a rumour . . .' from CSPV vol. 11, item 229.

Pages 145–6. The story of Jan Casten, including his hero's return to Venice, is related in Tenenti, *Piracy and the Decline of Venice*, p. 79.

Page 146. The hanging of Casten's men is described in CSPI vol. 3, item 470.

Page 147. The testimony of John King is quoted in Ewen, *Captain John Ward*, p. 9.

Page 147. 'furnished him with much artillery' from CSPV vol. 11, item 369.

Pages 147–9. Wotton's report from the sailor is CSPV vol. 11, item 268.

10: 'THE WAR AGAINST THE PIRATES'

Page 151. 'has been received, in appearance . . .' from CSPV vol. 11, item 248.

Page 151. 'the whole country is wild and woody . . .' from CSPV vol. 11, item 323.

Page 152. 'the nursery and storehouse of pirates' from Sir Henry Mainwaring, 'Discourse on Pirates' in *The Life and Works of Sir Henry Mainwaring*, G.E. Manwaring, ed. (2 vols., London: Navy Records Society, 1920), pp. 15–16.

Page 153. 'the pirates Bishop, Sakill and Jennings . . .' quoted in Ewen, *Captain John Ward*, p. 9.

Page 154. 'in the ocean, off Lisbon, is an English pirate . . .' from CSPV vol. 11, item 313.

Page 155. 'The two famous pirates . . .' Sir Charles Cornwallis in *Memorials of Affairs of State in the Reigns of Queen Elizabeth and King James I*, Ralph Winwood, ed. (3 vols, New York: AMS Press, 1972), vol. 2, p. 433.

Page 155. 'for some days past there have been reports . . .' from CSPV vol. 11, item 319.

Pages 155–6. 'the pirate followers of Ward . . .' from CSPV vol. 11, item 328.

Page 156. 'This man [is] now in England . . . from CSPV vol. 11, item 334.

Pages 157–8. Pepwell's letter to the Earl of Salisbury is found in CSPI vol. 3, item 470.

Page 159. 'the English corsair who recently . . .' from CSPV vol. 11, item 369.

Page 160. 'war against the pirates' quoted in John C. Appleby, 'A nursery of pirates: the English pirate community in Ireland in the early seventeenth century', *International Journal of Maritime History* 2 (June 1990), p. 25.

Page 160. 'a token of too much familiarity. . .' quoted in Appleby, 'Nursery of pirates', p. 21.

Page 160. 'it is thought that he will end ill' from CSPV vol. 11, item 363.

Page 160. 'too great lenity to offenders . . .' from CSPD vol. 8, p. 534.

Page 161. 'suspects that the officials of the admiralty . . .' from CSPV vol. 11, item 367.

Pages 161–2. Quotations are from 'A proclamation against Pirats (Whitehall, 8 January 1609)' in *Stuart Royal Proclamations*, James F. Larkin and Paul L. Hughes, eds (2 vols, Oxford: Clarendon, 1973), vol. 1, *Royal Proclamations of King James I, 1603–1625*, pp. 203–6.

Page 162. 'the hands of the very people . . .' from CSPV vol. 11, item 477.

Pages 162–3. The story of the mysterious gentleman assassin who approached Marcantonio Correr unfolds over several dispatches sent from the ambassador to the doge and senate. See CSPV vol. 11, items 417, 426, 431, 449, 463.

Page 164. 'the famous pirates Ward and Danziker . . .' CSPV vol. 11, item 556.

Page 164. 'The question of a safe conduct for the pirate Ward. . .' CSPV vol. 11, item 567.

Page 165. 'Under cover of the night . . .' CSPV vol. 11, item 628.

Page 165. For the governor of Zante's correspondence on Fijardo's raid, see CSPV vol. 11, items 586, 587 and 595.

Page 166. 'with allowance or rather procurement of the Council . . .' from Sir Charles Cornwallis in *Memorials*, Winwood, ed., vol. 3, pp. 15 and 39–40.

Page 167. 'were there a right course taken with him . . .' from Sir Charles Cornwallis in *Memorials*, Winwood, ed., vol. 3, p. 56.

Page 167. 'As the [Spanish] fleet was entering the Seville canal . . .' from CSPV vol. 11, item 663.

Page 167. 'Danziker has revolted against the Algerians . . .' from CSPV vol. 11, item 687.

Pages 167–8. 'has taken refuge in Marseilles with four great ships . . .' from CSPV vol. 11, item 712.

Page 168. 'he had rendered a service to Spain and other nations . . .' from CSPV vol. 11, item 725.

Page 168. The description of Danziker's demise is illustrated with quotations from Lithgow, *The Totall Discourse*, pp. 381–2.

Pages 169–70. 'The dinner was served in full state . . .' from CSPV vol. 11, item 801.

11: 'A CHRISTIAN TURN'D TURK'

Pages 171–2. 'To the Reader, which is as much to say . . .' from *Newes from Sea*, p. A4r.

Page 172. 'this notorious and archpirate Ward' from Barker, *True and Certaine Report*, p. 1.

Pages 172–3. 'the *York Bonaventure* of Hull, of the burthen of 180 tuns . . .' from *Newes from Sea*, p. B^{2}3r.

Page 173. 'whereas it was reported in a former book . . .' from Barker, *True and Certaine Report*, p. 27.

Page 174. 'Gallants you must understand . . .' from 'The Seaman's Song of Captain Ward', in *Naval Songs and Ballads*, pp. 25–7.

Page 175. 'Such wicked courses cannot stand . . .' from 'The Song of Dansekar the Dutchman' in *Naval Songs and Ballads*, pp. 27–9.

Page 175. 'There is confirmation of the news . . .' from CSPV vol. 12, item 151.

Page 176. 'Thou wicked lump of only sin and shame . . .' from 'To a Reprobate Pirat that hath renounced Christ and is turn'd Turke' in Samuel Rowlands, *More Knaves Yet: The Knaves of Spades and Diamonds: With New Additions* (London, 1612), p. B1r.

Pages 176–7. Quotations from Dekker's play are from the original published text: Thomas Dekker, *If it be not good, The Divel is in it* (London, 1612), pp. L4r–L4v. The play is generally known by its running title: *If this be not a good play, the Divell is in it*. Though published in 1612, it is likely that the play was written before December 1610, for in reviewing his file the demons make no reference to Ward's conversion. Had he been writing after 1610 perhaps Dekker would have been more willing to place Ward in the company of hell.

Page 179. 'that content this poor soul did know . . .' from Robert Daborne, *A Christian Turn'd Turk* in *Three Plays from Early Modern England*, Daniel J. Vitkus, ed. (New York: Columbia University Press, 2000), Scene 13, lines 153–4.

Page 180. 'I scorn to take from others to [achieve] my rising' from Daborne, *Christian Turn'd Turk*, Scene 4, lines 63–4.

Page 180. 'So that I rise, let the world sink, and heaven fall' from Daborne, *Christian Turn'd Turk*, Scene 4, line 81.

Page 180. 'with what brain can I think . . .' from Daborne, *Christian Turn'd Turk*, Scene 7, lines 274–80.

Pages 180–1. Quotations from Daborne's representation of Ward's conversion are from Daborne, *Christian Turn'd Turk*, Scene 8.

Page 181. 'Poor fellow, how he looks . . .' from Daborne, *Christian Turn'd Turk*, Scene 13, lines 52–4.

Page 181. 'our just Prophet hates false renegades' from Daborne, *Christian Turn'd Turk*, Scene 13, line 27.

Page 181. 'I condemn thee / As a most abject slave . . .' from Daborne, *Christian Turn'd Turk*, Scene 13, lines 27, 33–5.

Page 182. 'O may I be the last of my country . . .' from Daborne, *Christian Turn'd Turk*, Scene 16, lines 315–21.

Page 182. 'Do a woman to death, and she will be satisfied . . .' from Daborne, *Christian Turn'd Turk*, Scene 16, lines 85–6.

Page 182. 'Want of employment, not of virtue . . .' from Daborne, *Christian Turn'd Turk*, Scene 5, lines 17–18.

Page 183. 'Why, your thief is a gentleman . . .' from Daborne, *Christian Turn'd Turk*, Scene 6, lines 59–60.

Page 183. 'The slavery of man . . .' from Daborne, *Christian Turn'd Turk*, Scene 7, lines 201–3.

Pages 183–4. Daborne's preface was titled 'To the Knowing Reader' and is printed in Daborne, *Christian Turn'd Turk*, pp. 151–2.

Page 185. 'Captain Samson and Captain Wardiyya . . .' quoted in Nabil Matar, *Turks, Moors, and Englishmen in the Age of Discovery* (New York: Columbia University Press, 1999), p. 62.

Pages 187–8. Lithgow's journey into Ottoman North Africa, including his visits with Ward, are described in Lithgow, *The Totall Discourse*, pp. 358–81.

Notes

Page 191. 'the Moors knew scarce how to sail a ship . . .' from John Smith, *The True Travels, Adventures, and Observations of Captaine John Smith* in *The Complete Works of Captain John Smith* (3 vols, Chapel Hill: University of North Carolina Press, 1986), vol. 3, p. 239.

Page 191. 'without the help of which English . . .' from Barker, *True and Certaine Report*, p. A2r.

Page 191. 'in succeeding times Christendom must expect no traffic at sea' from Barker, *True and Certaine Report*, p. A2v.

Page 192. 'step by step how the germ planted . . . by Ward . . .' from Julian S. Corbett, *England in the Mediterranean: A Study of the Rise and Influence of British Power within the Straits, 1603–1713* (2 vols, London: Longmans, Green and Co., 1904), vol. 1, p. 294.

Pages 193–4. Quotations from 'The Famous Sea-Fight between Captain Ward and the *Rainbow*' are from the version printed in *Naval Songs and Ballads*, pp. 30–1.

Page 195. 'Captain Ward wrote a letter to our Queen on the 14th of February' from 'Ward the Pirate' (London: H.P. Such, *c.* 1875).

Page 195. 'He wrote a letter to our Queen on the third of January' from 'Captain Ward' (London: John Harkness, *c.* 1850).

Page 195. 'Loaded with silks and satins, a cargo of the best' from 'Ward the Pirate!' (London: John Harkness, *c.* 1850).

Page 195. 'O no,' says gallant *Rainbow* . . .' from 'Ward the Pirate' (London: J.O. Bebbington, *c.* 1856).

Page 196. 'Come on, come on,' said saucy Ward . . .' from 'Captain Ward' (London, John Harkness, *c.* 1850).

Pages 197–8. 'there was a John Ward, of course . . .' from the Preface of Thomas B. Costain, *For My Great Folly* (New York: Book League of America, 1942), p. vii.

Page 199. 'There was the bottom of a ship . . .' from Coxere, *Adventures by Sea*, pp. 83–4.

Bibliography

PRIMARY SOURCES

Barker, Andrew. *A True and Certaine Report of the Beginning,
Proceedings, Overthrowes, and now present Estate of Captaine
Ward and Danseker.* London: Printed by William Hall, 1609.

Boteler, Nathaniel. *Boteler's Dialogues.* W.G. Perrin, ed. London: Navy
Records Society, 1929.

'Captain Ward'. London: John Harkness, *c.* 1850.

Costain, Thomas B. *For My Great Folly.* New York: Book League of
America, 1942.

Coxere, Edward. *Adventures by Sea.* E.H.W. Meyerstein, ed. New
York: Oxford University Press, 1946.

Daborne, Robert. *A Christian Turn'd Turk* in *Three Turk Plays from
Early Modern England.* Daniel J. Vitkus, ed. New York: Columbia
University Press, 2000.

Dallam, Thomas. *The Diary of Master Thomas Dallam* in *Early
Voyages and Travels in the Levant.* J. Theodore Bent, ed. London:
Hakluyt Society, 1893.

Davies, William. *True Relation of the Travailes of the Most Miserable
Captivity of William Davies, Barber-Surgeon of London, Under the
Duke of Florence.* London: Printed for Nicholas Bourne, 1614.

Defoe, Daniel. *A tour thro' Great Britain (1742).* Samuel Richardson,
ed. 4 vols, New York: Garland, 1975.

Dekker, Thomas. *If it be not good, The Divel is in it.* London: Printed
for I[ohn] T[rundle], 1612.

Ellis, Henry, ed. *Original Letters Illustrative of English History*. 4 vols, London: Harding, Triphook and Lepard, 1825.

Firth, C.H., ed. *Naval Songs and Ballads*. London: Navy Records Society, 1908.

Hakluyt, Richard, ed. *The Principal Navigations, Voyages, Traffiques and Discoveries of the English Nation*. 12 vols, New York: A.M. Kelley, 1969.

Historical Manuscripts Commission. *Calendar of the Manuscripts of the Most Honourable the Marquess of Salisbury . . . Preserved at Hatfield House*. 24 vols in 18. London: Public Record Office, 1883–1971.

Howell, James. *Epistolae Ho-Eliane*. London: D. Nutt, 1890.

Lambarde, William. *The Perambulation of Kent*. London: Printed by James Flesherw, 1656.

Larkin, James F. and Paul L. Hughes, eds. *Stuart Royal Proclamations*. 2 vols. Oxford: Clarendon, 1973.

Lithgow, William. *The Totall Discourse of the Rare Adventures and Painefull Peregrinations of long nineteene Yeares Travayles*. London: Nicholas Okes, 1632.

Lives, Apprehensions, Arraignments and Executions of the 19. Late Pyrates, The. London: Printed for Iohn Busby the elder, 1609.

Mainwaring, Henry. 'Discourse on Pirates' in *The Life and Works of Sir Henry Mainwaring*. G.E. Manwaring, ed. 2 vols, London: Navy Records Society, 1920.

Marlowe, Christopher. *The Complete Plays*. J.B. Stone, ed. London: Penguin, 1969.

Newes from Sea of two notorious Pyrats, Ward the Englishman and Danseker the Dutchman. London: N. Butter, 1609.

Public Record Office. *Calendar of State Papers and Manuscripts Relating to English Affairs existing in the Archives and Collections of Venice and in other Libraries of Northern Italy* (37 vols, London: the Stationery Office, 1864–1947).

——. *Calendar of State Papers, Domestic Series of the Reigns of Edward VI, Mary, Elizabeth and James I*. 12 vols, London: the Stationery Office, 1856–72.

——. *Calendar of State Papers Relating to Ireland of the Reign of James I*, C.W. Russell and J.P. Prendergast, eds, 5 vols, London: Longman, 1872–80.

Purchas, Samuel, ed. *Hakluytus posthumus; or, Purchas his Pilgrimes*. 10 vols, Glasgow: James MacLehose, 1905.

Raleigh, Walter. *Judicious and Select Essayes and Observations by that renowned and learned knight*. London: Printed by T.W. for Humphrey Moseley, 1650.

Rowlands, Samuel. *More Knaves Yet: The Knaves of Spades and Diamonds: With New Additions*. London: [1612].

Shakespeare, William. *The Winter's Tale*. Stephen Orgel, ed. The Oxford Shakespeare. New York: Oxford University Press, 1996.

Smith, John. *The True Travels, Adventures, and Observations of Captaine John Smith* in *The Complete Works of Captain John Smith*. 3 vols, Chapel Hill: University of North Carolina Press, 1986.

Stow, John and Edmund Howes. *Annales, or a Generall Chronicle of England*. London: Richard Meighen, 1631.

Tawney, R.H. and Eileen Power, eds. *Tudor Economic Documents*. 3 vols, London: Longmans, Green and Co., 1924.

Verney family. *Letters and Papers of the Verney Family*. John Bruce, ed. London: Camden Society, 1853.

Walton, Izaak. *The lives of Dr. John Donne, Sir Henry Wotton, Mr. Richard Hooker, Mr. George Herbert. 1670*. Menston: Scolar Press, 1969.

Ward and Danseker: Two Notorious Pyrates. London: for N. Butter, 1609.

'Ward the Pirate!' London: John Harkness, *c.* 1850.

'Ward the Pirate'. London: J.O. Bebbington, *c.* 1856.

'Ward the Pirate'. London: H.P. Such, *c.* 1875.

Winwood, Ralph, ed. *Memorials of Affairs of State in the Reigns of Queen Elizabeth and King James I*. 3 vols, New York: AMS Press, 1972.

Wither, George. *Juvenilia*. London: for John Budge, 1622.

Wotton, Henry. *The Life and Letters of Sir Henry Wotton*, Logan Pearsall Smith, ed. 2 vols, Oxford: Clarendon, 1907.

Bibliography

SECONDARY SOURCES

Abun-Nasr, Jamil M. *A History of the Maghrib in the Islamic Period*.
New York: Cambridge University Press, 1987.

Andrews, Kenneth R. *Elizabethan Privateering: English Privateering
during the Spanish War, 1585–1603*. Cambridge: Cambridge
University Press, 1964.

——. 'Sir Robert Cecil and Mediterranean plunder'. *English Historical
Review* 87 (1972).

——. 'The Elizabethan seaman'. *Mariner's Mirror* 68 (1982)

——. *Trade, Plunder, and Settlement: Maritime Enterprise and the
Genesis of the British Empire, 1480–1630*. New York: Cambridge
University Press, 1984.

Appleby, John C. 'A nursery of pirates: the English pirate community
in Ireland in the early seventeenth century'. *International Journal of
Maritime History* 2 (June 1990).

—— and Mary O'Dowd. 'The Irish admiralty: its organisation and
development *c*. 1570–1640.' *Irish Historical Studies* 24 (May 1985).

Bennassar, Bartolomé and Lucile Bennassar. *Les chrétiens d'Allah:
l'histoire extraordinaire des renégats: XVIe et XVIIe siècles*. Paris:
Perrin, 2001.

Brown, Horatio F. *Studies in the History of Venice*. 2 vols, London: J.
Murray, 1907.

Cell, Gillian T. *English Enterprise in Newfoundland 1577–1660*.
Toronto: University of Toronto Press, 1969.

Chew, Samuel C. *The Crescent and the Rose: Islam and England during
the Renaissance*. New York: Octagon Books, 1965.

Corbett, Julian S. *England in the Mediterranean: A Study of the Rise
and Influence of British Power within the Straits, 1603–1713*. 2 vols,
London: Longmans, Green and Co, 1904.

Dan, Pierre. *Histoire de Barbarie, et de ses Corsaires*. Paris: Pierre
Rocollet, 1649.

Davies, Robert C. *Christian Slaves, Muslim Masters: White Slavery in
the Mediterranean, the Barbary Coast, and Italy, 1500–1800*. New
York: Palgrave Macmillan, 2004.

de Lisle, Leanda. *After Elizabeth: How James, King of Scots won the*

Crown of England in 1603. London: HarperCollins, 2005.

Earle, Peter. *Corsairs of Malta and Barbary*. London: Sidgwick and Jackson, 1970.

Ewen, Cecil L'Estrange. *Captain John Ward, 'Arch-Pirate'*. Paignton: 1939.

Eysturlid, Lee W. '"Where everything is weighed in the scales of material interest:": Anglo-Turkish trade, piracy and diplomacy in the Mediterranean during the Jacobean period.' *Journal of European Economic History* 22 (1993).

Farley, Edith Chapman. 'The Relationships of the Venetian Ambassadors in England with the Royal Family, Privy Council and Parliament, 1603–29'. Unpublished PhD dissertation. Mississippi State University, 1976.

Fodor, Pál. 'Piracy, ransom slavery and trade: French participation in the liberation of Ottoman slaves from Malta during the 1620s.' *Turcica* 33 (2001).

Froude, James Anthony. *English Seamen in the Sixteenth Century*. London: Scribners, 1895.

Fury, Cheryl A. 'Training and education in the Elizabethan maritime community, 1585–1603'. *Mariner's Mirror* 85 (1999).

Gardiner, Samuel R. *History of England from the Accession of James I to the Outbreak of the Civil War, 1603–1642*. 10 vols, London: Longmans, Green and Co., 1894–6.

Guilmartin, John Francis. *Gunpowder and Galleys: Changing Technology and Mediterranean Warfare at Sea in the Sixteenth Century*. New York: Cambridge University Press, 1974.

Handover, P.M. *The Second Cecil: The Rise to Power (1563–1604) of Sir Robert Cecil*. London: Eyre and Spottiswoode, 1959.

Harris, Tim, ed. *Popular Culture in England, c. 1500–1850*. New York: St. Martin's, 1995.

Harrison, G.B. *A Second Jacobean Journal: Being a Record of Those Things Most Talked of during the Years 1607–1610*. Ann Arbor: University of Michigan Press, 1958.

Inalcik, Halil. *The Ottoman Empire: The Classical Age, 1300–1600*. London: Weidenfeld and Nicolson, 1973.

Itzkowitz, Norman. *Ottoman Empire and Islamic Tradition*. Chicago: University of Chicago Press, 1972.

Julien, Charles-André. *History of North Africa: Tunisia, Algeria, Morocco*. John Petrie, trans., C.C. Stewart and R. Le Tourneau, eds. London: Routledge & Kegan Paul, 1970.

Karpat, Kemal H., ed., *The Ottoman State and its Place in World History*. Leiden: E.J. Brill, 1974.

Knolles, Richard. *The Generall Historie of the Turkes*. London: Printed by Adam Islip, 1603.

Lee, Maurice. *Great Britain's Solomon: James VI and I in his Three Kingdoms*. Urbana: University of Illinois Press, 1990.

Lloyd, Christopher. *English Corsairs on the Barbary Coast*. London: Collins, 1981.

MacCaffrey, Wallace T. *Elizabeth I: War and Politics, 1588–1603*. Princeton: Princeton University Press, 1992.

Marcus, G.J. *A Naval History of England: The Formative Centuries*. Boston: Little, Brown, 1961.

Matar, Nabil. *Turks, Moors, and Englishmen in the Age of Discovery*. New York: Columbia University Press, 1999.

Mattingly, Garrett. *Renaissance Diplomacy*. London: J. Cape, 1955.

Milford, Elizabeth. 'The navy at peace: the activities of the early Jacobean navy, 1603–1618'. *Mariner's Mirror* 76 (1990).

Oppenheim, Michael. *A History of the Administration of the Royal Navy and of Merchant Shipping in Relation to the Navy*. London: John Lane, 1896.

Parker, Geoffrey. 'The dreadnought revolution of Tudor England'. *Mariner's Mirror* 82 (1996).

Patterson, W.B. *King James VI and I and the Reunion of Christendom*. New York: Cambridge University Press, 1997.

Ramsay, G.D. 'The foreign policy of Elizabeth I', in *The Reign of Elizabeth I*. Christopher Haigh, ed. London: Macmillan, 1984.

Rodger, N.A.M. 'The development of broadside gunnery, 1450–1650'. *Mariner's Mirror* 82 (1996).

——. *The Safeguard of the Sea: a Naval History of Britain, 660–1649*. New York: W.W. Norton, 1998.

——. *The Command of the Ocean : a Naval History of Britain, 1649–1815*. New York: W.W. Norton, 2004.

Rowse, A.L. *Eminent Elizabethans*. Athens, GA: University of Georgia Press, 1983.

Senior, Clive. *A Nation of Pirates: English Piracy in its Heyday*. Newton Abbot: David & Charles, 1976.

Smith, Lacey Baldwin. *Treason in Tudor England: Politics and Paranoia*. Princeton: Princeton University Press, 1986.

Stiles, Andrina. *The Ottoman Empire, 1450–1700*. London: Hodder & Stoughton, 1989.

Stone, Lawrence. 'The fruits of office: the case of Robert Cecil, First Earl of Salisbury, 1596–1612' in *Essays in the Economic and Social History of Tudor and Stuart England*. F.J. Fisher, ed. London: Cambridge University Press, 1961.

Tenenti, Alberto. *Piracy and the Decline of Venice, 1580–1615*. Janet and Brian Pullan, trans. Berkeley: University of California Press, 1967.

Thorp, Malcolm R. and Arthur J. Slavin, eds, *Politics, Religion and Diplomacy in Early Modern Europe*. Kirksville: Sixteenth-century Journal Publications, 1994.

Wrightson, Keith. *English Society 1580–1680*. New Brunswick NJ: Rutgers University Press, 1982.

Index